Shrill Hurrahs

Shrill Hurrahs

Women, Gender, and Racial Violence in South Carolina, 1865–1900

❧

Kate Côté Gillin

The University of South Carolina Press

Published by the University of South Carolina Press
Columbia, South Carolina 29208

www.sc.edu/uscpress

Manufactured in the United States of America

22 21 20 19 18 17 16 15 14 13   10 9 8 7 6 5 4 3 2 1

Library of Congress Cataloging-in-Publication Data

Gillin, Kate F. C.
Shrill hurrahs : women, gender, and racial violence in South Carolina, 1865–1900 / Kate F. C. Gillin.
pages cm
Includes bibliographical references and index.
ISBN 978-1-61117-291-1 (hardback) — ISBN 978-1-61117-292-8 (ebook) 1. African American women—South Carolina—Social conditions—19th century. 2. African American women—Violence against—South Carolina—19th century. 3. Sex role—South Carolina—History—19th century. 4. Reconstruction (U.S. history, 1865-1877)—Social aspects—South Carolina. 5. South Carolina—Race relations—History—19th century. I. Title.
E185.93.S7G55 2013
305.48'896073075709034—dc23

2013014150

For Peter James Gillin

Contents

Illustrations

Acknowledgments

I wish to thank the two advisors who guided my graduate work: Helen Campbell Walker and Scott Reynolds Nelson. I am indebted to Professor Walker for her early influence on my studies, particularly for exposing me to the expansive range of literature that occupied her office floor. I am also deeply appreciative of the time and energy Professor Nelson spent reading and critiquing my work. Thank you for your humor and support, and for encouraging me to continue.

I am grateful for the work and support of Professors Leisa Meyer, Carol Sheriff, James Whittenburg, and Melvin Ely, whose scholarship and excellent teaching have made me a better student of history. I am particularly indebted to Dr. Barbara Bellows Rockefeller, a remarkable teacher and ally, and Beverley Whitaker and Beverly Smit, who started it all.

I would also like to thank the staffs of Swem Library at the College of William and Mary in Virginia; the South Caroliniana at the University of South Carolina in Columbia, South Carolina; the South Carolina State Archives; and the National Archives and Records Administration in Washington, D.C. To this list I must add David Mandel and the staff of the National Center for Civil and Human Rights; Chris Atwood, technology guru and patient teacher; and Alexander Moore of the University of South Carolina Press, who was always at the other end of an e-mail ready to help.

Special thanks to the Madeira School in McLean, Virginia, for funding my final research trip to South Carolina, and to former members of its history department Sara Cleveland, John Campbell, Shields Sundberg, Larry Pratt, and Lydia Nussbaum; they are excellent colleagues and great friends. A "chapel speech shout-out" must also go to the history department of the Pomfret School in Pomfret, Connecticut.

To my students, advisees, and dorm "children," thank you for teaching me far more than I could have taught you. And please note that I did not use the word "impacted" as a verb once in this book.

To my mother, a strong southern woman who faced adversity time and again, thank you for your courage and humor. I love you dearly and miss you terribly.

And, finally, to my beautiful family—Pete, Jack, Xander, and "the twins"—thank you for your faith in me. You make every day an adventure, and I love you all more than you will ever know.

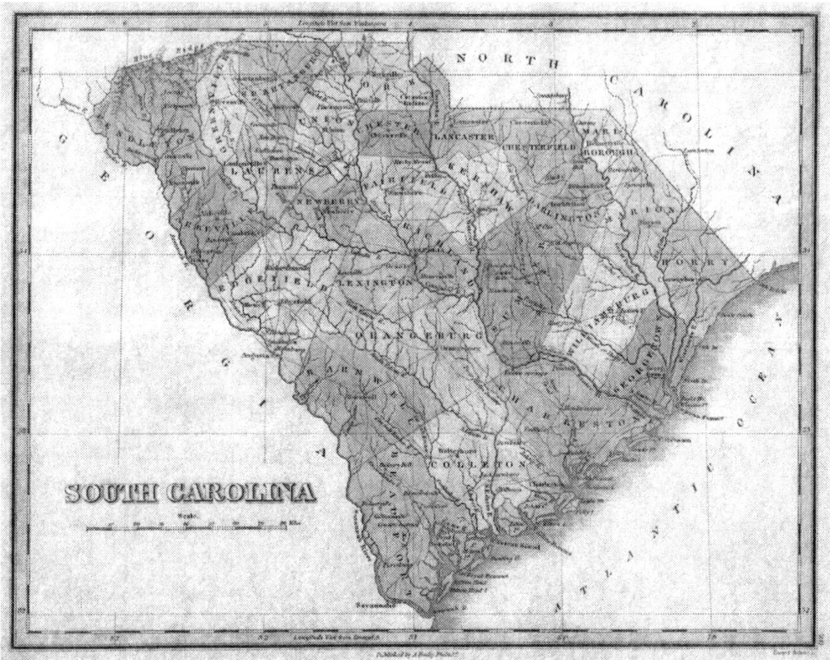

Introduction

Women, Violence, and South Carolina

In January 1871 members of the York County, South Carolina, Klan attacked the home of a local white woman named Skates. After a scuffle they pinned her to the ground, opened her upended legs, and poured a steaming brew of tar and lime into her vagina. They then spread the excess over her body and threatened to return if she did not leave the area within three days. Moments earlier Skates had assisted three black men who were themselves the targets of the Klan's violent predilections. The Klan found the men hiding under Skates's floorboards, dragged them from the house, and whipped them until the victims were able to escape. In their frenzy—and in response to her actions—the Klansmen then turned their attention to Skates. The penalty they chose for her was startling, not merely because it was cruel and violent, but because of its deeply gendered nature. They simply whipped the men, or at least that is all they were able to do before the men broke free. Skates's "punishment" was overtly sexual and played on her biological differences. It also far exceeded a whipping in terms of its brutality, and it was quite clearly premeditated since the Klan had brought the lime and tar with them. In an era of dramatic social, political, and economic upheaval, Skates was exempt from the protections promised to certain other southern women. Indeed many women in the South after the Civil War—white and black—found not only that their sex was no shield against the rampant violence of an undeclared racial war, but also that gender and sexuality were often the reasons for the violence. These women, however, were also empowered by this unstable period in southern history. Some found strength in their symbolic value; others chose to use their sex as a door to the wider world; still others embraced the brutality characteristic of the late-nineteenth-century South because it suited their individual and community goals. The following chapters will explore the rise of violent assaults on southern women of both races, the gendered reasons behind postwar violence, and women's own participation in acts of violence against others in the decades following the Civil War. The confluence of gender, sexuality, race, and violence was not original to the postwar era, but in a brief period of time, it achieved a heretofore unheard of level of intensity with repercussions throughout southern society.[1]

The Confederate surrender in April 1865 inaugurated a struggle throughout the American South: to what extent would the ruling class of wealthy white men allow newly freed black men and women to enjoy the right of self-determination? The process was complicated by a number of factors, including the rise of a southern middle class—both black and white—the weakening of elite hegemony during the war, black enfranchisement, and the physical devastation of the South. The postwar, Reconstruction, and Redemption eras were nothing if not unsteady as the South dragged itself toward the turn of the century. With each agonizing stage in the South's recovery, white southerners introduced greater social distinctions and restrictions that were designed to re-create order, but each of these measures contributed to tension and resentment among and between blacks and whites. That tension culminated in an era of unparalleled racial violence.[2]

South Carolina is an excellent source for new insights in the study of women, gender, and racial violence in the postwar era. As the hotbed of secessionist fervor in the antebellum period and the leader of the South's exodus from the United States in 1860 and 1861, South Carolina was both unique and exemplary of southern sentiments. The state that inaugurated four years of warfare in Charleston Harbor shared an economy and many social conditions with other southern states; but South Carolina set itself apart both before and after defeat. South Carolina's large black population was among its most notable distinctions: in 1865 black South Carolinians outnumbered their white counterparts 415,000 to 290,000. Blacks had in fact been a majority since the seventeenth century, but South Carolina's economic ruin, emancipation, and loss of 23 percent of its young white men during the Civil War highlighted the disparity. The state lost nearly thirteen thousand white men in the war, more than any other in the Confederacy, and defeat itself did little to assuage white citizens' resentment and fear of the freedmen. South Carolina had had a small free black population before the war—centered primarily in Charleston—but most whites were unfamiliar with the reality of black men and women accountable to themselves alone. These conditions, coupled with an uncertain future, provided a breeding ground for unstable social relations. Historian George C. Rable has in fact argued that white men and women in South Carolina feared blacks more intensely and acutely than did whites of any other southern state. As a result, in South Carolina, Reconstruction and the decades that followed would feature an explosion of racial turmoil.[3]

That turmoil, however, extended beyond the realm of race and into the delicate and deeply contentious arena of gender. In turn southern women, black and white, emerged as influential historical actors in the conflict. For white women the antebellum period, as Anne Firor Scott theorized thirty years ago, was not the haven of genteel southern ladies of lore. Regardless of their social status, they had very real responsibilities and interests that occupied their time. By and large, antebellum southern women did not participate in the burgeoning woman's movement taking root in the North, but they were active beyond the narrow confines of an imaginary "private sphere." The Civil War spurred developments in southern womanhood, both their idealizations and realities. In the absence of their fathers and husbands, women assumed greater responsibility for their families' political and economic survival. The new image of the ideal southern woman was more of a junior partner for her spouse than a porcelain doll or a complaisant mouse: deferential but not quite as fragile. Laws passed after the war reflected these changes. For example wives were finally entitled to own property in their own names. In part lawmakers intended this measure to protect a family's income from debts incurred by its patriarch, but such laws also indicated a subtle shift in both women's roles and gender prescriptions. The strengthened role of southern women in the economic and political realms was in many ways a reflection of the power of the debate over gender roles. Many white women sought to change those roles, and others did so inadvertently—ironically, often in the name of preserving antebellum gender traditions. Unfortunately these revisions could not be made without altering the idea of southern manhood, and such changes were as threatening to many whites as was the loss of the war itself.[4]

Black women were similarly empowered by the end of the war, beginning with emancipation and culminating in new roles in the economic and political life of South Carolina. As in the case of white women, these events went hand in hand with changing gender roles, and black women were even more consciously committed to that cause. Access to the privileges of womanhood—denied to them as slaves—would mean the strengthening of motherhood, marriage, and the right of black women to be safe from the antebellum privileges of white manhood, namely their unfettered access to the bodies of female slaves. As a result black women, as much as they desired the protections offered white women, constructed gender roles unique to their situation: "although defined by their race and status as freed slaves, former slave women . . . forged a gender identity that differed significantly from the gendered identities of white women." These changes, however, would not take place without a fight. Whites, male and female, found the elevation of black women and womanhood an ugly specter and resorted to violent measures—often in violation of their gender ideals—to defeat it. In fact Hannah Rosen, in her study of black women's responses to the Memphis riot of 1866, has written that "gender and sexuality became key sites for waging battles over race after emancipation, as . . . black women struggled to be free." They fought a legal system constructed by white men, one that denied them the privileges of motherhood and womanhood, and although they were frequently unsuccessful, their assertion of their rights moved them into a deeply gendered political sphere.[5]

Such developments were anathema to white southern men. Bertram Wyatt-Brown has argued that southern manhood hinged on mastery of slaves and a code of honor rooted in violence, and the men of South Carolina had already lost both the war and control of their slaves. The last remaining bastion of paternalism was the relationship between southern men and women, and postwar conditions threatened even that. Most elite, white men in South Carolina had portrayed the war as the field on which chivalry would demonstrate its superiority: individual honor exercised in defense of virtuous women and a righteous society. But the southern soldier had been conquered, and he now confronted the loss of his masculinity. The subsequent decline of southern manhood thrust women into the spotlight and pushed men toward a revised rhetoric of racism and violence. The end of Reconstruction did not signal a resolution to the question of gender. The struggle to claim and define both manhood and womanhood persisted through the end of the century. Historian Gail Bederman has concluded that by the end of the nineteenth century, the nature of civilization itself rested on the convergence of race and gender, even as each of these was a dynamic concept. The powerful influence of gender on the thirty-five years following the Civil War is reflected in the fact that its tentacles can be found in all the major issues that plagued the era, from labor and land, to democracy and political rebirth, and most particularly, to violent acts of every variety.[6]

In addition to the loss of so many of their men, white South Carolinians confronted the loss of a prosperous prewar economy, the devastation of extensive farm lands during Sherman's march from Georgia to Virginia, and the prospect of dispossession by the federal army. Rumors of land redistribution haunted white men and women as they looked east toward the Sea Islands. The islands, lost in the early years of the war, had been the site of an experiment in federal Reconstruction policies and by the war's end were occupied and farmed almost exclusively by free blacks. The specter of similar federal actions applied to the mainland cast an even deeper pall over the death of the Confederacy. In particular General Sherman's special field order no. 15 issued in January 1865, which promised to forty thousand black refugees forty-acre plots of land taken from the coast extending from South Carolina to Florida, was a source of much consternation for white landowners. In South Carolina, land had always represented wealth and status. A man who owned both land and slaves was doubly blessed. Indeed South Carolina was originally settled when its organizers promised additional acreage to those absentee landowners who sent servants and slaves to populate and cultivate the colony. By the mid-nineteenth century, a multi-crop economy dominated by cotton, rice, indigo, and slaves secured South Carolina's preeminence among its peers. As historian Gavin Wright has argued, now that white society had lost half of what defined wealth, status, and class distinctions—its slaves—the focus on land became even stronger. Such changes would ultimately become the foundation for the first round of widespread racial violence in South Carolina.[7]

Black women played a central role in the South Carolina economy both before and after the war, but freedom encouraged black women to use that centrality as leverage in re-creating their place in southern society as well as the economy. Jacqueline Jones wrote that the freedmen measured their freedom by their ability to control their labor and their families. The negotiation of contracts and labor arrangements was also a reflection of each family's private decision making, the heart of which was women's labor. All black women worked in some capacity, but they wished to concentrate on their homes and children whenever possible and sought contracts that would limit white oversight. Negotiating such arrangements became a difficult and often bloody process, putting women squarely in the middle of the violence surrounding the economic struggle. In particular black women themselves were at the heart of the process of defining freedom and shaping labor relations in one of the most valuable regions of the state because they were the backbone of the South Carolina lowcountry workforce. In turn these women and the malleability of gender roles in the postwar era were at the heart of the larger, more obviously dramatic political developments of the period.[8]

The political arena was hotly disputed throughout the South and particularly in South Carolina. Disfranchised Confederates, enfranchised freedmen, and the women of both races struggled to assert their primacy. The result was an erratic experiment that resulted less in true interracial democracy than in a brutal, increasingly gendered conflict. The powerful influence of women and gender on the politics of Reconstruction changed the nature of the skirmishes fought and the outcome of the larger war. Women, as the central figures of the household,

"Men Eating Watermelon, date unknown." From the Without Sanctuary Collection, National Center for Civil and Human Rights, Atlanta, Georgia.

were positioned to organize and mobilize the community, a sign of the deep interconnection between social, economic, and political worlds. The household, however, had such mutable boundaries that "within the internal political process women were enfranchised and participated in all public forums"; these women, including the freedwomen, saw political activism as a community right rather than a male prerogative. Gender roles among blacks were diffuse and changing during the Reconstruction and the Redemption periods, and black women joined the political fray without hesitation. This apparent "sexualization" of the political sphere meant that gender roles and the right to claim them were intimately wrapped up in the question of political power. Challenges to white men's political power were the equivalent of challenges to their sexual power, and politics became a battlefield on which white men fought to contain and control the sexuality of black men and women. Ultimately, however, the persistence of sexual insecurities beyond the question of politics—once Redemption was achieved—seems to indicate that politics was not sexualized, but that gender and sexuality were politicized.[9]

These events did not happen without a healthy dose of both aggressive and reactionary violence. In fact the late-nineteenth-century South was characterized by bloody racial conflict. From the Klan attacks of the 1860s and 1870s through the phenomenon of lynching in the 1890s, the issues of labor, land, politics, and power were riddled with acts of brutality. The violence itself was diverse, ranging from petty cruelties to murder and mutilation, and it was often disorganized, but it was always pointed. In the past historians attributed racial violence to the politicization of the freedmen or the battles over land ownership and labor arrangements, but more recently it has become clear that the violence of the period was inseparable from issues of gender and the roles of women. Violence was the medium through which southerners expressed their anxieties over the roles of men and women amidst the social, political, and economic changes of the day.

The thirty-five years after the Civil War demonstrate that the evolution of southern racial violence was inseparable from shifting gender roles and the emergence of a new southern woman, both black and white. Women influenced a racial dialogue that resulted in the abuse or death of hundreds of freedmen, just as race and violence altered notions of womanhood. Superficially, southern white men designed a system of oppression in response to emancipation, one that in part revolved around the idealization of white women and the vilification of blacks. But black and white women were not merely the passive objects of socially constructed race and gender prescriptions. They were both the victims of unfair systems—and their violent manifestations—and the architects of New South conventions. Women were active participants in a developing discourse of achievement and racial inequity. As mothers, wives, community leaders, and—simply—individuals, southern women were equal partners in the evolving relationships between the sexes and the races and often the violence that accompanied them.

Widespread violence began with emancipation and was used to deny blacks fair employment. It was a convenient weapon of the elite, used to protect their property and drive a wedge between blacks and poor whites. In many ways Reconstruction era violence amounted to a "counterrevolution." Violence in the late-nineteenth-century South, however, was too diverse for general assessments. Southern violence manifested itself in a variety of phases, each with its own unique qualities and each requiring independent analysis. At first that violence was spontaneous and disorganized: a manifestation of the white South's fear, rage, and humiliation. As time passed, however, racial violence took on an ironic and disturbing tone of order and thoughtful planning. Throughout this process women and gender were central actors. In an 1866 Tennessee clash in which black women were disproportionately victimized, "rioters acted out meanings of white manhood and insisted on 'unworthy' gender identities for African-Americans." By assaulting black women, they asserted their power over not just these women but also the black men who now defined their masculinity by claiming them as their own dependents. Women associated with black soldiers were particular targets because the military was traditionally a bastion of southern manhood. As time passed the violence became more "orderly," and its links to gender became increasingly clear.[10]

In South Carolina spontaneous violence in the period immediately following the war was followed by the reign of terror by the first Ku Klux Klan, the most well known of all violent postwar groups. With the exception of the short-lived black codes, the Klan was the first relatively organized expression of white racial anxieties in South Carolina. Its organization followed enfranchisement, and its activities coincided with political rallies and elections throughout the most hotly contested areas of the state. But Klan violence was not simply a tool of southern white politics. The Klan was the tangible realization of gender—as well as racial—insecurities. The Klan oath, for example, included a promise to "be of special protection to female friends, widows, and their households." The southern man chose to reclaim his lost chivalry—or bruised masculinity—through violence. Politics, economics, and the threat of racial upheaval were equally powerful motivations, but they too were wrapped up in a gendered tangle. The Klan attempted to fulfill the palpable goals of returning social, political, and economic power to white South Carolinians, but it also assuaged the damage that war and surrender had done to the southern male psyche. White southerners were preoccupied with gender and sexuality during the Reconstruction era, drawing a clear connection between Klan violence and these insecurities. The Klan was driven by the need to revive white manhood, and because of their abundant anxieties, all areas of southern life fused with issues of sexuality. Following the "death" of the Klan in the early 1870s, racial violence in South Carolina would become even more well-organized and deliberate, and because the reclamation of sexual power was a persistent problem, racial violence became more unmistakably gendered by the end of the century.[11]

The Red Shirts of the election of 1876 "redeemed" their state through the systematic intimidation and torture of black men and women, and their activities were even more openly influenced by gender issues. The race between Republican Daniel Chamberlain and Democrat Wade Hampton seethed with gendered rhetoric and male insecurity, but it was also the remarkable forum for the rise of the politically empowered women of South Carolina, black and white. Directly and symbolically these women breached the defenses surrounding the political arena. Some were even cheered by their male counterparts, which for white society was deeply ironic considering their desire to restore a sexual order that saw politics as an exclusively male world. The Hampton victory ultimately led to a reversal of many of the rights awarded to the freedmen during Reconstruction, but it did not end the struggle between and among the sexes. In fact the 1876 campaign transformed that undercurrent into a free-flowing torrent of violence in the decades that followed, with women at the heart of the fight.

The success of the Democrats in 1876 would lead to one of the most brutal eras in southern history and to the most open admission of South Carolina's obsession with gender roles and sexuality, the birth of the southern rape myth: the notion that savage black men would rape virtuous white women were it not for the intervention of heroic white men became the inspiration for the torture and lynching of hundreds of black men throughout the southern states. The phenomenon of popular lynching followed the fall of the Klan in the early 1870s as southerners embraced new methods for reclaiming their region and their identities. Throughout the period of "Redemption," racial violence remained a constant source of concern for the black community. Following the withdrawal of federal forces from South Carolina in 1877, white aggression against the black community escalated. The decline of black rights began in earnest, however, following the 1890s resurgence of radical white politics that advocated, among other things, the total subjugation of black southerners. White southerners used the rhetoric of virulent racism to eject the black man from southern political and economic life and confine him (once again) to a narrow code of behavior that, when violated, compelled a brutal punishment. Lynching was not new to the South, but never before had southerners used it so frequently or as the accepted tool of social control. By the turn of the century, violence had subdued much of the black community's public initiative, calming white fears of black domination. The lynch mob was a symbol of this transformation. Tragically the lynching phenomenon would also be the formal union in the long courtship of gender and violence in the Palmetto State. However, as lynching escalated, women were not merely passive symbols and good excuses. Women were as active in the shaping of racial violence as men, whether they acted as victims, accomplices, or perpetrators. As historians delve deeper into this story, they increasingly find women and gender—in any number of forms—at the trigger of the gun or the tip of the lash.[12]

On the surface white southern women do not appear to have participated directly in this process, but they were indeed influential actors in the events of the period. Ultimately white women shared responsibility for lynching. First, radical southerners developed the "rape myth" to justify the mutilation and murder of hundreds of black men. The idea that black men would—and did—rape white women if given the chance allowed white men to extend "protection" beyond the allged crime to its punishment. This symbolic representation of white womanhood was a traditional southern tool that, for example, helped rally men to enlist and fight during the Civil War, and although women were only indirectly responsible for it, they became a potent force in the lynching phenomenon as a result. Second, white women often complained of abuses by black men, fully aware of white society's probable reaction. Lynchings were also attributed to murder, theft, and assault—in fact studies have shown that such cases were more common than charges of rape—but accusations of rape drew the public's attention and generated stronger support for the lynchers. Third, many women promoted lynching by advancing the rhetoric of racism. Southern suffragists, for example, argued that the (white) female vote would secure the South against the black menace. By perpetuating the image of black man as aggressor and threat, they encouraged violent reactions to him. Finally, most white women simply acquiesced to the trend, and this silent sanction was as damaging as outright complicity.[13]

During the lynching era, black women were less frequently the victims of this new wave of violence than their male counterparts. Women were lynched, but there were fewer of these occurrences than the beatings and abuse they experienced during Reconstruction. Black women, however, were more instrumental than ever in seeking solutions to the problem. Black women had historically been the easiest targets of racial abuses, and although they remained victims of the practice, they also became its strongest opponents. Toward the end of the century, black middle-class reformers began to redirect their efforts toward the issue of lynching. They worked to transform lynching from an acceptable community activity to a liability for the ruling classes, associated with the lowest echelons of society and the most barbaric traditions. The most prominent of these was Ida B. Wells, a black journalist who used her skills at home and abroad to draw attention to the injustices practiced against the black community. Eventually black women shaped interracial cooperative efforts. By the end of the century, white society had disfranchised black men, re-creating a tyrannical system that suppressed their economic, political, and social opportunities. Black women moved more easily within that system and, in their constant contact with the white community, forged working relationships with white women who shared their agenda of social reform.

Even the earliest opponents of lynching saw the direct connection between sexual anxieties, gender roles, and the phenomenon. Ida B. Wells claimed that the threat of rape often had to do with white women's preference for the companionship of black men. She risked her life to argue that lynching was not an act of righteous manhood, but degraded savagery, and suggested that white men had better keep a closer eye on their own bedrooms. In 1929 Walter White, an antilynching activist and NAACP leader, connected lynching to the southern economy. He argued that violence against blacks was the means poor whites chose to assuage their economic woes; but White also blamed southern women for irrational fears of black men and blamed southerners in general for a preoccupation with issues of sexuality. Indeed the fluidity of definitions of manhood and womanhood was the issue that haunted southerners throughout the last thirty-five years of the nineteenth century. It was a powerful contributor to the rise of lynching, but constructions of gender had played a role in the politics, economics, and violence of the entire Reconstruction and Redemption eras.[14]

The explosive confluence of race and gender has been confined neither to the South nor to the last 150 years. The period from 1865 to 1900, however, highlights the most remarkable and drastic changes to confront southern women and racial issues in American history. In the decades during and after the Civil War, elite white southern men were forced to concede a measure of both power and status. As a result new variations of southern women emerged. White women enjoyed the strengths and relative independence they had earned, and while some forged new roles for themselves in southern society, most used these experiences to reestablish the authority of southern whites in the years following the death of the Confederacy. They insisted, however, that they share power more equally, a development that altered their role in society despite their claims to the contrary. The freedwomen experienced fresh opportunities and, although hindered by poverty and the resentment of former masters, developed new standards for black womanhood. Both struggled with these new identities, a New South, and often each other. Their activities, in turn, affected more than those people immediately around them. The home was not strictly defined by narrow and impermeable boundaries but exemplified changes throughout southern society, politics, economics, and culture. This household community became a field for negotiations between blacks and whites that included both men and women, and those negotiations commonly ended in violence. The fact that southern women of both races were inseparable from the development of racial violence is perhaps surprising, but their range of activities and the precedents they established are in fact representative of the parallel changes in gender roles and gender relations throughout the South in the late nineteenth century.

I.

Land, Labor, and Violence

Antebellum white South Carolinians used ideals of masculinity and femininity as yardsticks of worth for the members of their society. Those who qualified were among the wealthiest members, slaves were their antithesis, and poorer whites fell somewhere in between. These socially constructed paradigms were not inflexible, but they were often rigidly enforced. The basic definition of manhood included physical strength and prowess, the respect of one's peers, family and class loyalty, and in particular the defense of women ("ideal womanhood," rather than women in general). Womanhood applied to those demure, deferential, physically attractive, and socially adept silent helpmates of manhood's finest specimens. Although rarely an accurate representation of the practical realities of their lives, the ideal benefited those lucky individuals to whom it applied and continued to serve as an archetype for younger generations. Both its southern contemporaries and modern scholars commonly refer to the overarching system that encompassed these formulas as "honor."

Violence was a part of this gendered social code. Dueling, as historian Bertram Wyatt-Brown has written, was a ritual infused with all of honor's primary aspects, particularly constructions of the masculine. Dueling occurred between gentlemen only and usually was the result of an insult to the honor of one of the participants or his family. The most romantic of these involved women: wives, sisters, mothers, and targets of courtship. In other words, dueling was the height of idealized masculinity: a gentleman's pursuit, exhibiting his physical skill and bravery, and frequently in defense of a woman. South Carolina's young men volunteered for service in the Confederacy for many of the same reasons. During the war southerners believed their honor was at stake and that their superior martial skills would prevail. The argument that South Carolina's women required protection from the northern horde was also extremely popular among southern men. Many feminized the state itself, enlisting in the war effort with the intention of protecting "her" borders.[1]

Violence and gender were therefore long-standing companions by the end of the war, but the war had also rewritten the codes that defined gender norms, and southerners—particularly white men—were at a loss to find their place in society. Unconditional surrender gave southern masculinity a sound beating: South Carolina's favored sons had failed to defend both their state and their women. The fact that many southern women had survived largely because of their own resourcefulness was an additional ignominy. These women were now experienced in the maintenance of the family, farm, and plantation. They were one man's employee or the employer of another. They were accustomed to defending themselves, verbally and physically. The postwar southern white man and woman, therefore, bore little resemblance to antebellum gender constructions.

Labor had traditionally been an important component of prewar gender roles in the South. Masculine gentlemen controlled the labor of others. Among the elite, "real men" did not chop wood or plow fields but directed slaves to do so. Similarly "true women" avoided physical exertion in favor of moral strengthening. White men—regardless of social station—defined male slaves in contrast to their ideal: without honor or power because they were not masters of their own homes, they could not make legal claims to their families or defend their wives and daughters, and they could not determine when and where to labor. Female slaves were similarly denigrated. Slave owners forced them to work in the fields and forbade them to marry. They denied black women the roles enjoyed by white women and, in the case of fieldwork, forced them into male categories. Black women's physical appearance and dress—conditions that were imposed by, or the result of, their enslavement and the nature of the work they did—also stood in contrast to the angelic ideal of white womanhood. Slave women were considered physically strong, a product of their labor, while the idealized white woman was weak and required a man's strength. By providing little in the way of clothing, white masters denied slave women both modesty and beauty according to the standards idealized by white society. For many slave women, the absence of the protection that ideal womanhood provided white women led to assault and rape. Masters would not betray the system of honor in which men were responsible for guarding against the violation of southern women. By denying those qualities to slave women, masters also withheld from them the privilege of protection. Slave women were not entitled to defense since they possessed none of the qualities that demanded safekeeping. For slaves white gender constructions

"Negro Family Representing Several Generations. All born on the plantation of J. J. Smith. Beaufort, SC. 1862." From the Library of Congress, Prints and Photographs Division.

ended in abuse and violence. For whites this system upheld the status quo and its privileges, both social and economic.[2]

Emancipation and the ensuing Reconstruction legislation threw the racial and gender hierarchies of South Carolina into upheaval. Black and white, men and women had few precedents to guide them through the adjustment. The postwar revision of traditional racial and gender formulas left all concerned momentarily nonplussed. When South Carolinians recovered from their initial shock, they created new mediums and methods for contending with rising tensions between blacks and whites, husbands and wives, laborers and landowners, Republicans and Democrats, and men and women. As they did so, they re-created systems imposed by their northern conquerors in an effort to accommodate both traditional relationships and the modern context in which they now lived. The first and most obvious place to start was in the fields.

White South Carolinians could not accept the emancipation of the black population—the majority in their state—without alarm. South Carolina had had a small free black population before the war, but it was centered primarily in Charleston and subject to sweeping restrictions. In fact, only 2 percent of the black population in 1860 was free. Antebellum whites sought to thwart changes in their state's racial balance where they threatened and ignored examples of alternative social structures elsewhere, particularly in the North. Carolinians knew that larger populations of free blacks existed in other southern states and that those in the North lived free of many of the prohibitive legal codes found in the Palmetto state. They argued, however, that the conditions under which slaves lived were markedly better than those of free blacks in the North and South. They further asserted that the relationship between blacks and whites within slavery was more stable and resulted in their mutual prosperity. Thus antebellum white South Carolinians confined both their slaves and free blacks within complex economic and legal systems designed to assert white authority, limit black freedom, and perpetuate this "prosperity." The war changed and ultimately ended these systems, leaving South Carolina with a black majority eager to throw off the shackles of white oppression and a white minority weakened by four years of war and northern occupation.[3]

The Civil War, however, did more than simply alter the structure of the southern economy; it redefined the relationship between the races, breeding a spirit of resistance among the black population and inspiring violent retribution among whites. During the war slaves gave an indication of future labor disruptions, defying white authority in greater increments as the Union army made inroads into southern territory. Some slaves walked off their plantations, while others refused to work as directed, assuming the federal army would support their defiance. In some cases they even resisted the efforts of the same federal army to establish a free labor system within traditional plantation systems. Throughout the Sea Islands off the eastern coast of the state, slaves refused to accept the imposition of gang labor and pushed—however unsuccessfully—for family-based farming. Standing alone, Carolina's whites clung to the system that had defined them for decades. Even after the war's end, they resolutely resisted the changes freedmen and northern reformers openly advocated for the South. Their resistance demonstrated the power of their fears, a response to the loss of their former economic and racial dominance and the rise of an empowered black populace. This animosity had not always been so universal in the South. In spite of—and perhaps because of—slavery, blacks and whites had sometimes formed tightly knit relationships before the war. Although not common to every household, neither were these connections the postwar inventions of nostalgic conservatives. They were the very real product of daily interaction on a completely personal level. After emancipation, however, the basic structure of that relationship collapsed. Blacks sought independence and found it difficult to peacefully integrate a continued association with former masters into their new freedom. Whites were now without the systems that defined them as racialized individuals and the dominant force within the southern economy. Naturally, by undermining the premise of their social and psychological makeup, emancipation affected their attitudes toward blacks, even those with whom they had once shared an intimacy.[4]

White South Carolinians first reacted to emancipation with a mixture of horror and disbelief. The self-proclaimed saviors of the Confederacy returned home defeated and deflated, just as the source and evidence of the region's wealth left their masters' homes in celebration of their freedom. In some cases former slaves claimed those homes as the deserved reward for a lifetime of involuntary servitude. Whites observed the changes among the freedmen with dismay. Slaves who white slave owners had once believed were loyal rebelled at the earliest opportunity. Maids and cooks left their mistresses to wonder what had happened to established routines and the "trust" on which they were based. The once seemingly placid and obedient black figures characteristic of affluent white households became animated and anxious to dispel the illusions that had once shielded them from their masters' suspicions and ire. For most slave owners, shock and confusion quickly turned to anger. They came to characterize the freed men and women as ungrateful children who had betrayed them. The notion of betrayal was strangely less painful than admitting to having been cleverly deceived by a people less simple than whites who were dependent on racial distinctions could bring themselves to admit. Over time many would rewrite their history with blacks, blaming the losses of the war, the antebellum status quo, and their political hegemony on a weakness born of their formerly intimate relationship with their slaves. As one contemporary wrote, "we gave our infants to black wenches to suckle, and thus poisoned the blood of our children, and made them *cowards.*"[5]

The most immediate and tangible change for white South Carolinians was the elevation of blacks from the status of slaves to that of free laborers. This transformation affected whites at all economic levels. Planters, according to historian Gavin Wright, became landlords where they had once been "laborlords." Slaves were no longer the primary indicator of wealth; land ownership became the most concrete evidence of success. Control over the land now also determined power relationships. The freedmen were free to earn wages, but that, in turn, required employment. Most former slaves were unskilled farm laborers, and in seeking positions they encountered an embittered group of landowners, resentful of the black wage earner but desperate enough for workers to hire him. Mutual needs, however, did not translate into an equitable relationship between employer and employee. Historian Eric Foner describes what he calls a "Doctrine of the Harmony of Interests," in which mutual interests would theoretically aid the transition from slavery to contractual labor. While this was successful in certain cases, overall whites refused to bargain. Thus, for example, South Carolina's "black codes," enacted immediately following the war, placed extensive restrictions on blacks' economic freedoms. The codes established a sunrise to sunset workday, restricted the freedmen's movements, enabled whites to release them at will—frequently without compensation—and prevented them from seeking employment beyond farming or domestic work without a license purchased from a district court judge. Although eventually overturned once Congress invalidated the "new" state constitutions, even reform-minded occupation forces often settled for the appearance of a free labor system rather than fight for its full realization, allowing for the persistent exploitation of black workers. Blacks continued to struggle for their rights, and white landowners and white laborers met each attempt with determined resistance. The rise of the black wage earner, in fact, would initiate the first great wave of racial violence in the postwar period. Wealthier whites struggled to assert their former dominance, while poorer whites—also laborers—resented the economic and social competition from men and women over whom even they had once felt mastery. Whites' concerns, however, were not merely economic. Changes in labor relations highlighted changes in social relations, and the absence of slavery undermined whites' sense of self. White women did not want to share the privileges of womanhood with freedwomen, whose qualities—based largely on their status as laborers—they believed were decidedly unfeminine. White men understood southern manhood to mean control over blacks. For both groups assertive black laborers making claims to the rights of manhood and womanhood posed as powerful a threat to their identities as they did to traditional economic structures.[6]

Landowners turned to contractual agreements in their efforts to solve the "problem" of the black wage earner. The contract system was largely successful in curtailing the new freedoms of blacks in search of employment. Landlords drafted contracts that strictly outlined workers rights and responsibilities. Laborers were told the number of hours required, the pay offered, and the penalties suffered when rules were broken. Contracts also spelled out their duties explicitly. L. G. Miller of Edgefield contracted with several freedmen within a single document: Charlotte and her daughter Harriet were to work in the "house, yard, garden, and patches around the house," while the men, George, Lewis, Tom, and Isaac, "further agreed to stock and tend the horses on Sunday." J. D. Padgett, also of Edgefield, was so specific as to require the sons of his slave Spencer to hook up the carriage mules, Gin and Mike, "should Mrs. Padgett wish to ride in the carriage on the Sabbath or during the week." Freedmen were often prohibited from gathering in large groups, and many contracts even forbade visitors: "Fannie" agreed to J. P. Palatly's rule that she "receive no company without the permission of said Palatly." Charlotte, Harriet, George, Lewis, Tom, Isaac, and Fannie were also required to obtain permission from their respective masters to leave the plantation. Landowners commonly required their workers to conduct themselves in a manner eerily reminiscent of slavery, and the state's black codes called for the use of the word "master." Louisa, who was also employed by Mr. Padgett, was "to respect the family, obey all orders, and be kind and respectful to Mrs. Padgett and children" at all times and regardless of provocation. Refusing to do so would result in the loss of wages and possible expulsion from the plantation. Additional holdovers from slavery included painfully long days and whippings should a laborer's work and behavior not meet the landowner's standard, but in slavery, the laborer had little or no choice. The cruelest element of the contract system was that it asked former slaves to sign over their new freedoms to former masters and that necessity rather than enslavement drove them to comply.[7]

Freedmen's Bureau agents negotiated many of these contracts and often acquiesced to even the most egregious of the landowners' demands. Landowners considered many northerners their allies, particularly those who believed that putting blacks back to work was more important than ensuring their newly won freedoms. Many northerners were motivated by racism and held fast the assumption that blacks were lazy and would not work unless forced to do so. Others simply worried about the poor economic condition of South Carolina following the war and recognized the need to begin rebuilding as soon as possible. Many northerners further believed that the wealthier class of southerners was incapable of acts of violence or other abuses. Bureau sub-assistant commissioner J. M. De Forrest wrote in December 1866 that "the negroes are rarely wronged except by the lower class of whites." Unfortunately he overlooked the fact that most white employers were not of the lower class and were responsible for repeated abuses of black laborers. Overall northerners' concern for South Carolina's impoverished state allowed white landowners to reassert a disproportionate amount of control over black workers. Brigadier General Edward Wild wrote that his fellow agent, Brevet Brigadier General Molineux, repeatedly gave "countenance to obstructions, neglects, delays, and injustice."[8]

Some agents, however, insisted on greater equality of opportunity for the black laborer. The more liberal-minded among them forced landowners and whites in general to accept important changes in how they did business with blacks. Contracts often revealed the negotiations led by bureau agents. In binding her workers to her, Judith Kilerease at first required that they begin before sunrise and continue until after sundown. In the contract, however, the words "before" and "after" were replaced by "at" and "til" respectively, demonstrating that the freedmen sought to limit these constraints and that the agents complied.

Agnes Quarles, a white female landowner, was instructed that should she fail "to comply with her agreement that the said freedmen may demand the wages due them and leave the premises without any molestation." The fact that both of the employers in these cases were women and therefore subject to greater exploitation is intriguing, but a number of agents were indeed outspoken reformers and not just in those instances where they were negotiating with white women. Colonel James Beecher of the second sub-district wrote to Rufus Saxton at the central office of the bureau in July 1865 that he had always "identified with the freed people," and had "sacrificed all hope of promotion by coming into collision with my superior officers on this point and I do not regret it." Lieutenant Liedere, assigned to Moncks Corner, broke up a fight between a black woman and a white boy named Calhoun Nichols. Nichols had attacked the woman, Clara Anderson, while they were cleaning a local church because she had refused to call him "Mr. Nichols" while he insisted on calling her "Clara." Liedere arrested the boy and brought him before the magistrate. Although they let him off with a warning, Nichols was told that "he had no right to call other people, not in his employ, by their Christian names and require them to address him as master." Liedere had begun to rewrite the rules of behavior. White boys, regardless of age, had traditionally been able to call blacks by their first names, and in the Reconstruction era, those rules no longer applied. But Clara had begun to rewrite gender conventions: she demanded respect from a white male as an independent adult woman.[9]

In response to stubborn blacks and supportive bureau agents, landowners resorted to violent measures to force prospective laborers to accept their conditions. Slave owners had commonly used violence as a means to control their labor force: "in short[,] we kept them *in fear of us* by patrolling, lashing, clubbing or any means that would keep them under subjugation," testified Charles M. Wiggins, a former overseer. In the postwar era, beatings were similarly common and usually involved only the people directly concerned, but occasionally groups of landowners would act together to promote compliance on a broader scale. Their targets ranged from a single, defiant individual to entire communities of black laborers. In December 1866, in the Barnwell District, black laborers Mandy and Dennis Glover were attacked by seven white men. Two years later, in Pickens District, Frank Hench, a white man, assaulted Mary and William Blye "wholly without cause." Both cases were referred to the local authorities, but, more often than not, such local authorities disregarded bureau requests for action and justice. These "raids" on black neighborhoods and homes were the precursor to the activities of the Klan and similar organizations. The drive to reacquire their racial domination and the need to control the black labor market also led whites to establish "agricultural societies." On the surface they were forums for discussing new methods of scientific agriculture, price levels, issues of transportation, and similar concerns for the average farmer and planter. However, these white-only groups were equally useful for debating and organizing the best ways to intimidate and manipulate black laborers.[10]

Black workers, however, did not always accommodate white landowners, even when the latter began to organize to ensure their compliance. Freedom was a powerful motivator and a valuable commodity. Blacks were unwilling to give it up easily, and its rewards were compelling enough to convince many to hold their ground. Blacks fought for more liberal terms in their contracts. They also made good use of the Freedmen's Bureau to demand the fair fulfillment of those terms. When a white landowner of Unionville named Cook ran off to avoid paying the $7,000 he owed to local creditors, the workers on the Cook farm appealed to the bureau. Lieutenant A. P. Cavaher ordered Mrs. Cook to protect the rest of the crop from her husband's other creditors to ensure that the workers were paid. Cain, a black laborer from York County, sought support from the bureau when his employer tried to take away his gun. The agent informed the landowner that Cain was entitled to it unless expressly forbidden in his contract or he had "done some wrong with it." If a landowner needed workers desperately, former slaves had a modicum of leverage. Rare landowners recognized the benefits of cooperation and accommodated potential employees and tenants. A number, however, had neither the need nor the inclination to concede any of their antebellum control.[11]

To vent their frustration when it became obvious that their control was slipping away, whites again resorted to acts of violence against the freedmen. James Rast, a farmer in Moncks Corner, was fined $50 for assaulting one of his workers. Flora had left a tool in the fields and refused to retrieve it when he ordered her to. Rast struck her and demanded that she return the provisions he had paid to her. When she refused again, he took a gun and stormed into her house to enforce his will. In 1866 Grecian Murray was similarly convicted of whipping a twelve-year-old when his commands fell on deaf ears. When a black couple refused to return clothing—part of their wages—to William Cade of Darlington, he shot and killed the wife, "while in the arms of her husband." Laborers resisting the strict behavioral codes of the antebellum period routinely provoked already embittered landowners. The loss of their economic system, the illusion of regional superiority, and their social hegemony had driven most to the edge. Assertive and "ungrateful" workers pushed them over.[12]

Notably, black women were able to establish new parameters for their labor and black womanhood, and these changes affected the labor force as a whole.

Many black women refused to work in the fields following emancipation. They preferred to stay at home, caring for their children and their households. Black women wanted to redefine their role in the work force so that it reflected their own priorities and not those of white masters. Those priorities included reconstructing the black family. In addition to locating lost loved ones and legalizing their marriages, black women reclaimed black motherhood. In slavery their children were not legally their own and could be sold away on the master's whim. In freedom black women took their children back in hand, emphasizing—among other things—family unity, the politics of freedom, and the value of education. Freedwomen were particularly adamant about the last category. Education was a privilege that antebellum law had denied them. Black mothers recognized the social and political imperative of educating the younger generation of freedmen. Education was also a possible route out of drudgery. With a proper education, perhaps their child would have more options and a brighter future than they did. These goals, however, were long term. The most immediate concerns for black mothers were the role their children would play in the workforce and their right to chose for their children. As mothers waited for educational opportunities to develop, they defiantly protected the interests of their children within the changing economy.[13]

In slavery white masters had controlled the labor and lives of black children, but in freedom black mothers struggled valiantly to wrest control away from this exploitative system. The freedwomen fiercely guarded their children from the abuses of whites who stubbornly demanded their prewar control. Recognizing that they needed as much support from the authorities as possible, they avoided local law enforcement and went straight to the Freedmen's Bureau. The bureau investigated the case of F. W. Cooper in 1866. Cooper, of Darlington District, beat a black woman named Elizabeth simply because she had come to his house to visit her child who worked there. Delia Gray of York County complained to the bureau on January 6, 1866, that Jesse Young, a white man, had her daughter and "refused to give her up." Despite orders to do so, Young did not report to the bureau to return the child until January 28. "Dark," a freedwoman from Orangeburg, told an agent that the employer of her son Allen prevented him from visiting her every other Saturday. The white landowner had gone so far as to threaten the boy should he attempt to leave. Mothers stepped in to ensure that white employers did not exploit child laborers, insisting that all contract negotiations go through them, but even extended family sought to protect one another. Betsy Chapel filed a complaint against a white man named Dave Anderson who had hired both her son and her nephew without her permission. The agent determined that her son was to be returned, but that she had no legal claim to the other boy. Nevertheless the fact that she was confident enough to insist upon her rights to her white adversary and the federal authorities was a sign of massive social change, both racial and gendered. Ironically landowners also recognized the renewed importance of motherhood and children to freedwomen and used it to their advantage. Joe Flowers of Darlington punished his laborer Nancy for seeking employment elsewhere by refusing to release her children to her. The report she filed with the bureau, as well as her attempt to leave Flowers and find a better situation for her family, confirms the fact that emancipation had empowered the black mother and therefore redefined the black woman.[14]

Although the specter of the defiant black man had haunted white South Carolinians since the Stono Rebellion, the gender upheaval represented by assertive black women was almost more threatening. White men were accustomed to controlling the labor, families, and even sexual activities of black women. For black women to reclaim their rights as mothers with such intensity was an offense so great to the white community that they retaliated, once again, with violence. Joseph Baldwin of Chesterfield beat a freedwoman with a stick when she tried to prevent him from beating her child. Baldwin's frustration at being denied the right to discipline a boy who just a year earlier would have been his to buy and sell was evident. The woman was a target not because of the errors of her child, but her own "impudence" in standing between him and his employer. Similarly several white men broke into the home of Rachel Foster of Abbeville District in May 1868. The group included the acting constable, J. E. Bowie, who assaulted Foster and took her son. The boy had "unwittingly signed a contract of labor without his mother's knowledge," and the men were acting on behalf of their neighbor, the child's alleged employer, and indeed their society. Julia Calopton told the bureau that Mann Oxenn had taken her child and assaulted her when she tried to take the child back. Oxenn had beaten her with a stick and "choked her down." Calopton, however, was not just trying to reclaim her child from his employer; she was asserting her rights as a mother—regardless of race—in a culture formerly defined by both race and the powerlessness of the black woman.[15]

The initial withdrawal of a number of black women from the workforce resulted in a smaller pool of workers available to landowners. This gave former slaves a certain amount of leverage with prospective employers. Field workers were often able to force landowners to acquiesce to demands in their contract negotiations since the latter now had fewer choices available to them. Unfortunately even this limited power did not last long. Most freedwomen realized that the survival of their families depended on a second outside income. Although many continued to resist the fields, most went back into the workforce in some capacity. A large number returned to white households as laundresses, cooks, and maids. Ironically, since so many black women once again sought domestic jobs, white mistresses had a disproportionate amount of control in determining pay, hours, and treatment: with so large a labor pool, it was easy to replace an unruly maid demanding higher wages. Those who did return to the fields attempted to retain their independence by—among other things—keeping their own hours and behaving in a "saucy, insolent, intractable, disobedient, and dangerous" manner to their employers. George Leigh, a white man from Newberry, went to the Freedmen's Bureau in 1867 to file a complaint against his black laborer, Pauline, for being "saucy and impudent calling his wife 'red faced beth' [Beth]." Mary Chalmers caused enormous problems for her employer, John Mathis. He told the bureau that she "is very abusive to him, and . . . she refuses to work except when it suits her." Her obstinacy even angered the other field hands, but she would not relent. Mr. Zeigler of Orangeburg complained that "the freedwoman Charlotte has the most villainous tongue, and abuses himself and his wife"; the agent ordered her to "wag her tongue no more." For their stubborn insistence on their independence and civil equality, however rudely expressed, black women were commonly the victims of white landowners attempting, as they did with black men, to reclaim their hegemony through force.[16]

Acts of violence committed against black female laborers, however, were not new; the significance of postwar attacks on these women was that they were met with defiance and even retaliation. Black women were no longer going to take the abuses of the white community lying down. In effect they were claiming the prerogatives of womanhood: the right to defend themselves and be defended by the community at large. They commonly lashed out through the authorities. Within two weeks in July 1866, three black women of Unionville complained to the bureau that they had been attacked by white men. All three men were found guilty and either fined or imprisoned. Maria Palote of Abbeville complained that Ellis Turner, her white employer, hit her when she tried to leave his plantation and refused to return her belongings. A fellow Abbeville woman, Abbey Maddox, was forcibly removed from her home on her employer's plantation. She reported the incident to the bureau and the local authorities, although the recording bureau agent commented, "Squire McCord . . . has not and probably never will" serve the warrant. Panthenia reported her employer, Samuel Atchinson, after he "kicked and beat her badly . . . because she would not plow his wheat which she had nothing to do with." She insisted on observing the letter of her contract, but Atchinson, clinging to past prerogatives, was reluctant to abide by it. Sometimes a woman did not need to be stubborn or rude to earn abuse. A Darlington man named James Douglas shot at his servant, Silva, because she was too sick to nurse his family. She did not defiantly refuse to do her job; she was physically unable. But, to Douglas, she had said no, and that was enough. Others responded to violence with violence, as often reacting to a lifetime of abuse as to a single whipping. R. E. Hart of Moncks Corner became enraged when his worker Betsy Curtis did not bring home his cow "as usual." Curtis, however, did not simply complain to the bureau; she attacked Hart following the whipping, and although he claimed self-defense, the bureau fined him $25. For some black women, however, asserting their rights was not always easy. Sally Charles was assaulted by David Alison of Laurens in December 1866. He tied her to a tree and gave her thirty lashes with a hickory stick, but the attack was not reported for more than two weeks. When agents finally sent for Sally, she had fled to "parts unknown." Sally Charles had been cowed by centuries of abuse and submission, but more and more of her peers shed their fears quickly. While some were more comfortable with the support of the federal authorities, others brazenly asserted their interests at the tops of their lungs and even with their fists.[17]

Ironically, black women also needed to restructure their husbands' roles in their working lives. Coverture was an Anglo-American system in which a woman's legal existence was suspended during her marriage. She could not own property or sue in court in her own name: her legal rights fell under her husband's control. In the case of the freedmen, emancipation entitled black men to legally control their wives' contractual labor. According to Senator Charles Sumner, it was one of the defining elements of freedom for black men. Husbands—white and black—could negotiate and sign contracts on behalf of their wives and were entitled to any monetary compensation. Unfortunately, elevating the rights of black men meant a renewed oppression of black women. In response to their "new" legal status, a number of black women were forced to demand the right to control their labor from both former white masters and their husbands. Laney, a black woman from Orangeburg, reported her husband, Cesar, to bureau agents after he whipped her with a leather strap. Cesar defended himself by arguing that he had "whipped her for laziness & being indifferent to his comfort and welfare, and not working." He assumed the prerogative white men had enjoyed for centuries in trying to force his wife to work to his satisfaction. She, however, resisted and reported the abuse to a higher authority. William Griffin left his wife, Lizzie, because she would "not work or do anything for him," but she reported him to the bureau, which counseled him to return. Coverture was gradually dismantled state by state through married women's property acts and earnings laws. The process began in Mississippi in 1839 and continued into the 1880s. In the South individual debt necessitated the change: if property was held in the wife's name, the husband's creditors could not legally claim it as payment for his debts. After the Civil War, few southern white men lived without debt, and sympathetic state legislatures responded to protect their interests. For black women, however, the battle to determine their worth, work habits, and identity continued.[18]

Although also subject to coverture laws, many southern white women resisted restrictions on their public roles during and after the Civil War. With men at the front, wives and daughters went to work of necessity. Their activities reshaped the gender roles that defined southern women. South Carolina was no exception. During the war women ran plantations and smaller farms. Those with slaves often lived in perpetual fear of insurrection or desertion. Those whose labor force remained (and remained docile) learned to balance the work in the fields with the financial requirements of a large household. Women without slaves or hired help to work their land did it themselves, and landless women found employment in urban factories. Although South Carolina's industries were few and far between, existing factories were willing to hire women once the male workforce enlisted in the Confederate army. Most working women earned regular wages for the first time in their lives. For mothers, wages supported their families. For younger women, working outside the home and earning wages allowed them a measure of independence, even if most (if not all) of their money went toward the family's survival. Even in the midst of their suffering, the war exposed white southern women to new and empowering experiences. As they began to catch up with their northern counterparts, they asserted their interests in the private and public worlds of southern society.

The interests of white southern women, however, often clashed with those of black women, and their points of conflict led to violence as easily as did those between black and white men. In the postwar era, white women of the slave-owning classes were as disillusioned and angered by their slaves' abandonment as their husbands were. In fact women were perhaps more surprised by desertions because they had worked closely with their household slaves, in particular, and assumed they knew them well. In re-creating the economy in the postwar era, women played a stronger role than ever. Eugenia R. G. Leland of Ninety-Six, South Carolina, kept a diary in the postwar years. She wrote in June 1868:

> These times of trial bear especially hard on wives and daughters, for many of us were reared in luxury, and since we married have lived in comparative luxury, but besides being deprived of many comforts, we also have been deprived of our servants, on whom we had to depend for so much to make our homes comfortable. Now we toil on unmindful and unaided by them. . . . It is well that we can draw our daily supply of grace from above, but notwithstanding our trials, we have much to make us cheerful and thankful. . . . My dear Husband's means are greatly straightened and he is often worried and

> troubled as to how he will support us, but he has learned to cast his burden on the Lord, knowing He will sustain him. . . . But we should not murmer when we remember that our Savior was reproached and reviled by his friends.

Leland struggled with her husband to rebuild their plantation and reestablish their preeminence, but the hardship of living in a war-torn state was multiplied by the absence of formerly trusted slaves. South Carolina's white women, many widows among them, threw themselves into unpleasant economic realities to re-create stability for themselves and their families. In order to achieve that end, however, they confronted the fact that their former slaves had little interest themselves in that goal.[19]

Few white women were the demure, fainting victims of an oppressive northern regime and its black allies, as they would later claim. Most championed the interests of their race and class with vigor. In this way they both reinforced traditional gender roles and transformed them. In the arena of land and labor, white women contributed most in the developing world of labor relations. Women helped define the parameters of contractual labor, and they did not hesitate to speak up when they believed they were being wronged. George Simms, a black laborer, complained to the Freedmen's Bureau about Joseph Cofield of Newberry District in July 1867. Simms was in the process of negotiating his contract with Cofield when Mrs. Cofield, the landowner's mother, insisted that "she never knew Geo. to be out until half hour by sun" and that he was therefore unreliable. Mrs. Cofield was an active participant in the process, and her comments influenced her son's decisions. Unfortunately, when Simms attempted to contradict her, he made the mistake of referring to her as "'that woman' instead of 'that lady,'" which provoked her son to attack Simms with a chair and finally to shoot at him. Many white women were the actual employers rather than spectators and advisors, and they were as reluctant to give black laborers their due as the rest of white southern society. Miss Mary Pierce of York had to be instructed by a bureau agent to pay her servant, Louisa Summer, because she resisted the terms of Summer's contract. Ms. Hendrix of Newberry was similarly warned by the bureau to pay the wages due Lewis Boozer. Hendrix had ordered Boozer off her land because he had quit work early to go to the doctor. Pierce and Hendrix were in a difficult position: as women alone, they were at a distinct disadvantage within the chaos of Reconstruction. However, they acted brazenly, even if unjustly, which was new for most southern women. In insisting on the prewar social and economic hegemony and its standards of deference, some white women even lashed out at bureau agents. Mrs. George McCall sent a note to the local bureau agent in Darlington asking if he had intended to insult her "by meeting with her in his shirtsleeves." The agent decided that an apology was not required and dismissed her coachman who had brought the message. These women were as determined to re-create the antebellum economic hierarchy as their husbands and neighbors. But they were not above breaking the rules, the law, and especially the prewar gendered customs by which they claimed to abide. As a result, they forever altered the society they sought to preserve, and their moral flexibility led easily to greater injustices.[20]

Like their male counterparts, many white southern women wrestled with labor issues in a less genteel manner; many resorted to violent measures to subdue their laborers, assert their dominance, and even vent their rage. White women commonly allowed and in fact encouraged husbands and sons to "do their dirty work" for them, but they were not above committing acts of brutality themselves. Charles Moore, a freedman from Abbeville District, filed a complaint against Mrs. Burnett and her son, James, in June 1868. Moore's wife and daughter worked for the family, but Mrs. Burnett protested that she was not allowed "sole control over the daughter," as she would have enjoyed under slavery. In her frustration Mrs. Burnett ordered Moore and his family off the farm and assaulted the daughter when they argued. She later sent her son to intercept the women on the road where he beat them with a pistol. For reasons unknown Mrs. Frank Wright attacked her husband's employee, William Saxton, in August 1866. The Unionville woman "stoned him and cut his left arm" while he was completing a task for her husband. White women had resorted to violence against their slaves before the war, but the frustrations of the postwar era pushed many farther than they had or would ever have gone under slavery. Amerita Avinger of Moncks Corner accused Mary Preacher, her white employer, of both breach of contract and threatening to kill her. The agent ordered Preacher to bring the pistol with which she had threatened Avinger to the bureau, and when she refused, he was forced to seize her horse until she complied. Irvin Oliver brought charges against Catherine Mallard of Hickory Bend, "near Fourhole Swamp," for threatening to kill him. The federal government even brought charges against a white woman named Jane Willingsworth for assault and battery with intent to kill in October 1866. Slaves had been valuable commodities, but freedmen were, at best, expendable irritants and at worst, threats to the status and meaning of white womanhood. As such, they became easy targets for white women who were traumatized by the war and reluctant to submit to additional revisions of southern society. Ironically, in lashing out, they only added to the confusion of gender roles that characterized that changing society.[21]

One of the most explosive combinations in the battle to redefine labor and gender relationships was the struggle between white and black women. Black women had historically been victims of white women's abuses. As cooks and maids under the watchful eyes of their masters' families, black women suffered the rage of displeased mistresses. As freewomen, however, they did not hesitate to remind their mistresses that emancipation had forever altered their relationship. Black women were no longer simply slaves whose identities were defined relative to the white men and women around them; they were now citizens and independent women, on an equal footing with their white counterparts. They firmly declared that neither they nor the authorities would tolerate acts of violence. A black woman named Jane Moultrie filed charges against Mrs. Lordes of Ridgeville for "using forcible means" to keep her from leaving her service. Nellie reported Mrs. Peggy Berry for "beating her and threatening to drive her off." Siddy and Manda reported Mrs. David Wannamaker of Columbia for whipping them for not sweeping the kitchen. They argued that they were contracted to "plow three acres of land and do one month of spinning" only. White women, however, refused to be dictated to by former slaves and the federal menace. Caroline Virginia accused Aliza Ragsell, her employer, of assault and battery, but Ragsell produced an indenture of apprenticeship that "gave her the right to 'correct' Caroline whenever disobedient." This vague language restored some measure of her dominance and successfully defended her against the charge. White women were also not above using men to reinforce their supremacy. Freedwoman Caroline Sanders told the bureau that several white women on the plantation of Thomas Hyatt of Chester District threatened her life. She was later attacked by "some white people (names unknown)." Keziah Adams stated in a deposition on July 20, 1867, that Mrs. Rosanna Branyon threatened to "have her whipped wherever she went." Later that night, a group of men broke down her door, took her daughter, and whipped her. They then grabbed Adams, stripped her, tied her to a tree, and whipped her "unmercifully." For their part, black women were not always the innocent victims in these exchanges. Fiona filed a false charge against Mrs. Martha Witherspoon of Darlington for whipping her daughter until the child bled. She also claimed that Witherspoon had threatened to deny her the wages she had earned if Fiona reported her at the courthouse. The bureau dismissed the charges. Clara Edwards, a freedwoman, was arrested for stealing from Mrs. Ann Murray. When questioned, she admitted to taking a dress and stated that "she didn't know why she took it, since she didn't need it." Occasionally both parties resorted to less than just means to assert their interests. Katy Stoutmyer, a freedwoman, accused Mary Sweatman of breach of contract and threatening to kill her. When the bureau investigated, they determined that "both parties [were] guilty," confiscated a gun and a knife, distributed the wages, and ordered the freedwoman off the property. These dramatic exchanges were emblematic of the battle to determine the future of land and labor and of the war over gender and the power of womanhood. Their significance, however, is also in the prominent role women—black and white—played in the legal and violent interactions between the races.[22]

On rare but noteworthy occasions, white and black women rose above the racial upheaval of the postwar era to defend one another against increasing acts of violence. Three white Moncks Corner men were arrested and convicted of "forcibly, armed, and without a search warrant and against the will of the occupants entering and searching the premises of" a white widow named Mrs. Gibson, her employee Oliver Jenkins, and several other freed people. After the original complaint was filed, Mrs. Gibson was a witness on behalf of her laborers testifying against their white assailants. A black woman named Ebby Ann reported an assault by a freed boy named Armstead to the bureau. She claimed that he would not let her pass on the road and attempted to rape her. Mrs. Duckworth of Anderson Court House wrote to the bureau on Ebby Ann's behalf, supporting her account of the events and describing her as a "good well behaved girl." These events would set a precedent for more influential and equitable cooperation between white and black women later but, until then, were exceptions that proved the unfortunate rule that violence between blacks and whites and men and women was becoming a common response to economic and social uncertainty.[23]

"A rice raft with plantation hands, near Georgetown, South Carolina." By Strohmeyer & Wyman, 1895. From the Robert N. Dennis Collection of Stereoscopic Views, Miriam and Ira D. Wallach Division of Art, Prints and Photographs, the New York Public Library, Astor, Lenox, and Tilden Foundations.

Labor issues had emerged as the first truly contentious issue to plague blacks and whites in South Carolina. As land and control over the labor force had traditionally defined success and therefore the right to claim elite status, and elite manhood in particular, the upheaval of these systems inaugurated a much larger battle as well. White men and women had always defined themselves against the limitations imposed on slaves. Without those limitations former slaves could claim access to identities that whites were unwilling to share. White men responded with violence, not only a traditionally manly reaction, but one that also attempted to deny manhood and the rights of womanhood to their black victims. White women, however, followed suit, which not only illustrated the bold new southern woman created by the war, but also pushed the changes to southern womanhood even further. In addition black men and women resisted coercion and violence and even initiated it on occasion. Black men were laying claim to the rights of independent manhood, and their women were rewriting gender roles for themselves. They were now wives, mothers, and homemakers who would dictate the terms of their labor. The conflicts that emerged from these changes were the first in the evolution of postwar racial violence. Often spontaneous and disorganized at this stage, it would eventually grow more deliberate and openly gendered. For now, however, land and labor pushed changes in southern society and gender roles, leading—not for the last time—to violence between blacks and whites in South Carolina.

2.

Black Politics and Violence

Conflicts over land and labor helped reshape gender roles and led to racial violence in post–Civil War South Carolina, but other forces were at work as well. The politicization of the black community enraged and terrified white South Carolinians. A politically active black community in South Carolina violated not only long-standing southern racial traditions, but also the gendered traditions embodied by the master-slave relationship, honor and violence, and southern politics. In conjunction with the changing roles of women, southern white manhood and its privileges continued to lose ground. The confluence of black politics, the gradual liberation of southern women, and changes in gender definitions would have a dramatic effect, inspiring periods of racial violence from Reconstruction into the new century. The level of violence in South Carolina reached heights never seen before, and the combination of those elements was directly responsible. South Carolinians had paid among the heaviest prices in the Civil War; the losses experienced by white South Carolina were exceeded only by the gains of black South Carolina, the state's new political majority; and finally, South Carolina's gender constructions were now a shadow of their former selves. As South Carolinian John Leland wrote of his state following black enfranchisement, "her seat and name has been usurped by a brazen-faced strumpet, foisted upon her 'high places' by the hands of strangers." He characterized both the state and the black voter as feminine in an effort to illustrate their "weakened" condition and his belief that only white manhood could redeem South Carolina. He and others like him would do so at any cost.[1]

Black southerners found their political voice after the war, and land and labor prompted the movement. Land and labor issues were the focus of black political debates in post–Civil War South Carolina. According to historian Martin Abbott, three issues dominated public meetings among blacks during Reconstruction:

freedom (how to use it and how to preserve it), labor (fair practices and the rise of the free labor system), and politics. Their role in politics would determine the future of freedom and labor. Shortly after Appomattox blacks organized political meetings throughout South Carolina. Most had been either praying or preparing for this moment for years. For example, in 1864 a number of black men who would later emerge as leaders within South Carolina politics participated in a national black convention in Syracuse, New York. Among them were Richard Cain and Jonathan Wright: a future South Carolina congressman and a future state supreme court justice respectively. They discussed the future of black southerners and their priorities, the need to secure their rights once attained, and the deteriorating rights of their counterparts in the North.[2]

These themes reappeared after the war, but they also soon moved beyond strictly economic issues. In July 1865 a black mutual aid society met in Charleston to address freedmen's concerns. Predominant among these were land and labor. Two months later the freedmen of St. Helena met to compose an appeal to the state legislature for changes in the state constitution. In September 1865 blacks again met in Charleston to debate the issue of suffrage. They agreed that a lack of education should not bar black voting since ignorant whites already had the privilege. The Colored People's Convention also assembled in Charleston that November, the first organization that included all of South Carolina's black leadership. The convention issued a series of documents intended for both local and national audiences. The "Declaration of Rights and Wrongs," "An Address to the White Inhabitants of South Carolina," "A Petition to the State Legislature," and "A Memorial to Congress" outlined the goals of black South Carolinians, as well as their needs and their perceived rights. The documents reveal a young but relatively advanced political consciousness among South Carolina's black leaders. Although largely conservative—arguing on behalf of basic human and civil rights rather than social revolution—the authors did not fail to express the belief that their state and country had obligations to black citizens, and that as political leaders of the black community, they would oversee the transition.

These grassroots movements were organized largely by skilled laborers, local churches, blacks who had attained freedom before the war, and those who had acquired at least a basic literacy. This is not to say, however, that the mass of freedmen did not rise to the occasion. On the contrary their political activism followed hot on the heels of their freedom. Historian Eric Foner wrote of Reconstruction that "the remarkable political mobilization of the black community is one of the most striking features of the period." Blacks made use of their antebellum institutions—formal and informal—in order to develop their postwar politicization and leadership. Church groups, in particular, were precursors for

Republican organizations and served as forums for political issues. In addition religious leaders came to play an invaluable role: many were literate, already had an established following, and were compelling speakers, able to draw new members into the political fold. The role of the church in the struggle for black civil equality would continue into the twentieth century. In the nineteenth, congregations were readymade audiences for Union League and Republican representatives. The churches themselves were meetinghouses for political rallies and sites where groups could meet to brave the dangers of registration and voting together. As the most important black institution both before and after slavery, the church brought the poorest freedmen into the political process.[3]

After Congress passed the Reconstruction Act of 1867, blacks throughout South Carolina began electing members of their own race to official government positions on the local, state, and federal level. Blacks were—nearly uniformly—members of the Republican Party, and South Carolina blacks were therefore in a position, as their state's racial majority, to transform Palmetto State politics. Blacks accounted for 61 percent of the state's representatives and 42 percent of the senators between 1868 and 1876, and they occupied 52 percent of all state and federal offices open to South Carolinians in that period. Blacks in no other southern state came near such political successes. According to historian James McPherson, "only in South Carolina did blacks hold office in numbers approaching their proportion of the population." Alonzo J. Ransier was elected lieutenant governor of South Carolina in 1870, and Francis Cardozo became the secretary of the treasury in the same year, and Jonathan J. Wright became the only black member ever of a state supreme court. Black South Carolinians, however, never elected one of their own to the governor's office or the U.S. Senate, and the only freedman to be elected to a position in Charleston government was a Democrat. Historian Steven Hahn has also noted that more impressive than the numbers of freedmen in the state government was the number of those elected to smaller but regionally powerful local offices. However, while blacks in South Carolina were certainly the numerical majority and did achieve a measure of political primacy, tales of a powerful "Black Majority" designed to frighten more recent generations and discredit Reconstruction-era black politicians were more myth than reality.[4]

Black leaders in South Carolina directed their nascent political consciousness toward a variety of concrete but relatively conservative goals in the early years of Reconstruction. Meetings such as the Colored People's Convention indicated freedmen's interest in politics and their commitment to participating in it, but the platforms they developed were not designed for social upheaval. They betray a desire for revision rather than revolution and illustrate the philosophical divisions within the larger black political community. The convention's leaders,

"Radical Members of the First Legislature after the War, South Carolina." From the Library of Congress, Prints and Photographs Division.

for example, did not call for the redistribution of land in South Carolina, even though the majority of the black population desired it. After a lengthy debate, they agreed to table the issue until a later date. Most argued in favor of its omission in order to avoid provoking panic among and retaliation from the white community. But, by contrast, they did not shy away from other controversial issues. Black leaders openly and aggressively attacked the black codes of 1865, which served to restrict the social, economic, and political lives of South Carolina's black citizens. The reason behind the different approaches, Thomas Holt argues, is that the black codes were far more detrimental to black political leaders, a number of whom were former free blacks and therefore unaccustomed to many of the prohibitions the black codes outlined. For them destroying the black codes was a battle to preserve their personal freedom. Land was a thornier issue because the goals of the larger black community necessitated divesting whites of property in order to redistribute it. For many within black leadership circles, retaliation by the white community was—like the black codes—potentially devastating to their survival as free, upwardly mobile citizens of South Carolina. Unlike most blacks they were not bound to the white community through labor contracts, and their need for land was limited. They were also not subject to the increasing violence of the new labor system and to an extent condemned the freedmen to a landless future to preserve their own security. Despite their best efforts at restraint, however, the mere fact of black political activity was enough to provoke an edgy white populace.[5]

Democratic clubs were the white response to black enfranchisement, the rise of the southern Republican Party, and the subsequent danger to white political hegemony. Black South Carolinians outnumbered their white counterparts, and their potential political advantage necessitated a response from the white community. With the vote blacks were in a position to dominate local politics, particularly in the southern half of the state and along the coast. Whites organized the Democratic clubs to fight what they perceived as a battle for survival on two fronts: economic and political. Not coincidentally, membership in the local Democratic clubs was commonly identical to that of the all-white agricultural clubs that also emerged in South Carolina in the 1860s. The agricultural clubs were, at least nominally, designed to help revive southern agriculture by giving farmers a forum to discuss their problems and possible solutions. In reality white landowners used the clubs to compare methods for coercing blacks into bad contracts and to organize more general local efforts to oppress the freedmen. Their Democratic counterparts would serve a similar purpose. Historically, politics, land, and labor in the South followed contiguous paths. Most recently they had helped lead southerners to war. Now they would initiate a system of political abuse that would evolve from blackmail to terror.

Economic coercion was the first line of defense against black politics in South Carolina. The freedmen were largely dependent on white landowners for employment, and although many resisted bad contracts and abusive situations, whites persisted in using the economic weakness of the black community to try to keep them from the ballot box. In June 1868 James Scott, a freedman from York County, complained to the bureau that Daniel Carter, his white employer, had thrown him off the plantation without pay for attending a Republican meeting. The responding agent reported that Scott returned in July to say that Carter still refused to let him to return. The agent wrote to Carter, ordering him to allow Scott to work and eventually earn his share of the crop, "unless he had a good reason to turn Scott off." Political disagreements did not merit his expulsion. William Simpson, also of York, reported that J. A. Workman turned him off his farm for distributing Republican leaflets. In this case the agent determined that Simpson had indeed broken his contract but was entitled to wages earned to that point. Whites often went further. Roland James threatened to have Ludy Henderson jailed because Henderson sympathized with Republican "principles."[6]

In spite of these threats, the freedmen flocked to the polls in the late 1860s, but white landowners did not give up hope that poverty and desperation would ultimately conquer black suffrage. Walter King complained to the bureau about Noah Besley, who expelled him from his Newberry plantation for voting in June 1868. King returned two days later to report that he could not find work: "parties will not hire him because he was turned off for working against their interests as well as Besley's." When efforts to prevent blacks from voting failed, some whites simply tried to get them to vote for the other ticket. Occasionally this strategy worked. Richard Huggins of Abbeville complained to a bureau agent that when he went to vote, he was told he would lose his job unless he voted for the Democratic candidate. Rather than succumb to this indignity, Huggins chose to not vote at all. Overall, however, economic coercion was not enough to keep most blacks interested in a political voice from participating in the process. Their resistance to pressure would encourage many white South Carolinians to sink lower in their efforts to protect their dying monopoly on southern politics.[7]

Political violence in the postwar era ranged from threats to barbaric acts of cruelty. Indeed historian Richard Zuczek has written that these activities were "integral components of state politics as whites began an eight-year effort to regain political power." Stories of white assaults, both verbal and physical, flooded local government offices. Samuel Bayley of Marion complained that two white men, Rob Rogers and John St. Moody, told him that if he "should vote the radical ticket . . . [they] would pick away his god damned sole and throw [him] in the river." Three freedmen in Greenville District were all threatened with hanging by a group of white men in May 1868 if they voted for the Republican candidate. According to the bureau, "innumerable" black men "were prevented from voting by violence. . . . Death would be visited on any one who attempted to vote the Republican ticket." Others had been hiding in the woods since "some time before the Election to save being murdered in their beds." In November 1867 in Abbeville District, a group of white men tried to keep up to 150 black men from voting by bribing the freedmen with whisky, and when that did not work, threatening them with death. Eventually the freedmen discovered that being affiliated with the Republicans was enough to bring vigilantes to their doors. Henry Moore, Nelson Martin, Moses Martin, and Josh Wardlaw were all stripped, whipped, and shot at one night by white men in Abbeville County in September 1868, not for voting against the Democrats, but simply for being Republican Party members, or "radicals." Allen Pickens and Samuel Buck accused Soloman Walls and David Bailey of assault and battery in April 1868 "because of some political differences and without any just provocation." Pickens was struck in the head, and the white men fired a pistol at Buck. These acts of vengeance, however one-sided, were a sign not only that whites were planning to resist further changes imposed by the government, but that blacks were also breaking away from deferential habits and asserting themselves in the political sphere. Were they not a realistic threat to white power, white South Carolinians would not have responded as aggressively as they did.[8]

White aggression, however, often went further than mere threats. Their efforts to prevent and punish the rise of the black voter left casualties across South Carolina. There was a riot at the polls near White Hall in November 1867 when Dr. Moses Taggert "instigated a melee." One freedman was killed and five others were wounded; all were prevented from voting. In November 1868 an unknown black man was shot at in Abbeville, which "thereby kept the freedmen from voting" near Calhouns Mill. White vigilantes did not discriminate between their victims. They would as easily attack a party official or member of the state government as they would a landless black laborer. B. F. Randolph, a black member of the South Carolina legislature, was on his way to deliver a speech in Anderson when he was shot and killed at Hodges Depot, "while changing cars." One suspect was arrested as an "accessory before the fact." The assassination of a political leader and elected official indicated that many white South Carolinians were willing to do almost anything to keep their politics from becoming color-blind.[9]

The escalation of white responses to black politics from economic coercion to violence was not due simply to whites' desire to keep blacks and Republicans from political office. Both agricultural and Democratic clubs were compelled by more than just the problems surrounding the upheaval of traditional land, labor, and political systems. White South Carolinians were consciously responding to the threats posed to gender systems by emancipation and Reconstruction. Southern men had traditionally defined masculinity as a white man's province. The antebellum rituals of southern manhood incorporated a variety of practices, including politics and violence. Election days were, in fact, among the best opportunities for southern white men to gather in town and exercise their manly customs. They drank, gambled, and showed off their horses as they discussed politics and voted their choice. The closest black men came to these rituals were as drivers and body servants to their white masters. Following the passage of the Reconstruction Act of 1867, however, black men seized the opportunity to participate in the process, chipping away further at the exclusivity of white definitions of manhood. A South Carolina convention asked "that we should be recognized as men . . . that the same laws which govern white men shall direct colored men." A few years later, Alexander P. Wylie of South Carolina testified before Congress that "ever since—I am thinking of 1868—ever since the Negroes got to voting they have been very domineering over men." By men he meant white men—black men did not qualify. The white response to black politics was not merely a reaction to sharing the ballot box with men they deemed racially inferior; it was a rebellion against the redefinition of masculinity. Historian Scott Nelson has written that this transformation of the public sphere was taken by white men as an equally threatening transformation of the private sphere. He has argued that many white men in South Carolina came to associate the evolving rights of blacks and women as a symbolically sexual relationship between the two, "a public penetration of white womanhood." In response to what they perceived as a direct attack on both their political power and sexual hegemony—and because it was traditional—they lashed out at the black community with violence. Equality before the law and its related privileges implied far more than racial equality to many southerners, and centuries of oppression and cultural traditions would not die easily.[10]

In keeping with gender traditions, whites often tried to use their power over black women to deter the efforts of politically active blacks. These abuses of the freedmen's rights were reminiscent of the antebellum power of white masters. White men had once stood firmly between black men and black women, destroying families, reserving the sexuality of black women for their own use, and denying black men the prerogatives of manhood. Asserting their control over black women both punished politically active black men and stripped them of their rights as husbands and fathers, reinforcing the gendered nature of the struggle over South Carolina politics. Dolly Hunter of Abbeville District was released from her contract for allegedly beating a mule. Hunter, however, told the bureau that she believed that she was driven off because her husband worked for the Republican Party. A freedman named Norman of Newberry was released from his contract in October 1867 because he took a day off to register to vote. Because he had been unable to keep Norman from participating in politics, his employer, Hillard Graham, refused to allow Norman to see his wife, Emily, who had also signed a contract with him. The bureau agent was eventually forced to remove Emily from the plantation because Graham refused to relent. Keeping Norman from Emily was an unpleasant reminder that black men had once lacked even the right to call a woman their wife, and a sign that white men did not divorce gender politics from state politics.[11]

In response to white mobilization against black political activity, blacks joined organizations designed to promote black manhood and protect their rights. The 1860s witnessed the rapid growth of both the Republican Party and the Union League movement in the South, each of which played a role in the effort to create an informed black voting block. The league began in the North in support of Lincoln's administration during the war. It spread south in response to the interest and needs of southern unionists, particularly white yeomen from the mountain regions. The National Council funded the growth of the movement following the war, and it began to attract black members in increasing numbers. Blacks found a forum for their grievances in the league, which became an arena for debating community issues and political solutions. They met in churches, private homes, and even in the woods when an alternative venue was unavailable or tensions with whites called for caution. The league was particularly active during elections. White southerners associated the league with the Republican Party, and although they were compatible, they were technically not affiliated. Where both the party and the league were politically active, the league was also a place for airing personal grievances and resolving labor problems. For example, in March 1868 the league petitioned on behalf of members on Edisto Island that planters who were paying their workers in goods be required to pay them in cash instead. The league was powerful because it was backed by the North and unified the interests of the freedmen under a single banner. In addition the league in South Carolina instructed blacks in the new gun laws and encouraged them to organize for their own defense. These contributions to the Reconstruction South were therefore invaluable to the freedmen but horrifying to white South Carolinians.[12]

The Union League frightened white South Carolinians on several levels: it promoted black political participation, it educated the freedmen on their rights in the postwar era, and it encouraged armed resistance to white abuses. In short it bolstered black citizenship and manhood. In turn the league became an easy and obvious target of white anxieties and violence. An agent of the Freedmen's Bureau wrote a letter to John Williams on behalf of his employee, Robert Counts, in 1868. The agent commented that "you told me the other day that Robert was doing very well. . . . Now you are going to turn him off your place for going to a public meeting." Once again economic coercion was the first resort of a frustrated white community. The bureau, however, took a strong stand against such actions throughout the state. Sub-assistant commissioner J. M. De Forrest reported to his superiors in July 1867 that "some trouble may be anticipated from the unwillingness of many of the planters to have their employees join the Union League. In the two cases of this nature which have been referred to me I have taken the position that no employer shall turn off his hands for attending any political meeting or holding any political faith." Economic coercion was therefore only relatively effective, and whites soon turned to violence to solve their problems. Several white men assaulted Andrew Walker and a friend while they were attending a wedding because Walker belonged to the Union League. Walker refused to tell them about the league's activities, and the assailants beat both men severely. One month later Berry and Irvine Garrett, William Jones, and Edgar Case of Greenville attacked brothers Thomas, James, and Levi Henry. The white vigilantes "broke into Levi's house, beat all three men, threatened to hang James, and forbid them from voting the Republican ticket in the coming election." The invaders admitted to targeting the men because they were all members of the league. The league represented the transformation of politics, society, and, as a result, gender, in the South. To respond to such threats with anything less than their all would have been a failure on the part of southern white manhood. Unfortunately, in their reduced condition, the only resource white men believed was available was violence.[13]

Eventually both the Union League and the Republican Party took their service to the freedmen and their threats to white society a step further. On March 16, 1869, Robert Scott—former bureau official and now the governor of South Carolina—signed the militia bill into law. The bill made legal the establishment of an interracial state militia. Whites, of course, could not accept the integration of their militia, and most promptly resigned. With the exception of their white officers, South Carolinians had thereby created all-black militia troops throughout the state. Both the league and the Republican Party fed the black militia: they were instrumental in the politicization of blacks, they taught organizational skills and encouraged self-defense, and their membership rolls were routinely duplicated within militia companies. In turn the black militia guarded black political—Republican—rallies and protected black voters at the polls. As racial violence developed in the Reconstruction era, they were often at the heart of local bloody conflicts.

The mere idea of a black militia frightened white South Carolinians, and it hung like the sword of Damocles as soon as the war ended. Although not legally until 1869, blacks bore arms as soon as the federal government dissolved South Carolina's postwar constitution and the black codes. Before the end of the war, however, the laws forbade blacks from possessing weapons. Guns were the understood privilege of white men. This was amply illustrated in 1865 when freedman Mack Gibson told the Marion bureau agent that before emancipation, "colored people would no more have dared to use guns or speak of wanting to be free than they would stick their heads in the mouth of a cannon." After the war whites panicked at the unfamiliar sight of armed freedmen and repeatedly violated the law to keep blacks from their guns. In September 1866 "a party of white men" broke into the home of Joseph Macbeth "and demanded his fire arms which he gave to them." A white man in Darlington met Gilbert and Patsy Braddy as they came in from the fields. He demanded Gilbert's gun, and when the latter put it down but held onto the barrel, the white man grabbed Patsy and demanded the gun again. He then shot Gilbert in the face, picked up the freedman's gun, now lying on the ground, and said according to witnesses, "now dam you go that will learn to cock your gun on a whiteman." Although generally supportive, the bureau did not always uphold the rights of the freedmen to keep and bear arms. When D. E. Hart complained that one of his workers carried a loaded and concealed weapon and "fires it off at every opportunity near his employer's house," the agent ordered the worker to hand the gun over to Hart until the end of the year. Gun-toting freedmen were a legal but shocking development in the postwar era. Organized black men carrying guns were therefore anathema to white South Carolina.[14]

The prospect of a black militia posed a double threat to southern whites: organized groups of armed blacks trained to kill, and protection of black political activity and the Republican party in the South. Many whites believed that the militia was actually a tool of the Republicans that would help them take the elections each fall. But the specter of physically strong, armed, and confident black men was perhaps more disturbing. Terrified white witnesses reported blacks drilling with weapons as early as 1866, and it drove a number of them to plead for help from, of all places, the Freedmen's Bureau. The citizens of Walterborough complained to the bureau that "certain colored persons were raising and drilling a military organization at that place." They begged for assistance and received it: the four black ringleaders were arrested and sent to Charleston for trial. Blacks near Edisto Island were arrested for "forming military companies . . . mustering, drilling, and refusing to disband" in 1867. Some freedmen looked to the bureau for permission to form militia companies before Scott's 1869 law, but all were rebuffed. In August 1866 a black laborer named Ryerson requested the authority to organize his fellow freedmen "for the purpose of exercising themselves in drill." Only days later, a former sergeant in the United States Colored Troops, William M. Viney, asked the bureau if he could "form a company of colored soldiers . . . [in] Lewisville," to protect the interests of the freedmen. Both applications were denied outright. The bureau recognized the potential for violence a black militia would create in those early years: white southerners believed in the onset of a race war, and the bureau did not wish to hasten it. Many whites recalled the terrifying days of Nat Turner's rebellion of 1831, during which Turner fashioned himself a general and sent his lieutenants from farm to farm, killing the inhabitants. A black militia led by trained black soldiers was therefore even more distressing, since black soldiers had fought the Confederacy and, as occupying troops, completely overturned the authority of white southern men. The bureau received a number of complaints from white South Carolinians with tales of plots for a military takeover by the freedmen. In August 1866 John Palmer, a white resident of Orangeburg District, told a harrowing story to his local bureau agent. A neighboring black man had confessed to him that a former soldier in the Fifty-Fifth Regiment of the U.S.C.T. named John Thomson approached him about forming a military company. Thomson planned to gather his soldiers on the night of September 2 and march to Orangeburg Court House, dividing only to take the Cannon's Bridge and Bennaker's Bridge Road. The freedmen's army would then "kill every white man they could find, and take what they wanted." The rebellion never materialized, but as long as the militia existed, rumors of such plans persisted. Palmer, in fact, further believed that "it is the object of the Radical party of the North to bring about collisions between the negroes and whites." The militia would continue to go hand in hand with black politics and eventually become the main crossroads for black politics and the rise of racial violence.[15]

Blacks were drawn to the militia for several reasons. It offered a form of self-defense, allowed them to publicly demonstrate racial pride, and attracted eager members by virtue of having been outlawed prior to 1869. Most important, the militia was also a means for black men to reclaim a sense of manhood from white society and the system of slavery. In slavery black men could not determine how and where they spent their time, could not assert themselves as the legal masters of their own homes, and could not protect their wives and children from the suffering associated with being the property of others. Following emancipation and enfranchisement, black men looked to family, labor, and politics for their independence. Many also looked to the militia to reclaim their manhood. As of 1869 the militia accepted all those who chose to join, regardless of race or economic status. In addition, for the first time in recent southern history, blacks could legally bear arms in the protection of their state. More important, they could also legally protect their families, neighbors, and interests. Finally, the militia was a physical, historically male activity, and one that restored black masculine pride. Membership in the militia became a celebrated ritual for the black community because it encompassed so much of what they had been denied under slavery. Characteristically, white South Carolinians resented it for both that reason and the threat it posed to their control over their society.

Whites did not react well to the rise of the black militia after 1869, even if they were indirectly responsible for its creation: Scott had legalized an interracial militia, but they had made it almost uniformly black by resigning. Many white militiamen offered their continued services to the governor, provided they could remain segregated, but the governor refused. In response whites began to organize "social clubs": essentially militia groups that were not sanctioned by the state. Many formerly white militia companies kept their membership rolls and simply changed their identity. Rifle clubs were groups of armed whites that, like the state militia, drilled in formation, took target practice, and planned for the day they would rally against their black counterparts. Saber clubs were similar, but their members were mounted on horseback. Both organizations were indeed social—an excuse to blather with friends and neighbors—but their purpose was also distinctly racist and violent in nature. Their targets were necessarily unlimited. They included the black militia, individual black men as well as women, and whites who had—in their opinion—betrayed their race by associating in some "inappropriate" way with the black community. The all-white rifle and saber clubs were designed to enforce a racial hierarchy of which white men were in command. They sought to dictate social mores, political affiliations and rights, and economic strata. But their motives were also deeply rooted in more intangible concepts: gender and gender roles. Just as the desegregation of the militia enlivened black manhood, it altered the definition of southern masculinity. For blacks the new definition was more inclusive. For whites it was diluted, weakened by the presence of black men for whom manhood and its privileges had never been an entitlement. As the perceived military arm of the Republican Party, the black militia brought the gendered nature of southern politics to the fore. South Carolina politics became, more than ever before, an arena for the struggle to determine not simply the economic and political future of the state, but also the gender roles of men and women of both races. The combination set the stage for unprecedented violence.

The black militia rarely incited violence, but their efforts to assert their local power and intimidating but innocent celebrations involving firing weapons into the air often led to large-scale vigilantism on the part of white South Carolinians. Ultimately the black militia would set a new wave of racial violence in motion and, in some cases, start the race war whites feared, but this was never their intention. Established to protect black voters during elections, its existence provoked whites to lash out at what they perceived as a hijacking of the political system. One of the most brutal exchanges took place in Laurens County in 1870. The black militia was organized there in the spring and summer of 1870. Residents reported that they "made the night hideous by the discharge of firearms and their savage yells." By the fall whites suspected its leaders were hatching an insidious plot to overtake the county. Smaller skirmishes took place throughout the autumn, but a larger conflict was brewing. In anticipation of violence, white merchants ordered shipments of rifles, and the local Democratic club appointed leaders. On the day of the November elections, militia leaders brought the ballot boxes from all the county's precincts to the center of Laurens so that they could protect black voters. Some whites reported that this made it difficult to reach the polls, but the votes cast for the conservative party were appropriate to their numbers. In Laurensville, the day passed without incident, in spite of the fact that bands of armed whites patrolled the streets looking for an excuse to start firing. A day later, however, the tension broke. Witnesses claimed that following a skirmish between a white conservative and a black constable, a black militiaman's weapon discharged accidentally. At the sound, the Columbia *Daily Phoenix* reported, the armed freedmen fled to a makeshift armory, believing the whites were firing on them, and themselves started firing into the square. Eventually whites stormed the armory, and the "battle" was over by the end of the day. White citizens, however, were not going to allow this breach of the social order to pass without comment. Men from surrounding areas poured into Laurens County to put a stop to the "race war" they believed had been started by the black militia. At least three black elected officials and ten others were murdered, and over 150 citizens fled their homes in what deteriorated into a "Negro chase" by mounted white vigilantes. Eventually the white renegades dispersed, leaving the town and the black community in chaos. Republican members of the state house of representatives proposed legislation to strengthen the power of the militia or impose martial law in several counties, but none of the bills passed. The Laurens riot became an infamous example of the volatile nature of politics during Reconstruction; volatile because of the connection between black politics, the militia, and the fears they engendered. This connection persisted throughout the 1870s but would ultimately inspire the rise of more organized white responses to blacks armed with rifles and the vote.[16]

Ironically South Carolina politics in the 1860s was so explosive that it defied even the traditions of racial violence. Whites and blacks who betrayed their respective race in the political arena would pay the price, and in this case, both races were responsible for inciting acts of brutality. Benson Hallam and his son, Burris, charged two other freedmen, Cato Hallam and James Ladd, with assault in April 1868. Ladd and Hallam had attacked Burris, they claimed, "because he would not promise to vote for their man, a Democrat." While black-on-black political violence was not uncommon, white-on-white political violence was perhaps more pervasive since the number of white Republicans running for and winning elected office in South Carolina was higher than that of black Democrats. White-on-white political violence was also generally more excessive. Two white men assaulted a white member of the South Carolina legislature named J. B. Hyde for making a political speech that favored Republican principles. A white Republican named Cornell was driving with a freedman in Abbeville in September 1868 when an unknown white man stopped them, overpowered Cornell, tied him to a tree, and "riddled [him] with blows." Two months later another white Republican was grabbed by a white mob while he was encamped near Laundsville, tied to a tree, and shot. These abuses defied racial tradition, but the alliances that brought them on did as well. The black community perceived blacks who voted Democrat as traitors to their race and its interests. Whites who voted Republican, particularly white southerners, were perhaps more threatening to their race because by siding with black political interests, they were also, however indirectly, betraying long-standing gender codes as well. In a society resisting change as violently as South Carolina in the postwar era, such actions earned notice and retribution.[17]

Although South Carolina politics was traditionally a man's activity, more than black men transformed its gendered nature following the Civil War. Black women reshaped the political sphere to better incorporate their own needs. Although not legal voters themselves, black women found more creative ways to involve themselves in the rites of the southern citizen. First, within the black household, there was a relatively equitable system of decision making. The nature of slavery in the South had forced husbands and wives to share what few responsibilities were left to them by white masters and the law. This arrangement lingered into the postwar era. Although the Fourteenth and Fifteenth Amendments gave men the more direct role in politics, black men did not necessarily exclude black women. Historian Elsa Barkley Brown writes that the black community did not assign politics to the male sphere because the boundaries between men and women were not absolute. As a result black women were enfranchised within the community. Many considered the vote a family decision, in which husbands and fathers submitted a ballot agreed upon by wives and mothers. Although reaching a consensus within the family was simple—the vast majority of blacks were Republicans—their common political affiliation did not detract from the valuable role women played within the process. Their opinion was valued.[18]

Black women were also active political participants in the public arena. The Rollin sisters of South Carolina, daughters of a successful black lumberman, hosted a political salon in Columbia. One of the sisters married William Whipper, state senator and future judge, and another was engaged to a white senator who, sadly, died before the wedding. A third sister addressed the South Carolina House of Representatives on the issue of universal suffrage, and the fourth was elected secretary of the South Carolina Women's Rights Association, an affiliate of the American Women's Suffrage Association. South Carolina's black women also attended political rallies, cheered their candidates, berated their opponents, and voted at mass meetings. In many instances their presence so unnerved white Republicans that the latter encouraged black men to—like white society—keep their wives and daughters at home. Observers of Republican rallies frequently commented on not only the presence of black women but also their active role in the proceedings. For example attendees were required to leave their weapons "at the door" when they arrived at political rallies, and black women often guarded the weapons while men entered the debate. Their role was not passive. They were not participating directly, but given the hostile climate in which black politics was developing, it was a vital post. White South Carolinians resented black enfranchisement; they feared large congregations of blacks to such an extent that such gatherings had been outlawed since the antebellum period; and most blacks in South Carolina owned and carried weapons with enthusiasm. The combination repeatedly led to violence. For black women, guarding the weapons was therefore an indication of the trust that their community had in them and the potential power they wielded within their race's embryonic political rituals.[19]

Occasionally black women came closer to the polls than was perhaps legal. The wife of a Democratic leader in Union County wrote that black women were "the head and fount of the opposition. Some going to the polls to see that the men voted right, threatening them with assassination if they did not vote as they wished." Black women were known to have incited violence not just against black men who voted "wrong" but also against those whites who stood in their way. Henry Thomson wrote in 1927 that "it was noted everywhere that in their bitter hatred and denunciation of the whites and the Negro Democrats the women were even more violent than the men." Some freedwomen even attempted to vote. Since the black militia guarded the polls after 1869, black women had easier access to the ballot box. Instances of voter fraud were certainly not as common as contemporary whites insisted, but black women were frequently suspected of padding the votes for the Republican Party. Rumors abounded in Laurens Country in 1870 that Joseph Crews, a very controversial local militia leader, encouraged black women to disguise themselves as men and vote. Although the papers could not say if it had happened, the Columbia *Phoenix* related that, "of the 1,000–1,200 blacks on the Square all day, there were 1,900 votes." In

Abbeville in 1867, Tess Calhoun filed a complaint at the Freedmen's Bureau that Ned Maherion, another freedman, had deceived her and a friend by handing them Democratic ballots and "telling them they were radical." Perhaps Calhoun was picking up the ballot for a male family member and perhaps she submitted it on her own; regardless, she felt so much a part of the process that she went to the bureau when she believed fraud had been committed. She did not seem to recognize her own role in possible voter fraud but emphasized her political entitlement over any potential rule bending on her part. E. W. Seibels testified before Congress in the early 1870s that "women and children voted. Women gave votes for their husbands, or their brothers, who they said were sick." Such events demonstrated that black women embraced politics as powerfully as their men. Although not legally enfranchised, they participated and would defend that perceived right even in the face of white retribution.[20]

Because of their activism, black women were targeted by white vigilantes in the 1860s. Their sex afforded them little or no protection from reprisals, economic and violent. In keeping with their treatment of black men who joined the ranks of the Republicans, employers similarly abused freedwomen who became politically active. Many black women were also punished in lieu of their husbands and brothers. Freedwoman Hariet Hernandes told Congress that by the 1870s, black men and women lived in a fairly constant state of fear "because men that voted radical tickets they took the spite out on the women when they could get at them." The same was true in neighboring states. In Georgia a massacre in Camilla left over forty casualties, including eleven dead. One of the victims, a young black girl, was attacked by a white man named John Gaines. He cut the back of her head, neck, and arm, and he split each of her fingers from the tip to the palm. Gaines hurt her because she and her aunt had attended the political rally that had started the massacre. This girl, despite her youth, posed a threat to the white ruling class because she took an interest in politics, previously reserved for whites and men only. For black women in South Carolina who took more than a mere interest in politics, the violence necessary to quell their passion would need to grow before it would be able to keep them from participating. Unfortunately white South Carolina would rise to the occasion.[21]

Despite these constant threats, black women continued to play a role in South Carolina politics, but they also found more indirect ways to participate in the process. Black women were partisan political animals, and many focused on the role of education in the politicization of the black community. During Reconstruction black mothers sought and supported schools for their children, and black women eventually filled southern schools as teachers. Historians Darlene Clark Hine and Kathleen Thompson wrote in 1998 that black women were largely responsible for the education of their race: between 1890 and 1900, the number of black women teachers nearly doubled, and by 1910 two-thirds of all black educators were women. For blacks education was a route to economic success, and they invested in its future. Southern blacks, in fact, spent over one million dollars on education from 1865 to 1870. More important, education was a privilege of citizenship—one that had been withheld from blacks by white society—and would provide access to political leadership. Robert Brown Elliott, a black politician in South Carolina, remarked of the connection between education and political activity that "if they are compelled to be educated, there will be no danger of the Union. . . . The masses will be intelligent, and will become the great strength and bulwark of republicanism." Even bureau agents recognized this connection, and many sought to support blacks' efforts to become more educated. In requesting funds for school construction and teacher salaries, Brevet Major C. F. Allen of Abbeville wrote to his superior that "the education of the freedpeople is of the utmost importance, and their future success depends wholly upon their preparations for the higher duties in life." Most blacks did not need encouragement; school attendance in South Carolina rose rapidly in the early Reconstruction era. Freedmen's Bureau sub-assistant commissioner J. M. De Forrest reported in 1867: "The most hopeful sign in the negro is his desire for education. During last winter the highest number of scholars on the roll of the Greenville Freedman's School was about 400. This summer the school was continued by Mrs. Belden, one of the white teachers, and Rev. Charles Hopkins, colored teacher, with a roll of 200 scholars." The numbers went down in the summer months because children were needed in the fields, so two hundred students was a promising beginning. By 1876 almost two fifths of black children in the former Confederacy were enrolled in school. For black women, educating their children was both a reinforcement of their newly empowered maternal roles and the politicization of the black community. To white South Carolinians, the freedmen's education was therefore a sign of a new, and unwelcome, era in southern history.[22]

Because of the connection between black education and changing political roles, black schools were frequently targeted for violent reprisals by fearful southern whites. Historian Martin Abbott has argued that opposition to black education became more pronounced in 1867 because of the rise of "Radical Reconstruction," but 1867 also marked the enfranchisement of the freedmen in South Carolina, and the connection between the two issues was as clear to the white community as it was to the black. Black schools were a symbol of emancipation and a tangible route to social, political, and economic advancement in postwar southern society, but South Carolina's schools could not long endure the barrage of assaults from local whites. Vigilantes burned schools, terrorized teachers, and threatened parents who persisted in sending their children. This was true of neighboring states as well. In St. Mary's Parish in Louisiana, white vigilantes raided the area, killing and torturing members of the black community. They concluded their visit by setting the local black school on fire. The bureau agent assigned to the region reported that "this was done on the eve of an election for the purpose of intimidating the freedmen and . . . there were many freedmen deprived of the vote through fear." The school was a symbol of black political activism, and burning it was a warning to those who planned to vote. It was also a convenient way to disrupt future political meetings, as many took place in black churches or schools, and was a long-term reminder that black votes would be met by white violence. The results of attacks like these were devastating in South Carolina. In June 1866 Oliver Howard of the Freedmen's Bureau listed seventy-five bureau schools in the Palmetto State. By November the South Carolina assistant bureau commissioner, Robert K. Scott, counted only thirty-eight. By October the number of black schools in Edgefield County had been reduced to just one. According to historian George Tindall, white opposition to black education, in conjunction with the white supremacy movement of the last decades of the nineteenth century, would eventually promote a shift among blacks toward industrial and agricultural education and away from more classical studies. By 1880 only one-quarter of black children had received enough education to read. Violence against schools and teachers, however, did not stop the black community from pursuing their political rights and did not stop black women from preparing their children for their civic responsibilities.[23]

Like their black counterparts, white women found a stronger political voice following the Civil War, in spite of the fact that they too were excluded by the Reconstruction amendments. This process actually began during the war itself when white women, left to their own devices, acted on developing political beliefs. White women were forced to deal with civic officials during the war in order to defend their interests. Many took grievances or opinions out of the realm of correspondence and private conversations and into letters to newspaper editors and with public demonstrations of frustration. Women wrote to Jefferson Davis with requests ranging from the return of husbands and sons from military service to an outright end to the war. Others declared their support for the Confederacy in newspapers from Charleston to Richmond. Following the war this relatively untried political activism of South Carolina's white women would find new venues.[24]

A primary political role for white women during Reconstruction was as liaison between their husbands and sons and an angry federal government. Women, together with their lawyers, made pleas for family members incarcerated for their role in the Confederacy. These petitions were made to the U.S. Congress and, early in the process, to President Johnson himself. White women also fought for relatives convicted of crimes committed against federal soldiers and the freedmen. One of the most notable South Carolina cases in the 1860s was that of James Keyes, his son Robert, Francis Stowers, and Elisha Byron. These white men were convicted of the murders of three soldiers in October 1865. The soldiers, stationed in Anderson, South Carolina, were shot and drowned in the Savannah River. Following the convictions Mrs. Keyes and Mrs. Stowers, "two old women, the wives of the two old men who were under sentence of death," appeared before President Johnson, who told them that the case was out of his hands. Before the war southern women did not generally venture far from their farms and plantations unless they were visiting family and friends. They certainly did not go to Washington, D.C. on business with the president. Following the war these activities became far more common, and many women acquired, of necessity, a better understanding of both the law and the political process. Some women were not above using their sex to manipulate the system. Keyes and Stowers, it appears, played on the sympathy of a man for two elderly southern women when they wrote to complain that their husbands had been moved by the military and they "could not ascertain where; that they were in great distress of mind about it." The recipient of the telegram later learned from the secretary of war, Edwin Stanton, that the telegram was false and that the ladies had been informed of the move and had been told that their husbands were imprisoned at Fort Delaware. These machinations made use of the stereotype of helpless white women of the South but reflect a savvy understanding of the strategy necessary to free their husbands. Eventually their efforts were rewarded when a federal judge discharged the men from the custody of the military.[25]

Unlike their black counterparts, however, South Carolina's white women did not immediately dive into the political fray on the local level. In the 1860s and early 1870s, white women did not generally attend meetings of the Democratic Party, and even white Republicans tended to stay away. This does not mean that they ignored the events of the era. Most were invested deeply in their state's political future, particularly since politics was so intricately wound together with social, economic, and gender changes. Most were also sympathetic to the efforts of white men to keep blacks from the polls. They perceived the rise of the empowered black man as a threat to both their political and physical security. In neighboring North Carolina, an election toward the end of the century led to a riot and massacre. Shortly before the election, Rebecca Cameron wrote that "it has reached a point where blood letting is needed for the health of the common wealth, and when the depletion commences let it be thorough." Alternatively some white women were not unsympathetic to the freedman's cause. Following the same massacre, Jane Cronly confessed that "it will be a day to be remembered in my heart with indignation and sorrow. . . . I waited hoping a stronger voice than mine would be lifted up in defense of a helpless and much injured race, but such has not been the case." Cronly recognized both the injustice of racial violence and her own relative helplessness to stop it. Most white women were in a similar position, and they simply kept watch from a distance, at least for the time being.[26]

White women were also enmeshed in politically motivated racial violence by their male relatives who committed acts of cruelty against the freedmen. Ella Aiken, the daughter of Confederate colonel David W. Aiken, wrote down her memories of the Reconstruction era and passed them onto her descendants. In 1868 her father was arrested for the murder of black politician B. F. Randolph, who was shot and killed at Hodges Depot by three white men. Randolph was a minister, former assistant superintendent of education under the bureau, and Orangeburg representative to the state senate. Unfortunately he had been "making most incendiary speeches . . . [and] to a man of Father's high sense of justice, impetuosity, & perfect fearlessness, there was nothing so hard as to keep quiet." Colonel Aiken, allegedly a member of a "secret committee of the Democratic Party," confronted Randolph at the train station and warned him not to make any speeches in their area. "He even told him it would not be safe. . . . Mother and I were near the depot and heard the conversation," Ella naïvely wrote. She did not know—or chose not to know—that Aiken had been encouraging Randolph's assassination. Witnesses later testified that he told the Anderson County Democrats "never to suffer this man Randolph to come in your midst; if he does, give him four feet by six." In spite of this, Aiken's daughter became his most ardent supporter, interpreting the threat at the depot as a generous warning. This reinterpretation—or denial—was an invaluable skill that white southern women used in the face of unspeakable and undeniable horror. They maintained a sense of order while their sons and husbands were busy disrupting it. Women also maintained the home front, much as they had during the war, and Ella and her sisters were evidently also the people who kept their home together after his arrest. After he was taken into custody, Aiken wrote to them that "poor 'Mother' does not know that 'Father' is in jail or she would go crazy," leaving them in charge of the domestic front. Aiken did not return until much later after the case against him had been dropped, despite the fact that he had been released on bail provided by General Wade Hampton and Colonel L. D. Childs. Such was commonly the case when acts of violence against the freedmen were prosecuted.

Although not necessarily the aggressors, white women were the confessors, advocates, and pillars of strength for the men who left them behind. As Reconstruction-era violence intensified, the white women of South Carolina would be called on again and again to fill these roles.[27]

The emergence of the black voter, the presence of blacks in the Republican Party, and the development of the black militia overturned the lives of white South Carolinians, and each one successively prompted a more extreme reaction. In keeping with their recent history, whites lashed out at the black southerner first through the economic system and eventually—and perhaps predictably—through intimidation and violence. This new system of abuses began immediately following the surrender at Appomattox, but in South Carolina, racial violence would take decades to evolve. Its first, primitive stages were marked by disorganization and the perpetuation of old habits. It was a sign that the old regime was still clinging to life, despite all evidence of its destruction. Blacks, however, were not always passive victims. Many responded aggressively in an effort to retain their hard-won freedoms and avenge years of poor treatment. As rapidly changing circumstances necessitated fresh methods, white and black South Carolinians found new ways to hurt one another. White society, however, had had more practical experience and would ultimately emerge as the clearly dominant aggressor.

While men were commonly the main participants in episodes of politically motivated racial violence, women were consistently a part of the larger picture. Like their male counterparts, black and white women were both aggressors and victims. But, unlike men, women were also often the motive or excuse for racial conflict. In addition gender itself was a participant. A politically active black population redefined the political sphere—a traditionally male and decidedly manly activity—as interracial, bringing black men a new measure of masculinity and white manhood on par with its black enemy. Postwar politics also changed ideas of womanhood to include partisan support for husbands, sons, and their party of choice. While black women were more active publicly, white women were no less invested. In some cases these changes led women directly into acts of racial violence. Politics, gender, and racial violence therefore became inseparable in the 1860s. And, while this relationship would not change over time, the methods used within it would. As the 1870s dawned, racial violence in South Carolina escalated and became relatively well organized. As it did, so too did the role of women.

3.

Getting Organized

The Ku Klux Klan in South Carolina

Early in "radical" Reconstruction, southerners took their rage and made more structured attempts to intimidate and punish blacks for the impudence of acting on their civil rights. The most widespread of these early efforts was the Ku Klux Klan. The Klan emerged in Tennessee in 1865 or 1866 and spread quickly throughout the former Confederate states. Its diverse membership shared a single goal: the subjugation of black men and women to a condition reminiscent of slavery and the revival of the old southern racial hegemony that elevated whites, regardless of class, above their newly freed neighbors. The Klan has been examined for its role in southern politics and the economy but rarely recognized for its direct participation in the evolution of gender roles and the impact it had on southern women of both races. The Klan's activities, regardless of their stated purpose, were inherently gendered, which further advanced the connection between racially motivated violence, South Carolina's women, and the meanings of male and female in the postwar South.[1]

The Klan was born in the law offices of Judge Thomas M. Jones in Pulaski, Tennessee. The pet project of six former Confederate officers, the organization was originally an answer to boredom but became one of the most fearsome and violent groups in American history. There are a number of false stories about the Klan's beginnings, including the theory that its members were really a secret group of Chinese opium smugglers. Another rumor suggested that the name Ku Klux Klan was from "some ancient Jewish document referring to the Hebrews enslaved by Egyptian pharaohs." The name actually derived from the Greek word for circle, kuklos, and the Scottish tradition of family clans; and its members were no more exotic than most well-educated young men from rural

Tennessee looking for an interesting way to pass the time. To add to their amusement, the group created an elaborate structure with outlandish titles. Each local group was known as a "den." The head of each den was known as the Grand Cyclops; his assistant, the Grand Magi; and their secretary, the Grand Scribe. The Grand Turk greeted candidates for membership, and the members themselves were Ghouls. Other titles were Night Hawks (messengers) and Lictors (guards), as well as Goblins, Furies, Hydras, and Geni. Eventually the head of all Klan dens nationwide was known as the Grand or Imperial Wizard; and on a statewide level, the Grand Dragon.[2]

The Klan's early activities were in keeping with these self-consciously absurd rituals but quickly degenerated into more purposeful violence. In the haze of rage and frustration caused by the loss of the war and emancipation, the original members of the Ku Klux Klan decided to use their new fraternal order to manipulate the freedmen of Tennessee. The first raids were designed to frighten blacks, during which the Klansmen played "tricks" on their victims. One of the most popular involved a Klansman on horseback in full regalia riding up to a freed person's house and asking for water. The Klansman would "drink" several buckets, more than a human could consume, by funneling the water through a tube under his robe. Once finished, he would remark that he had been so thirsty because he had not had a drink since he had died at Shiloh, Gettysburg, or Chancellorsville. The prank was an effort to create the illusion that the Confederate dead were haunting the living, particularly those freedmen who sought a station in life above the one to which southerners had kept them before the war. Ultimately the trick failed to fool the black community, but it did convince them that whites were beginning to organize against them. That was enough to put them on their guard. Unfortunately black resistance to Klan abuses escalated the tensions. Tricks soon advanced to beatings and, in many cases, murder, the immediate ends of which ranged from political power to social control.[3]

The chaos of the postwar era and the dramatic and rapid nature of social, political, and economic change made an organization like the Klan an attractive option for southern men frustrated by their loss of control and what they perceived as the perversion of the natural order. Joel Williamson has argued that the first Klan grew out of a "rising confusion of identity" on the part of whites and has noted that South Carolinians in particular "lost their sense of self and [their] ideals became blurred." Their subsequent desire to cling to smaller groups or organizations led to a distinctive "clannishness or Klannishness" within the Palmetto State. Historians have estimated that at the height of its popularity during Reconstruction, the Klan had as many as five hundred thousand members throughout the South. That membership spanned all classes within the white community.

Although early historians of Reconstruction blamed the lower classes for the Klan's rise and reputation, subsequent analyses determined that the bulk of the Klan's leadership came from the upper class. The Klan was therefore largely representative of southern society, with the social elite at the top and poorer whites at the bottom. Although many white nonmembers would privately disapprove of the Klan's tactics, few would take an active stand against it, and "the silence of the most prominent white southerners spoke volumes . . . [and] fostered a climate that condoned violence as a legitimate weapon in the struggle for Redemption."[4]

In 1868 the Tennessee leadership sent R. J. Brunson, a member of the original Pulaski den, to South Carolina, where he organized dens in several areas of the state. The Klan would take root and become most violent in nine upcountry counties: Chester, Fairfield, Laurens, Newberry, and Union in the lower Piedmont; Lancaster, Spartanburg, and York in the upper Piedmont; and Chesterfield in the sand hills region. Historian Richard Zuczek argues that the Klan thrived in South Carolina because it incorporated two of its more popular traditions: community-based, extralegal responses to events perceived as a threat to its society, and organizations such as the slave patrol and black code patrol designed to placate the fears of its citizens. The Klan in Reconstruction-era South Carolina would have two major phases. The earlier of the two would occur as a result of the election of 1868, which convinced whites of the need for dramatic action. The second phase began in 1870 and continued until the federal government pursued prosecutions of those responsible two years later. Contemporary witnesses later attributed the Klan's popularity to the "brutality" of Reconstruction and pointed to developments such as the Reconstruction Acts, the creation of the black militia, corruption in the Reconstruction government of the state, and the power of carpetbaggers to illustrate their point. Whites argued that their way of life was under siege by northerners, the federal government, and their social and intellectual inferiors. As the Charleston *News and Courier* later wrote, "the brutal deeds of the Kuklux in South Carolina grew out of the organization of a society for strictly defined defensive purposes. Its objects . . . were eminently proper." However, the reasons for the Klan's growth in South Carolina were more complex and far less justifiable than its members and supporters would ever admit.[5]

South Carolina's white population did not wait for the introduction of the Klan in their state to act on fears of a social revolution. Retributive actions against the freedmen began as early as the surrender at Appomattox, but most early efforts were conducted by individuals or small vigilante groups acting spontaneously. Eventually South Carolinians sought greater efficacy through organization, and the Bushwacker was born. Also known as Deadheads, the Bushwackers were pre-Klan organizations that grew in response to the black community's efforts to assert their civil rights and achieve some measure of economic independence. Many were former Confederates who chose to resist federal occupation as early as the spring of 1865. In March Brigadier General Judah, stationed at Rice Hope Plantation, wrote to request an entire battalion to combat "the guerrillas which infest the vicinity of this post." Ultimately, however, service in the Confederate army was not a requirement for membership. In February 1866 a freedman named Tolliver complained to the Freedmen's Bureau that Bushwackers in Newberry District "infest the vicinity of Frog Level," and planned to raid the plantation of a local white man named Kinnard. Kinnard had sent Tolliver to beg for protection from the bureau. The following month Corporal Daniel E. Knox, a representative of the bureau, was actually attacked by a member of "a gang of outlaws and murderers that infest this state." Although shot through the lung, Knox survived the attack. The language chosen by all three chroniclers was appropriate: these pre-Klan groups did indeed infest South Carolina and swarm the countryside like insects. Later in 1866 they shot a U.S. soldier in Newberry when he refused to hand over the keys to the jail so that the Bushwackers could free two white men accused of killing a freedman. Although the federal government was an attractive target, the victims of the Bushwackers were more often black than white. Freedman Irvin Poe of Orangeburg reported that a black man named Isaac had been murdered in November 1866 by a group "calling themselves dead heads." The bureau agent reported the matter to the civil authorities, and by December three Deadheads had been arrested and were locked in jail. These attacks continued through 1867 and into 1868, as the Klan began to establish a foothold. South Carolinians had yet to realize the value of better communications and cooperation among resistance groups, and the Bushwackers competed for their loyalty. Their methods, however, were building to those that would eventually resemble the Klan's. Threats and coffins left in doorways bore symbols and strange language, playing on the mysticism so attractive to the Pulaski founders. A freedman named David Macy, for example, accused two white men from Greenville named Bowers and Ward of leaving threatening notes on his door. One such letter read:

> ALIVE TO DAY AND
> DED TO MORROW IF
> YOU DONT LEAVE
> 6 unplucks Plan Have nothing
> To Eate but the flesh of man, Band
> of Knight and Banish By Day auld
> Dave gett out of the way

The men believed Macy had reported their illegal still to the government, which had seized it. Bowers had already appeared at Macy's house, where he confronted Mrs. Macy, silently lit his pipe, and left. Since such actions were intimidating but not illegal, and since Macy had no proof that Bowers and Ward left the note, he was advised to be on his guard and return to the bureau if he believed he was in danger. Macy undoubtedly was, but overall the Bushwackers were little more than a name adopted to give the appearance of greater organization and power. The violence was real, but the perpetrators lacked focus and a chain of command that the Klan would soon provide.[6]

The Bushwackers served their purpose until a more efficient alternative came along. Although historians continue to debate the extent of the Klan's connectedness den by den, both within South Carolina and the South as a whole, the order offered greater formal organization than any other group up until the point of their first great period of activity. Certainly, as the Klan became more widespread, their connection to Pulaski faltered, and even within individual states, larger membership rolls challenged dens' ability to control their neighbors and even their own members. But regular communication between and within dens, a highly structured hierarchy, well-ordered assaults on entire communities, and a successful campaign of terror indicate that despite obstacles, the Klan's central purpose and devoted following kept the organization on track. This sense of order was imposed on each den at its inception. When white citizens of Rock Hill met to form a new den in the summer of 1868, they received instructions from J. K. Chambers, the Chief of the 6th Division, at the "Head Quarters" of the Chester Conservative Clan. "By virtue of the authority in me vested," he began, "to organize a division in the vicinity of Rock Hill to be known as Division no. 13," the new den would elect four officers and recruit between twenty and fifty members. These numbers and their respective titles were prescribed by the larger group. The letter also included an oath that all members were required to take. The final paragraph included the phrase, "we do furthermore swear that we will render true and faithful obedience to the constituted authority of this organization and to the best of our abilities carry out and perform all orders emanating from said authorities." Chambers was perhaps ambitious, but not without good reason. Historian Allen Trelease has argued that, although state and national connections may have been more tenuous, countywide organization in South Carolina was perceptible; within each county, thousands of Ghouls faithfully reported to superiors up through the Grand Cyclops. A former member interviewed by the *New York Times* in 1871 confessed that "we were sworn to protect each other, and anything done against a member of the Klan would have been brought before the Grand Klan . . . the principle or head of the county—all subordinate Klans reported to the Grand Klan." These powerful leaders wielded tremendous influence throughout the upcountry. Among the most notable of South Carolina's high-ranking Klansmen was James W. Avery, a former major in the Confederate army and the chief of the York County Klan. Avery sent detailed instructions to his followers in order to ensure that their goals were met. In October 1868 he wrote to provide direction to the local dens, including issues as minor as their appearance: "It is impossible for all the members of any Klan to obtain Regalia, the Cyclops will have as many as possible." But Avery's policies were more than simply decorative. He ordered them to survey "all meetings or proposed meetings by negroes" and warned them that "no Klan or members of this organization . . . will undertake to redress grievances of a general character or act in any manner calculated to produce a breach of the peace without orders from these Hd Qrs." Avery's control may have been extraordinary, but York County became one of the most volatile regions of the state, and eventually one of the Klan's success stories. In fact John Hubbard, Chief Constable of South Carolina, later testified that by 1868, the Klan had "achieved a considerable degree of organization," in York and nine other upcountry counties. Without at least a small measure of organization and deliberate planning, the Klan would not have been able to begin the process of reclaiming South Carolina for its white citizens alone.[7]

The mission of the South Carolina Klan also helped keep individual Klansmen and local dens in line with the objectives of the wider group. As Major Avery wrote, "Whenever it may be necessary to act, let us do it deliberately, firmly, with concentrated power and strength, demoralizing our opponents by the overwhelming display of our strength and with an eye single to the good of our Cause and Country." The South Carolina Klan would follow this advice, and although its leaders eventually met exposure and prosecution, they were able to fulfill many of their goals. Historian Eric Foner has written that the Klan's overarching goals were to dismantle the Republican Party in the South, "undermine the Reconstruction state," control black laborers, and restore the racial hierarchy of the antebellum era. South Carolina's objectives were identical, but in facing a black majority, the imperative to silence the black voter and interrupt the work of the state legislature was perhaps even stronger. In fact the Klan first appeared in South Carolina following the passage of the new state constitution, written by a biracial convention. According to Richard Zuczek, their failure to defeat its ratification, and the obvious nature of their new minority status, led whites directly to Klan recruitment. The activities of the Klan in the Palmetto State therefore included interfering with elections by intimidating the black community and punishing Republicans of both races for their role in Reconstruction.

Among their main targets was the Union League. As the Klan itself stated, "we will do all in our power to counteract the *evil* influences exerted by a certain secret *Radical* organization known as the *Union League.*" "Whatever may have been its original intent . . . it has become a political organization whose purpose . . . is to put the democratic party up and the radical party down," wrote the joint congressional committee that investigated Klan atrocities in the South. However, such aims were shared by the Democratic clubs, which had already begun to respond to the advent of black male suffrage. Since South Carolina's Democratic clubs were not generally the province of the lowest classes, early Reconstruction historians claimed that the clubs were an outlet for the elite and the Klan for the uneducated masses. They also argued that the clubs were a less violent alternative, appealing to the more genteel members of society, but later prosecutions and more recent analyses would demonstrate that the Klan and the clubs often shared members and that "it was impossible to draw a distinct line between the Klan . . . and the Democratic clubs. . . . Their operations were remarkably similar." The Klan's operations, however, were to become more gruesome with each passing month as the organization fought to reverse the advances made by the freedmen.[8]

The Klan's threats and intimidation began in earnest during the election of 1868. Freedman Frank Talbert was stopped in the road in Abbeville County in late October by the Klan and made to swear that he would vote Democratic. Talbert also told the Freedmen's Bureau that he knew of several black men who were physically prevented from voting. A few days later, the Klan attacked Talbert, Henry Coke, and Spencer Coltrain as they slept in their home. Mason Parker, their neighbor, was forced to hide in the woods for over a month. Unfortunately such actions would seem innocuous compared to the violence that followed. Klansman Shaffer Bowens of York County confessed that the goal of his den was to destroy the Republicans by any means necessary. He described his first raid, during which the Klan killed a black man named Tom Roundtree. When Roundtree defended himself and shot one of his attackers, they brought him down with gunfire and slit his throat. They also smashed his skull with the butt of a gun, cut his body open, and "after thrusting into it ploughshares [the blade of a plow] for sinkers . . . threw it into a stream." When James H. Goss was interrogated by members of Congress, he was asked if the outrages he knew of were politically motivated. Goss responded that they were "all political." The success of black and Republican candidates at the polls in 1870 led to the second and more brutal phase of Klan violence. The renewed violence "dwarfed the terrorism of 1868." Klansmen left a note in Union demanding the resignation of the members of the legislature, the school commissioner, and the county commissioners: "and if they, *one and all,* do not *at once and forever resign* their present inhuman, disgraceful and outrageous rule, then retributive justice will as surely be used as night follows day." Such "justice" followed in abundance.[9]

The Klan, however, was not solely motivated by political change. George C. Rable wrote that the Klan was more than a "military adjunct" of the Democratic Party; it sought to reclaim white hegemony in the economic realm, in addition to addressing more specific local needs. J. C. A. Stagg has further argued that historians have relied too much on politics and demographics in their analyses of Klan growth. The South Carolina Klan was as anxious to reassert control over the black labor force as it was to destroy the Republicans: "There is a good deal of evidence to suggest that land tenure problems in the South Carolina up-country were instrumental in creating a situation in which relations between the two races deteriorated to such a degree that violence was either resorted to or condoned by all groups in white society as a method for settling their grievances." Both white landowners and their black employees were dissatisfied with the contract system, and both felt they were forced to concede too much to the other. In response the Klan rose to defend white economic power.[10]

The economy had been a sensitive subject and had inspired violence since emancipation; the Klan merely gave the violence a greater sense of order. Early on Democratic clubs combined the issues of the economy and politics by passing resolutions refusing to rent land to Republicans. Others stood at the polls and wrote down the names of freedmen who voted the radical ticket, "for the purpose of giving preference in the renting of land to Negro Democrats." The tactic worked in some areas, and a number of freedmen stayed away from the polls out of concern for their financial future. The Klan, however, went beyond the connection between politics and economics to enforce the will of the white landowner on the black laborer. Former bureau agent and local business owner Leander Bigger testified that, in his area, the Klan destroyed the property of people who rented land to blacks or made monetary advances to them to help them get on their feet. From the Klan's perspective, providing aid to the freedmen was the equivalent of injuring the white laborer and threatening the power of the white landowner. Some freedmen were attacked for refusing to work for whites. One freedwoman reported that when she declined an offer from Augustus Williams to work for his family, she was told, "you'll be Ku Kluxed for that." The Klan assaulted her shortly thereafter. The Klan was therefore not confined to the political realm but asserted its will on many aspects of southern society. It was, in fact, the social element of Klan activities that is perhaps the most interesting and least examined of their history.[11]

Historians have consistently viewed the revived Klan of the early twentieth century as a mass movement designed to arbitrate the social mores of World War

I–era America—a time of rising immigration and diversity—but the first Klan was as much a mediator of southern society as its later incarnation would be of the nation at large. Both groups defined the true American citizen narrowly, and both persecuted groups that could not or would not conform to that ideal. Both sought to limit the political and economic power of nonnative, non-Christian, nonwhite citizens, but these issues ultimately spoke to whites' fears of larger social changes. In the late nineteenth century, for example, the Klan fought the black voter and the black wage laborer, but the Klan also targeted the men and women who crossed the social or racial parameters established under slavery. As E. W. Seibels testified, "some negro burns a gin-house, or commits a rape; or some officer conducts himself in such a way that he becomes so perfectly odious and obnoxious to the community . . . then a parcel of dare-devil young men get together" to put them in their place. Their attacks were, ironically, an immoral response to a perceived violation of morality. For example the Klan threatened H. M. Turner, a white man from Spartanburg, with a whipping if he "continued to abuse his wife." Turner was a Republican, and it was possible his political affiliations drew the Klan's attention in the first place, but not all of the Klan's victims were Republicans. James Steadman of Unionville told the authorities that the Klan assaulted several white Democrats for beating their wives and "doing mischief in the community." Similarly James Steele of Rock Hill was whipped for getting drunk and beating his wife. These white men had breached the moral code of postwar South Carolina, but they had also provided the Klan with a reason to assert their vision for the state on its people. That vision was decidedly antebellum in tone. For that reason the freedmen remained the primary targets of the Klan's attempts to dictate South Carolina social customs.[12]

Black men whose actions deviated from the social order drew the Klan's special attention. A black fiddler named Willis Smith of Limestone played at a ball hosted on the land of the widow Smith. The Klan visited him because, although she had given permission for the ball, Mrs. Smith was white, and the fiddler and the guests were not. A black preacher named Isaac and his pregnant wife were beaten because they had said publicly that they "would raise [their] children as good and as nice as anybody's children." Statements and actions asserting freedmen's equality or rights brought the Klan down on the heads of the freedmen, but Klansmen were particularly violent when such violations of social and racial boundaries crossed the line into the realm of love and sex. In such cases not even race was a guarantee of safety. White South Carolinian Joseph Herndon stated that he had "heard of their visiting white men who were living in adultery with black women, and black men who were living with white women." Similarly, in Chester two white men were whipped for living in "open adultery" with a black woman. But in the end, the Klan reserved its worst punishments for blacks. A band of Klansmen killed a black man in York because he was living in adultery with two white women. Although the adultery was certainly a factor, it was a minor breach of social mores compared to his relationship with not one, but two white women. In one of the more gruesome events of 1869, Tilman Ward, a freedman from Unionville, was executed by the Klan because his stepdaughter gave birth to the child of a white landowner named Lemasters with whom she had been having an affair. Ward did not keep the child's origins a secret, and in response, the Klan beat the girl and murdered the stepfather. The congressional joint committee sent to investigate Klan abuses asked Joseph Gist, a witness to Ward's murder, "why does not your virtuous community down there indict this man [Lemasters] for adultery with a negro woman," if their intent was indeed to punish those who violated the moral standards of the community. Gist had no answer for the committee, and no action was ever taken against Lemasters.[13]

The Tilman Ward incident was also indicative of the most overlooked element of the Klan's reign of terror: the gendered nature of Klan abuses and the sexual undertones of racial violence. The Ku Klux Klan was not simply the result of social, political, and economic insecurities on the part of white southerners; it was a response to the diminished power of white manhood, the rise of black manhood, and the changes imposed on the ideals of womanhood by the experiences and actions of black and white women. Ward's stepdaughter had been having a sexual relationship with a white man, and Ward had the temerity not only to openly acknowledge that relationship but also to claim the child's white lineage. Antebellum sexual relationships between white men and black women were rarely for public consumption, and the offspring of those relationships were equally rarely acknowledged. In fact the children were commonly property, and the relationship to the father purely economic. The antebellum order stressed two essential white male prerogatives: access to black women's bodies and ownership of slave property. Ward and his stepdaughter had asserted a new order, one that publically cried out for Lamasters's accountability and connection to both the girl and her child. The Klan responded by punishing Ward and the girl, but in taking Ward's life, they tried to silence both his claim of a new order, and his right as a man to do so.

In order to reclaim their power, the Klan asserted the masculinity of white men figuratively as well as literally. For example the order often chose gendered language to convey their message. A common Klan warning read, "justice was lame, and she had to lean on us." By characterizing the state and its systems as feminine and therefore weak, Klansmen presented themselves as stalwart saviors, boosting their masculine self-image. The fourth principle of the Klan constitution, under "The Obligation," stated more directly, "Female friends, widows and their households shall ever be special objects of our regard and protection." By using such language, the Klan laid claim to not only racial dominance, but sexual as well, putting both blacks and women in a subordinate position to white men, and especially white Klansmen. Perhaps more disturbing, they often used highly sexualized forms of punishment, a sign they were at least subliminally aware of the gender insecurity that motivated them. Forty members of the Klan attacked Republican William Champion, a politically active white farmer from Limestone Township, one night in 1870 in order to give him a lesson in "nigger equality." After a prolonged beating, Champion was made to kiss the "posterior" and genitalia of a black acquaintance named Clem Bowden. He was then forced to do the same to Bowden's wife. Champion was whipped again when the Klansmen ordered him to rape Mrs. Bowden and he refused. The sexualized nature of the attack, which had been brought about by political differences, demonstrated that for the Klan, politics was intricately connected to the issue of sexuality and the struggle to reclaim and rebuild white southern manhood. However, since white manhood necessitated the suppression of black masculinity and the control of black womanhood, the assault on Champion and the Bowdens was designed as an exercise in the domination of black sexuality as well as a reminder to white men of where the Klan thought they existed within the hierarchy. The ritual was intended to shame Champion for his political activities and beliefs, but in trying to make him rape Mrs. Bowden, the Klan also asserted their idea of the acceptable order of things. White men were "entitled" to the bodies of black women. In addition Mr. Bowden's involuntary participation sent the equally powerful message that white men could dictate black men's sexual contacts as well. As brutal as this assault was, however, the Klan often went further. The goal of robbing black men of their masculinity occasionally went beyond mere metaphor. A black preacher named Lewis Thompson was murdered and his body thrown into the Tiger River because he had failed to heed the Klan's warnings against preaching about freedom and opportunity. His body remained in the river because local blacks were too intimidated to retrieve it for burial. The significance of Thompson's death, however, is that he was castrated before he was killed, physically and symbolically robbed of that which made him a man.[14]

Because sexuality played such an important role in the rise of the Ku Klux Klan, southern women were naturally central to their activities. South Carolina's women variously inspired the Klan's retributive justice, supported the efforts of husbands and sons, testified against husbands and sons, and were among the most victimized of their targets. Of the last, the most common were South Carolina's black women. As during slavery and the years immediately following the war, black women were easy targets for whites bent on reasserting their authority and punishing the freedmen. Black women were, in fact, often targeted for the actions of others rather than any "misbehavior" of their own. Freedman John Lipscomb was hiding in the woods near his home when the Klan came to his house one night. Because Lipscomb was unavailable, the Klansmen beat his wife as well as her sister, tied her hands, whipped her, and hit her in the head with the butt of a pistol. Andrew Cathcart of York had bought himself out of slavery in 1850. In 1871 the Klan came to his home, where they pistol-whipped his neighbor's wife before turning on him. As they left they stopped to tear down and burn his daughter's house, which also served as a school. When the Klan came for Elias Hill, a "crippled" freedman from Clay Hill in Yorkville, they beat him and then dragged his sister-in-law into the yard, forced her to carry Hill into the house, and beat her as she struggled with his nearly unconscious form. That night they also whipped J. P. Hill's wife and whipped and raped Julia Barron, wife of Miles Barron. The night Samuel Bonner of Limestone in Spartanburg County was kluxed for his radical politics, the Klansmen beat and whipped his "mammy" and sister as well. They returned two weeks later and assaulted the women again, "on principle . . . just for being a nigger." Jefferson Huskins was similarly attacked for being a radical. The Klan beat his entire family, including his wife and his nine-year-old daughter. By taking out their rage on the wives and daughters of the men for whom they had come looking, they punished the freedmen twice: with their own physical suffering and with the emotional and psychological wounds of watching their loved ones being victimized and not being able to stop it. The latter in particular was devastating for black men because it was reminiscent of their powerlessness and emasculation under slavery.[15]

Many black women were attacked not just for their indirect role in the Reconstruction saga, but also for their proactive participation in the freedmen's struggle for justice and equality. Samuel Poinier reported that a black woman was whipped by the Klan in Limestone Springs for helping the Republicans. Another freedwoman was beaten so badly she could not get up the next day. The Klan accused her of having talked about killing a Democrat and warned her that she should have "taught" her husband better than to be a radical. The Klan burned Lucy McMillan's house in Spartanburg to the ground because she had attended a political meeting. Fortunately McMillan escaped both the fire and the Klan. Politics, however, was not the only excuse the Klan used to victimize South Carolina's black women. The economy was nearly as dependent on the labor of black women as it was on that of black men: York County in 1870 suffered from a labor shortage many blamed on the refusal of black women to perform fieldwork. In defense of their economy and its control by white men, Klansmen resented black women's resistance. In turn freedwomen were frequently beaten for refusing to work for certain white families or in positions they did not want. Lucretia Adams of Yorkville claimed to have been kluxed for leaving her husband, who had taken up with another woman, but her husband argued that Lucretia was attacked because she refused to work for a local white family. Mrs. Adams undoubtedly sought a measure of revenge against her husband for leaving her, and she used the Klan's attack to bully him, but her estranged husband's account is more plausible. Mrs. Adams, however, was not wrong in claiming that the Klan also targeted black women for reasons more social than economic. Again, when Tilman Ward's stepdaughter bore a white child, the Klan beat her in addition to killing her stepfather. When the preacher named Isaac was attacked for announcing that he would raise his child to be as good as any white person, his pregnant wife was beaten as well. The issue at hand was control over the daily and personal activities of the freedwomen, and those who attempted to assert their new freedom of choice in the home, the workplace, and the polling place were punished for it. They did not, however, surrender in the face of Klan atrocities. For many it was a galvanizing rather than a repressive force.[16]

These women faced their attackers bravely, often attempting to defend their husbands or themselves, however vainly. In Union county in 1870, a black woman tried to fight off a band of Klansmen who had chased a freedman into her home. When Isham McCrary was assaulted, his wife ran to the door to confront the Klan. She attempted to volunteer to take the beating in order to save her husband—the Klan told him that they would whip him to death—but in her haste, she slipped and fell so hard she was lame for two weeks. The Klan mocked her efforts. Black women also defended their community by bearing witness to Klan atrocities. After Tom Roundtree was brutally murdered by Klansmen who shot him and slit his throat, his wife identified several of the fifty or sixty men who had committed the crime. She was soon driven from her home and forced to rely on the federal army for food and shelter. The Klan threatened John Lipscomb repeatedly, leaving notes on a tree outside his church, but it was Lipscomb's wife who badgered him to grab the notes and report the threats to the authorities. The wife of Wallace Fowler, a freedman in his seventies, confronted the Klansmen after they shot her husband in the doorway of his home in 1871. She later testified that she "raised up my right hand and said, 'Gentlemen, you have killed a poor innocent man.'" Black women often stood up to the Klan in spite of the fact that the authorities were commonly unresponsive. When Jane Surratt and her daughter were whipped together with her husband and son in a Klan assault in Spartanburg, she remained in her home after the attack even though her husband went into hiding. She also testified before the congressional committee and bravely identified her landlord as having said he was "a friend of Ku-Klucking" the day after her attack. Such bold stands reflected the strength of South Carolina's black women, but their actions were not always defensive. A number of freedwomen took a page from the Klan's book and resisted their reign of terror with acts of violence against their would-be oppressors.[17]

Neither centuries of being cowed by the system of slavery nor their sex precluded South Carolina's black women from seeking to wreak their own bloody vengeance on the white community. Most resorted to threats and driving their husbands and sons to commit the actual violence, but their encouragement was tantamount to participation. Alexander Wylie, a white man from Chester Village, bemoaned the fact that three black women he had known a long time turned to such rhetoric: "one of them has been treated most kindly throughout her life by an old aunt of mine; she raised the cry, 'Now is the time to burn.'" He was particularly dismayed by a young woman who, he said, "had been treated just as a white person," but who apparently stated that she would love to be in hell, "to have a churn-paddle, and churn the whites to all eternity." Wylie could not comprehend the deep resentment felt by the black community, and particularly black women, toward South Carolina's whites. But what was equally disturbing for Wylie and his contemporaries was that it was the women, not simply their husbands and sons, who were so eager for violence. Although never credited with the attributes of the truly feminine, black women had raised white men, fed and cared for them, and had been the objects of both love and lust for centuries. They may not have been able to lay claim to so-called "true womanhood," but neither were they often associated with the kind of violence particular to men. That they wanted to physically hurt the white community, after a long history of nurturing, was certainly a shift greater than many whites could anticipate or accept easily.[18]

It was, in many ways, truly absurd that white South Carolinians were surprised by the resentment of black women. The brutality slave women endured before the Civil War was unspeakable, and the violence heaped on them following the war was often as devastating. Whites should have expected such remarks as Wylie related because black women had long been common targets of their own rage and frustration. These remarks were also further evidence that racial violence in the postwar era was increasingly the realm of women and gender. The Klan's activities raised the number and frequency of black female victims, encouraged the desire for violent retribution by South Carolina's black women, and illustrated more profoundly than ever that racial violence was an attempt by the white men of the state to reassert their power and sexual dominance over the black community. Nowhere was this more evident than in their treatment of many black female targets. When the Klan visited Harriet Simril for the second of three times in 1871, they tore apart her home, ate her food, dragged her outside, and raped her repeatedly. Their first act was to desecrate her home, the domestic haven most black women tried to reclaim once free; their second was to desecrate her body. As a free woman, she was no longer the property of another man without the right to defend herself against sexual attacks. By denying her power over her own body, the Klan attempted to convince her—and themselves—that white masculinity was as strong as it had ever been, that she was still subject to the whims of the white male libido, and that she was therefore not entitled to claim the benefits of femininity and womanhood. Rape became a common method for conveying this message. Throughout the South, whites adopted it with greater frequency as time passed, but the Klan would find it difficult to lead the charge. In spite of—or perhaps because of—their success in reclaiming southern manhood at the expense of black South Carolinians, the Klan invited a third party into the racial and sexual dialogue of Reconstruction: the federal government.[19]

By the early 1870s, the Klan's behavior in South Carolina was so out of control that President Ulysses S. Grant finally chose to act. Unfortunately his first steps were tentative. In March 1871 Grant commanded the Klan to suspend its activities. The Klan's members, however, denied its existence, and Democratic newspapers argued that the violence was either exaggerated or outright lies told by Republicans. Whites pointed to a directive composed by Nathan Bedford Forrest, the organization's first Imperial Wizard, which ordered the Klan to disband in January 1869. This may have been the moment when any interstate organization ceased to exist, but the Klan certainly survived throughout the former Confederacy. One month after Grant's faint declaration, Congress strengthened his position by passing the Ku Klux Klan Act, also known as the third Enforcement Act. The first of the Enforcement Acts, passed in 1870, was intended to prop up the Fifteenth Amendment by imposing penalties ranging from fines to imprisonment for interfering with a citizen's right to vote. The act put such offenses under the jurisdiction of the federal government and authorized the president to use the army or navy to enforce it. The second Enforcement Act of February 1871 intensified these measures. The third, the Ku Klux Klan Act of 1871, listed a number of common Klan activities, such as forming conspiracies and traveling in disguise with the intent of hindering an individual's civil rights, and made them federal crimes. It also, by defining such actions as components of a rebellion, gave the president the power to suspend the writ of habeas corpus following a proclamation or warning that the "insurrection" would be addressed by force. The first arrests of suspected Klansmen began following the first Enforcement Act, but Klan activities continued unabated, and South Carolina's carpetbagger governor, Robert K. Scott, was reluctant to ask for greater assistance. To support their legislative efforts, however, Republicans in Congress called for a joint committee to investigate the problem of Klan violence, providing Grant the incentive and evidence he needed to move forward. The committee formed in April 1871 and sent a subcommittee to South Carolina in June and July. Throughout the summer over one hundred witnesses, both black and white, testified before the committee about Klan atrocities or in defense of the organization. In Spartanburg alone so many witnesses came forward that the committee's planned three-day stay was extended to eleven. Thousands of pages of evidence were compiled into a report completed and submitted to Congress in February 1872, but Grant finally acted before the document was finished. On October 12, 1871, the president proclaimed the existence of a conspiracy in South Carolina and commanded the Klan's disbandment. Five days later he suspended the writ of habeas corpus in nine upcountry counties. On October 19 the government began mass arrests of suspected Klansmen and their supporters. By the end of the process, over thirteen hundred indictments had been issued, and the Klan in South Carolina was destroyed.[20]

The trials, however, did not move forward as smoothly or as successfully as their proponents hoped. Major Lewis M. Merrill was the officer in command of the troops sent into South Carolina in the early 1870s. As the commander of the post at Yorkville, he witnessed numerous crimes against the freedmen and struggled to sort through the wreckage after Klan raids. He despised the Klan and devoted himself to its eradication, pushing for federal intervention and overseeing hundreds of arrests once given the authority. Merrill supported the work of D. T. Corbin, the United States attorney for South Carolina, who was in charge of the prosecutions. Corbin would share this responsibility with Daniel H. Chamberlain, the South Carolina attorney general and future governor of the state. The men responsible for the defense were Reverdy Johnson and Henry Stanbery, both former attorneys general of the U.S. Henry Stanbery had also been involved in the defense of Andrew Johnson during his impeachment ordeal, and Reverdy Johnson had participated in the landmark Dred Scott case. Altogether the men involved were highly qualified, but the extent of the Klan's reach and its violent history presented obstacles that even the most well-intentioned officials could not overcome. First, in 1871 alone over two thousand Klansmen fled South Carolina, leaving plenty of guilty men, but often allowing the worst offenders to successfully evade prosecution and imprisonment. Second, many of the most awful Klan atrocities were committed before the Ku Klux Klan Act of April 1871, and it was not retroactive. Third, the federal government failed to understand that southerners were fighting for principles beyond political power; they were struggling to salvage their social and economic futures as well as pursue the unspoken war on black masculinity. As a result their commitment was difficult to break through mere legal actions: "Republicans—at the state and federal levels—dealt in bluff, while conservatives dealt in blood." Finally, the sheer number of suspects and indicted persons overwhelmed the relatively unsophisticated mechanism put into place to prosecute the cases. In the end over one thousand cases never made it to court. The trials began in November 1871, but ultimately the government was forced to focus on only the most extreme cases and egregiously guilty men because they were the most straightforward cases to prosecute. Although they secured a number of notable convictions, the vast majority of Klansmen at all levels of the organization escaped punishment. In addition those Klansmen who had fled the state to evade prosecution were allowed to return without fear of arrest in 1873, and many of those convicted and imprisoned were released by the 1880s.[21]

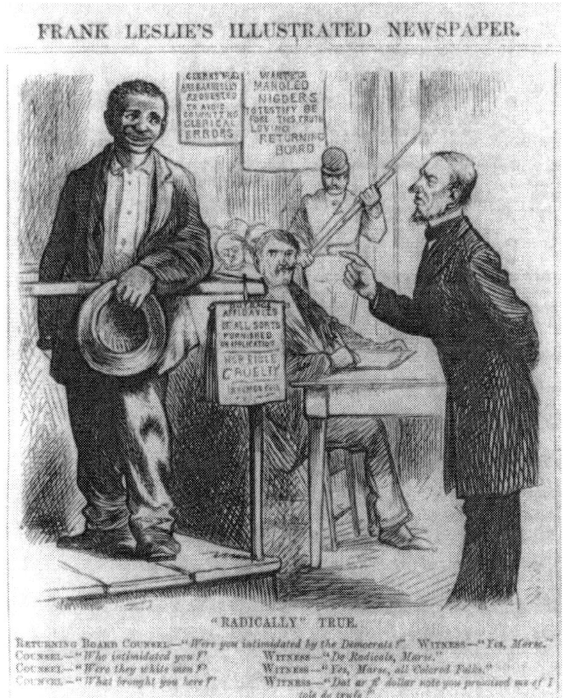

"'Radically' True." The conservative press insisted that reports of outrages were fabricated. Here a freedman testifies before the Klan Hearings, with a sign behind him that reads, "Wanted: Mangled Niggers." From the Library of Congress, Prints and Photographs Division.

Such evidence might imply that the South Carolina Klan trials were a failure, and some historians have indeed made that argument. Richard Zuczek claims that the trials were a weak exercise, that Klan violence was on the wane before the prosecutions began, and that the federal government was not truly committed to the process. Eric Foner is more generous. He grants that the prosecutors were unable to punish most of those responsible for Klan violence and that racial violence in South Carolina would continue to be an effective tool of the white community, but he argues that the trials restored the confidence of South Carolina's Republicans and encouraged blacks to continue to assert their rights for the time being. Alternatively Lou Falkner Williams claims that despite the federal government's eventual retreat from such defenses of the freedmen and their rights, the trials succeeded in dismantling the Klan in South Carolina. Allen Trelease adds that, "if the history of the Ku Klux Klan begins at Pulaski, Tennessee, it ends most fittingly at Yorkville, South Carolina." Yorkville was the site of some of the Klan's greatest acts of terror and violence, the southern county more overwhelmed by Klan activity than any other, and one of the two primary targets of the federal prosecutions in the state. Ultimately the Klan's reign of terror in South Carolina ended, and the trials of suspected Klansmen, although thwarted at almost every turn, contributed directly to its demise.[22]

Lou Falkner Williams makes a deeply gendered argument in her analysis of the Klan trials when she contends that while the first goal of the trials was to prosecute Klan abuses, the trials were also intended to "bring women and children under the protection of the Federal government." Washington, she contends, entered the struggle to command authority over southern women—an ironic step for an institution seeking to prevent the Klan from doing just that. Williams focuses on those black women who were victims of the Klan's abuses, stating that although the Enforcement Acts confined the government to voting rights and other political issues—from which women were excluded—the government tried to move beyond the simple political framework by zealously indicting South Carolinians suspected of a variety of crimes. Most of these efforts lost ground because the earliest presiding judge recognized that the federal government did not have the legal right to prosecute crimes not related to voting, and the defense continued to make strong arguments to that effect, but Williams is right in placing the Klan trials squarely in the South's gendered dialogue. Williams accurately demonstrates the victimization of women by the Klan, but in the end, neither the black women nor the white women of South Carolina were merely passive victims or bystanders of Klan violence.[23]

South Carolina's white women were involved in the rise of the Ku Klux Klan from the beginning. As always, white women served as an excuse for violence, and the Klan never failed to call on the defense of white womanhood as a motivating force and excuse for their most brutal assaults. Again, the Klan's constitution listed it as a primary reason for its formation, indicating members' desire to both restore white manhood and resurrect more traditional notions of white womanhood. But white women were more than a fixed background against which the turmoil of Reconstruction played itself out. Women aided and abetted Klan violence, and although many of their activities seemed quaintly domestic in tone, the brutality of the organization they were supporting could not have gone unnoticed by them. In addition their actions took them beyond the womanly ideals embraced by the Klan, once again stretching the boundaries of womanhood despite the organization's intentions.

One of the first tasks of the good upcountry South Carolina housewife was to clothe her husband and sons. For the Klan's women, this extended to the ceremonial dress of its members. One Klansman from South Carolina described the diverse and often intricate designs worn by men in South Carolina as well as in his own den to a newspaper reporter from New York: "The masks, as a general thing, were not all alike; in some places the mask covered the whole body, but in our section we had masks made of red flannel which covered the head and neck. Horns were made of this flannel, stuffed with cotton; pieces of white cloth was sewed about the eyes to make it look horrid at night. Cow tails, horse tails and the like, were fastened to the mask, and sometimes the horns were trimmed with ribbons; anything that would make us look ugly was added to the masks." These outfits were the responsibility of white women throughout the state. Christina Page, a black woman from Union, told the congressional subcommittee that her employer, Mrs. Brock, made Klan outfits, which she called "dominoes." Ironically, and perhaps cruelly, Brock instructed Page to assist her on more than one occasion. Most white women denied such activities, and some, like Miss Laura Gowan, who made her own appearance before the subcommittee, claimed to have been sewing "costumes" for local balls. In fact "costume balls" became code for Klan raids. Once the danger of prosecution had passed, however, few women denied their role. Susan L. Davis, the author of *Authentic History: The Ku Klux Klan,* published in 1924, dedicated the book to "My Mother, Sarah Ann (McClellan) Davis, and the Other Southern Women Who Designed and Manufactured with Their Own Fingers the Regalia for the Ku Klux Klansmen and the Trappings for Their Horses." Clothing the Klansmen of the South was no small task but a significant contribution to the violent rituals of the day. This role was evidently so important to the white community that Davis was eager to celebrate it in her dedication. White women therefore took pride in assisting the work of the Klan because, after all, it was often done on their behalf.[24]

The women of the first Klan also continued to hold down the home front in the absence of husbands and sons. This became particularly important once the third Enforcement Act was passed and the mass arrests began. The resultant community of women had run and protected their homes during the war and on those occasions when the racial violence of the early Reconstruction era left them to their own devices, but the Klan trials presented new challenges. In particularly violent counties like York and Spartanburg, hundreds of arrests threatened not just short-term absences but also the possibility of lengthy prison terms for a large percentage of the region. These families would also now bear the emotional burden and cost of a prolonged legal fight. Both were commonly alleviated by the support of fellow South Carolinians, but the overall ordeal was draining and often debilitating nonetheless. For many of the women who subsequently ran these households, supporting the Klan came with new sacrifices that they were willing and even eager to make to endorse the agenda of white—and ironically male—supremacy.

One of the most infamous families to come under scrutiny during the South Carolina Klan trials was the Bratton family of York County, and Harriet J. Rainey Bratton's career is an excellent example of the roles white women played as the Klan deteriorated. John S. Bratton and J. Rufus Bratton were elite members of South Carolina society. Both had attended South Carolina College, pursued medicine, and served in the Confederacy. Rufus was a respected local doctor, and John focused on his plantation and the family he built with Harriet. Following the war, John Bratton reluctantly adjusted to the new labor system, dividing his crop among his employees fairly as early as 1865, and in 1870 he incorporated the Columbia Oil Company, indicating his personal recovery from the economic struggles of the postwar era. The Brattons' acceptance of the new status quo, however, did not linger. When the Klan arrived in South Carolina, both became local leaders, and Rufus in particular was responsible for a number of devastating raids and abuses.

The most notorious of the Brattons' activities was the murder of Jim Williams, a local black militia leader. Williams was a former slave of John Bratton's, and white rumormongers claimed he had been making threats to "kill from the cradle up." The white community, fearful of the black militia regardless of the language of its leadership, sought redress. The Klan was also interested in the weapons Williams and his unit had been stockpiling and refused to relinquish. As one carpetbagger later wrote, "Whether Captain Williams made that threat or not, he certainly did refuse . . . 'to disband his company or give up their guns.'" The last of Williams's suspected crimes was the most haunting for

Yorkville whites. William K. Owens later informed the congressional subcommittee that Rufus McLain had told him that Williams announced "what he would do to white girls if he had the power to do it." Again, it is entirely plausible that Williams never made the remark, but the fact that white men believed that a black man threatened the virtue of their women was the perfect incentive for Klan violence. This was one of the guiding principles of the Klan: to reassert white manhood in the face of black empowerment, particularly in defense of white women. To ignore this comment, however suspect, would be to hand their masculinity back over to the freedmen. Therefore, on March 6, 1871, at least forty mounted men attacked Williams's home, marched him to the woods near his house over the pleas of his wife, hanged him from a tree, and riddled his body with bullets. As a last indignity, the Klansmen hung a note from his chest that read, "Capt. Jim Williams on his big muster." Rufus Bratton himself was said to have placed the noose around his neck, and perversely, the coroner brought the body to Dr. Bratton's office for the inquest.[25]

Williams's murder did not go unnoticed by local blacks, but justice was less than swift. The dead man's militia company swarmed the area promising retribution, but another Klan leader, Major J. W. Avery, arrived with men and weapons to counter the threat. The case remained unresolved for several months although it was common knowledge that the Klan and the Brattons were responsible. Their galling lack of remorse was evident when Rufus, mere weeks after the murder, acted as the secretary at two public meetings for local blacks, few of whom attended, to determine how best to address the rising violence. A week later both Brattons were present at a meeting for local whites that declared, "without intending to justify the acts of violence which have been committed in this county, it is proper to set forth the fact that the Negro radical government of this State is responsible for all the evils that are upon us," and that "we earnestly express the hope that peaceful relations between the races may be reestablished; that there will be no further violence; and we respectfully invoke all law-abiding men to cooperate with us in the attainment of these end." The first hint that Williams might receive justice came when the congressional subcommittee arrived in York in July. Rufus Bratton and his brother stayed in town and testified. The recent murders were a main topic for discussion, and Dr. Bratton denied involvement to the last. He even denied the existence of the Klan but stated that "this Ku-Klux business is certainly a terrible remedy; but if the motive be to keep down dishonesty and rascality, and place honest and virtuous men in power . . . we all ought to sanction it." Seeing that arrest and prosecution were imminent, the Brattons fled the area in October, Rufus going as far as London, Ontario.

Their flight, however, left John's wife, Harriet, the unofficial head of the family, responsible for not only supporting it in a time of crisis but also for leading the defense of her husband and his brother in their absence.[26]

Like many of South Carolina's Klan wives, Harriet Bratton confronted unfriendly circumstances largely alone. In November 1871 the very first Klansman to come to trial was Robert Hayes Mitchell, a white Yorkville man who was, together with the Brattons and several other men, indicted for creating a conspiracy to deny Jim Williams his constitutional right to vote. Mitchell was convicted of the conspiracy, but not for the overt act that brought the case to the forefront of the trials—the murder. He was sentenced to imprisonment and shipped off to jail, and his conviction sent a cold shiver through the white community, particularly those homes with absent members. Harriet Bratton, although remarkably strong, was no exception. At the beginning of his exile, John Bratton hid in Memphis, Tennessee, at the home of Colonel Hiram Tilman. To prevent detection and throw off the authorities, C. D. Melton, the family's lawyer and friend, forwarded Bratton's copy of the local paper to Baltimore. Harriet, desperate to see her husband, made inquiries through Melton as to the danger of visiting Memphis. She was justifiably ill at ease: the prosecutions were proceeding apace, her household was in disarray, and she was spending yet another Christmas away from her husband. Bratton had also sent the clear message to his wife that the situation was perilous, which undoubtedly kept her unsettled. Earlier in 1871 he had written to her to instruct her to use a code in case their periodic telegrams were intercepted. He explained, "If you want me to come home immediately in case of sickness or death, write 3.8.9 circled. If I want you in case of sickness I will write the same way 3.8.9M circled. The M will stand for Memphis or A for Augusta. . . . If you want me to be secluded + guarded, write this way 9 circled + if you are certain they are in pursuit of me write 9.9 circled." Figures and explanations followed to designate sickness of varying degrees and the different children and relatives in question. Such correspondence must have reminded her that his future and that of her entire family was totally uncertain.[27]

Harriet Bratton's first problem was financial. To alleviate some of the burden of managing her home alone, Harriet brought her daughter Julia home from boarding school in Virginia. Julia, however, was withdrawn also because Mrs. Bratton was struggling to make ends meet. The headmaster of the Virginia Female Institute in Staunton wrote to apologize: "The bills had gone home to you before we heard Miss Julia was to be withdrawn. I will see the bookkeeper tomorrow and send you a corrected statement. . . . We are greatly moved by the Infamous proceedings of the Govt + beg to assure you of our deep sympathy with the people of your state, particularly your own household." It must have been deeply humiliating for a woman like Mrs. Bratton to bring her daughter home under such circumstances. Unfortunately she also faced greater economic threat from Jim Williams's wife Rose, who was in a position to file a lawsuit for damages. "Rose not being his legal wife, but radical judges override Constitutions, laws and all established precedents," a friend wrote to John Bratton. Finally, Harriet confronted a problem involving her husband's brother Robert, to whom he owed money. Harriet needed to preserve the integrity of the plantation in the face of Rose's suit and Robert's threats, and although Robert agreed to set aside their differences temporarily, John Bratton was advised by a friend to transfer title of the land to his wife, protecting it against suits filed against him and making her the official family breadwinner. Such was the fate of the wife of a Klansman: facing ruin and suddenly independent of her husband, physically and economically.[28]

Finally, like many Klan wives, Harriet Bratton was at the forefront of the quest to bring her husband home safely. S. P. Hamilton, an attorney in Chester who had defended another of the men indicted for the Jim Williams murder, was solicited by Bratton's allies to draw up a petition for his pardon. Rather than respond to the applicants, he turned to Harriet Bratton. He informed her that the president would not consider the pardon of a man who had not yet been convicted, but he added that the evidence of which he was aware was not enough to build a sufficient case against her husband: "if the only thing they have against Mr. Bratton is what has come out in the trial there is no reason in my opinion why he shall not return." However, Hamilton cautioned her, "if he knows of anything else to connect him with the Ku Klux Organization or any raids upon any negros . . . then I advise him not to come home." Needless to say, Bratton chose not to return, and Mrs. Bratton pursued the pardon. A petition was submitted to the president on her behalf on June 10, 1873, and in the week that followed, Bratton came home to be with his wife, who had fallen ill. T. J. Robertson handed the last petition to the attorney general eighteen days later, and while they waited for a response, he advised Bratton to "remain peaceably at home with his afflicted wife." By July 3 Corbin had agreed not to prosecute him. The news was indeed a relief to a woman who had endured family crises, legal struggles, and personal suffering because of her husband's involvement with the Klan. In spite of her troubles, however, she stood by his actions and affiliations. Her personal papers were uncritical of Klan activities, and in supporting her husband she endorsed its racist and violent agenda.[29]

The white women of South Carolina followed Harriet Bratton's example from the home and into the public spectacle of the Klan trials. When minister John A. Leland was arrested in March 1871 for conspiracy and murder, the women of Laurens, Columbia, and Charleston rallied around him and his fellow inmates.

In an article that appeared in the *Southern Presbyterian* and a book called *A Voice from South Carolina,* Leland chronicled the key role white women played in the Klan trials of the 1870s. Leland was arrested for his participation in the Laurens riot of October 1870, in which several people were killed, including Wade Perrin, a black member of the state legislature. Leland later wrote of the riot, "the severe lesson taught our colored fellow-citizens on the 20th of October, 1870, had proved most salutary. They then found out . . . there was a limit beyond which they could only go at the peril of their lives; past that limit, and he [the white man] would not only resist, but he would kill." He believed that the Klan was a response to immorality and not its embodiment. For this reason, he had little sympathy for the victims of racial violence. South Carolina's women embraced Leland's plight wholeheartedly. The prisoners were first brought to Columbia. The ladies of the town, including Leland's own stepmother, Mrs. Clara Leland, and his sister, Mrs. N. W. Edwards, rallied to their aid. From the beginning, the women dove into their work, preparing supplies for the imprisoned, financing bail, supporting the families of the "victims," and collecting contributions to sustain their efforts. When the men suffered from illness, "the ladies were about the first to 'minister to us,' and soon saw to it that our back-rations should be abundantly supplied." Leland referred to these women as "Mothers in Israel," and once it was determined that the men would be held indefinitely, the women organized their efforts systematically: "some would collect contributions . . . others would purchase and see to the preparation of the supplies, and a third party would see to their safe delivery. . . . Mrs. Dr. John B. Adger was the indefatigable supervisor and treasurer. . . . Mrs. Dr. Woodrow was the most constant of all our lady visitors." This material support was invaluable to the men and their families. But the work of these women fell into the realm of the emotional as well. As they had so often before, southern women demonstrated enormous fortitude in the face of hardship. Their grit fed the prisoners: "that *Mother's* arm around my neck, and that warm Mother's kiss, meant more than all she could have said, and I went in the strength thereof for forty days at least."[30]

White women often went further to demonstrate their support for the accused Klansmen. Such public displays were remarkable given the nature of southern womanhood and the stigma public activism would have brought in the past. When Leland and his friends were informed that they were to be moved to Charleston for trial, they were given the opportunity to attend church services before their exodus. Leland later waxed rhapsodic about the scene, but what is significant is the women's actions: "When the communicants were invited forward, I hastened to reach the very seat my sainted mother had occupied on such occasions for more than a generation. But when I saw her life-long friends, Mrs.

Peck, Mrs. McFie, and Mrs. Howe, come forward and take the seats nearest me on the right, on the left, and immediately in front, my heart swelled; and for the first time since my arrest, my eyes began to overflow." Defiance of the evil northern horde undoubtedly earned these women the respect of their neighbors, but such public declarations of their association—or at least sympathy—with the Klan once again stretched the limits of southern womanhood beyond its old constraints. In Charleston it was "not as fashionable here for ladies to visit the jail, as it was in Columbia," but white women found alternative ways to support the prisoners. In some cases the methods of the Charleston women went further than those of the Columbia ladies. Perhaps it was appropriate; they were endorsing the violence of the Klan, so why not embrace violent acts of their own? Leland and the others processed through Charleston under guard. This humiliating spectacle raised the hackles of a number of women: "Miss Gussie took her stand at the window in our room, to see the processional pass out of the gate. As the leaders first appeared . . . she swayed herself backwards . . . and bringing both clenched fists down on the window-sills with all her force, and as though there were no bones in them, she *hissed* out, 'Oh, that I could smite you all to the centre of the earth!'" Others were more aggressive. As the men marched to the courthouse to post bail, several women walked with them. Local blacks watched the procession, many of them encouraged by the sight of federal justice in action. The women, however, were less appreciative: "Mrs. Chapin was noticed to stoop down and pick up a rough looking brick-bat. Upon being asked what she intended to do with it, her reply was loud enough to be heard by the parties threatened; 'Just let one of those darkies on the opposite side of the street dare to hoot at these gentlemen, and I *will* show you what I will do!' We at once promoted her to the chief command, among our lady champions. . . . " Klan violence, regardless of its motivation, seemed to have inspired many southern women to embrace not merely the agenda of the Klan but its practices as well.[31]

Similarly many white women took their anger toward the freedmen's northern allies out in less than genteel ways. White teachers in freedmen's schools were favorite targets. Snubbed by white society, they were treated to worse by the Klan's "ladies auxiliary," who chose such expressive phrases as "damned Yankee bitch of a nigger teacher" to address their visitors. One such teacher reinforced their poor opinion of her when she married D. T. Corbin, the U.S. attorney who prosecuted the Klan. But the wives of northern officials received no better. Louis Post, an attorney sent south to assist Corbin in the Klan trials, brought his wife to South Carolina. Local women so despised her that they refused to go near her. As she walked down the stairs of their hotel, the women of Columbia clung to the walls to make sure that their clothing never brushed against hers. On another evening a woman from Baltimore fainted, and when Mrs. Post went to assist the woman who had rushed to help, the latter stood up and walked from the room, leaving the unconscious woman helpless on the floor, rather than work near or with Mrs. Post. Such displays were perhaps less violent than those of their Klan husbands and sons, but they were designed to punish and were, relative to the scope of their gender and experience, no less aggressive.[32]

These developments, however, violated the Klan's purpose from the beginning, and some women paid a price for it. The Ku Klux Klan taught many white southern women to relish violence against their enemies and, in some cases, perpetrate it. Yet, at the same time, the Klan had sought to reinforce its own limited definition of womanhood, which certainly did not entail women's adoption of traditionally male behavior. The Klan stated from the outset that white women were the "special objects of our regard and protection"; South Carolina's women were weak, inferior, and in need of the Klan's services. Empowered white women did not fit that image. Black women were not deserving of this protection, but they shared something important with white women: the Klan's desire to dominate them socially, economically, and sexually. The Klan was therefore never simply about enforcing white power and "superiority"; it was always also a tool of men for the subjugation of women. Because of this, white women became the targets of the Klan when they violated its ideals of southern womanhood. The most commonly abused were those white women who breeched sexual boundaries. Women of "ill repute," for example, often received visits from the Klan. In June 1871 a woman in Sumter County was tarred and feathered by local Klansmen for keeping "a low house." In York the Klan descended "upon a disreputable house maintained by white women whose naked bodies were daubed with tar by the raiders and the women driven from the neighborhood." White women in relationships with black men were particularly abhorrent to the Klan, as were the products of any interracial union. Such liaisons sent the message that southern white men had failed on the battlefield, in the statehouse, and in the bedroom. For example Alexander P. Wylie told the congressional subcommittee that in Chester, a white woman was attacked for living with a black man. Furthermore Eric Foner has argued that "those most certain to suffer abuse were interracial couples in which the male was black," indicating that violations of the racial and sexual order by white women were more abhorrent than those of white men who both determined these rules and had been engaging in such behavior throughout slavery. Even white women who sympathized with black victims of the Klan became its victims. Mrs. Skates of York (whose story was described in the introduction) was attacked because she tried to protect three black men from the Klan. She was abused because her choice of alliances implied more than mere sympathy: white women were not allowed to form friendships with black men because it threatened white masculinity and sexual dominance. The Klan claimed to be the salvation of South Carolina's white population, but its purpose was equally to preserve the hegemony of white men.[33]

Overall the Klan changed South Carolina, but its effects on women and gender roles were as startling as those on the political and economic realms. In the nineteenth century, the Klan was an all-male organization designed to promote the reversal of Reconstruction legislation and the resurrection of southern white manhood. Women and gender were instrumental to its organization, motivation, successes, and failures. The Klan targeted black men for asserting their civil rights, but they were attacked as often for reclaiming the rights of manhood and trying to restore black masculinity. Black women became victims of the Klan indirectly and directly. Black women were targets when the Klan's intended victims fled—a symbolic blow to the black household, black manhood, and their own claims to womanhood. But they were also as defiant as their men, stubbornly demanding the privileges of citizenship for their husbands, their sons, and even themselves. In so doing they rewrote racial and gender roles for southern society, a task previously reserved for whites, and particularly, white men. For this presumptive behavior, they were beaten, raped, and murdered. Finally, white women ran the gamut from the Klan's staunchest allies to its most pitiful casualties. South Carolina's white women sewed, wept, cheered, scourged, and suffered to forward the Klan's agenda. They were first used as an excuse for violence, but in the end, they too embraced it as an appropriate response to the changes brought about by the Civil War and Reconstruction. Because they were women and therefore subordinate, however, white women were also among the Klan's victims. When they broke the codes of race and sex, Klansmen were anxious to punish white women and remind them that these codes were inviolate under their watch. But white women's activities—for or against the Klan—ultimately breeched the traditional female role the Klan was trying to enforce. Like black women, white women rewrote the rules, whether they intended to or not. These events reinforced and advanced the connection between racial violence, women, and gender. As they did, each of the three was transformed by the process. In the end the federal prosecutions destroyed the Ku Klux Klan in South Carolina, but its legacy endured. It was the first coordinated effort by white southern men to press their agenda through violence since the Civil War. By the mid-1870s white South Carolinians would embrace their example and its lessons and lead the state into its "redemption."

4.

Sin and Redemption

The Election of 1876

On November 7, 1876, Mary Gayle Aiken wrote in her journal, "Election Day[,] mostly bright and cold." A day later she commented, "cold[,] good news of the election[,] party at Miss Harper." By the fifteenth she was—for Mary—nearly buoyant: "still cloudy[,] Hampton certainly elected." Mary Aiken devoted most of her remarkably brief entries to the weather and local social events, but like most South Carolinians in 1876, the eleven-year-old was preoccupied with the election of that year. For South Carolina the election of 1876 represented a turning point. Politically, whites looked forward to a future free of "radical" Republican rule. Economically, they sought to deprive blacks and "carpetbaggers" of their gains and what they perceived as the wasteful corruption of an illegitimate government. Socially, however, South Carolinians had the most at stake. On the outcome of the election of 1876 hinged not just the racial order, but also the last important battle in the war for white manhood.[1]

Politics continued to be an avenue through which southern men asserted their sense of honor and masculinity, but one that took on even greater importance after the interference of the federal government during the Klan trials of the early 1870s. Strictly speaking, violence alone had not reversed the order prescribed by the Reconstruction government. The violence had, in fact, provoked the ire of northern Republicans, brought a renewed occupation of the state, and landed a number of leading white citizens in jail. White South Carolinians, however, learned a valuable lesson from the experience. The key to their salvation was political control of the state. Violence with a social and political agenda was a temporary salve; an expression of rage rather than an active solution to the "problem." Politics and social renewal reinforced by selective violence, however, might get the job done.

At the heart of this process was the continued need of South Carolina's white men to recapture their ability to define gender roles for both white and black citizens. Their gender insecurity had not been assuaged by the Klan. Black men continued to vote and work independently; together with their wives, they asserted their right to protect themselves and their children from white encroachments. Through the election of 1876, white men began to win back their antebellum privileges. Ironically, however, the election also gave voice to the nascent politicization of white women and the continued political growth of their black counterparts. These unintended consequences illustrate the gendered nature of this election: women participated in unprecedented numbers and in a variety of ways. The terms of their femininity—as well as the meaning of masculinity for both races—were rewritten once again in the process. In addition, throughout the election its participants used overt and symbolic references to the deeply sensitive nature of their battle. The 1876 election in South Carolina was never simply an issue of political power, but a struggle to assert a more complex racial and sexual hierarchy.

The roots of the election of 1876 grew from the seeds of the 1874 contest. A reputation for corruption overshadowed the state Republican Party by the mid-1870s, alienating many of its more conservative members and further enraging native whites. White Democrats had chosen to remove themselves from state politics in 1872, assuming that nonparticipation would highlight the illegitimate nature of Republican rule as they saw it and drive a wedge between feuding factions of the Republican Party. The strategy had failed, and they were now confronted with continued Republican control and legislation that failed to meet their needs. In response white Democrats began to listen more closely to the cries of conservative Martin W. Gary, a Confederate veteran and leading citizen of the state. Gary proposed importing whites from western European nations, specifically Germany, until they outnumbered the black population throughout the state and could vote a straight Democratic ticket into office. Gary also proposed a return to violent methods, and it was this half of his plan that received widespread support. Former Klansmen and Bushwackers reunited under the flags of rifle, gun, and saber clubs, participating in a number of social functions to camouflage their true purpose. Since the federal government had been preoccupied with vigilantes in costume during the Klan troubles, they were confident—with good reason—that their current activities would go relatively unnoticed. The state government, however, did notice, and the general assembly issued a call for a state militia in the spring of 1874. Blacks responded in droves, and, as before, most whites stayed far away, preferring extralegal methods.[2]

The result was a resurgence of violence throughout the state, including the famous "Ned Tennant riots" in Edgefield, and the nomination of Republican Daniel Chamberlain. Chamberlain represented the interests of Republicans eager for reform. Ironically Chamberlain had a reputation for misdeeds committed during his tenure as the state's attorney general, but he had since rejected graft, as well as his radical abolitionist past, in favor of compromise. He and his supporters hoped his candidacy and promises of an end to corruption in government would win the hearts of white voters. His nomination, however, split the Republicans, and the bolters—calling themselves Independents—chose John T. Green, a native South Carolinian, as their candidate. Green's running mate was Martin Delany, a black man whose presence on the ticket was balanced by the appeal of a conservative—albeit Republican—white southerner as governor.[3]

Despite the fact that they did not field a candidate, the election of 1874 signified the return of both white Democrats and violence to the center of the state's political process, setting the stage for the state's redemption two years later. Abandoning the abstinence policy of 1872, white Democrats—members of the Conservative Party in the absence of a statewide Democratic organization—voted for Green as the lesser of two evils. Polling places exploded on November 4, 1874, as each side claimed to struggle for the soul of South Carolina. It was "as bloody an election as South Carolina had seen," and although Chamberlain won by a healthy margin, the Democrats were reenergized by the experience. Throughout the nation Democratic candidates took seats in state legislatures, governors' offices, and Congress. South Carolina remained in the hands of Republicans, but the opposition party began to rebuild under the leadership of men like Martin Gary. Sadly, Chamberlain found it hard to live up to his campaign promises of good government. He tried to remove reputedly corrupt officials and thwart their supporters in the legislature. His efforts, however, won him only enemies within his own party. Whether Chamberlain was corrupt, or whether they were wary of his courtship of native conservatives, or resentful of cuts he made to programs favored by blacks, many Republicans came to mistrust him. In addition the majority of whites remained relatively unimpressed and unmoved. By the eve of 1876, many had determined that cooperation was out of the question. The remainder would follow along shortly.[4]

The Democratic meteor, once ignited, ascended the skies above the Palmetto State and glowed with relentless rage. In the months before the election, a few outspoken white men pushed loud and hard for a home-grown, Democratic candidate, one whose worldview would not have embraced a black running mate. Led by Gary, they rejected compromise with the Republicans, even the reformer Chamberlain. This faction was not immediately successful in convincing Democrats at large, but events in 1875 and early 1876 bolstered their plan. In the Mississippi election of 1875, a racially based "People's Party" overturned the Reconstruction government using a variety of extralegal methods, the favorite of which was violence. Their example convinced Gary and many others that a "straight out" Democratic ticket could win in a state with a high percentage of black voters. Back in South Carolina, the nomination of two Republican candidates, whom whites considered particularly odious, to the state's judiciary branch illustrated the helplessness of Governor Chamberlain and the futility of compromise. Franklin Moses Jr.—a former governor known for a weak and allegedly corrupt administration—and William J. Whipper—a black northerner—would not have been the choice of the white population. But neither were they the choice of the current governor, who refused to approve their appointments. Although some conservatives applauded Chamberlain's strong stance, the nominations outraged whites and convinced them fully of Chamberlain's weakness, dooming Chamberlain's plan to draw moderates to his camp. Many whites determined not to give ground to a party dominated by radical and black members because they were convinced that the nominees were designed to, as the *Charleston News and Courier* editorialized, "Africanize South Carolina." These two events sent white South Carolinians to the revitalized Democratic Party in droves. Local chapters began to spring up throughout the state with the kind of energy and determination not seen since the secession crisis. This rapid growth, however, was not haphazard. South Carolina Democrats organized within and between townships and counties. They marshaled their forces and declared war on Reconstruction. Their armies were led by a gentleman of the "Old South"; however, the campaign was often driven by the women of the new, and fueled by the gendered rhetoric characteristic of a struggle for racial and sexual hegemony.[5]

The candidates in the election of 1876 were truly symbolic of the mood of the state. The Democrat's nominee was Wade Hampton III, a war hero and elite son of South Carolina. He was chosen in August and quickly came to represent a "glorious" past of white supremacy and black subjugation. White South Carolinians eagerly pinned on Hampton their hopes for victory in November, and for rescue from the Republican horde: "with a leader they could love and trust with a definite hope[,] the white man and woman would rise like a tidal wave." Hampton was a moderate compared to Martin Gary, but Gary orchestrated Hampton's campaign and often deferred to the candidate. Hampton publicly scorned political violence, which Gary would quietly use to great effect, and courted the black vote. As one awed contemporary wrote, "General Hampton had strong faith in

"The Hon. D. H. Chamberlain, Governor of South Carolina." From *Harpers Weekly*, January 15, 1876. Courtesy of South Caroliniana Library, University of South Carolina, Columbia.

the power of persuasion and kindly reasoning with people of that race. He overlooked the malign influence of the Union League and the vicious leaders of both races, the devilish cunning of the carpetbaggers." His gentility and the genius of the party under Gary's leadership created an atmosphere of triumph before the first ballot was cast. By contrast, Chamberlain struggled to unite Republicans and bolster the courage of black voters. The Republican reputation for corruption and inefficiency alienated even some former slaves. More damaging, however, were some of Chamberlain's conservative efforts to retrench state finances and win the support of native whites. Although black legislators supported many of his "reforms," other Chamberlain programs sought to cut the militia, remove black justices and officials, and limit funding to education. These did not appeal to most Republicans and made it difficult for devout radicals to generate enough enthusiasm for the candidate to still the Democratic whirlwind: "There was Hampton, wherever he went cheered and glorified, the bone and sinew, substance and character and refinement and beauty of the state thronging to do him honor and shower blessings and flowers on him. The Republican speaker, the offscourings of their own party, sneaked about." As the year progressed, Hampton's popularity only grew, increasing the confidence of white South Carolinians, and although Chamberlain's followers continued to rally support where they could, these developments foretold a close race up through November.[6]

The campaign of 1876 was characterized by coercion, fraud, and violence. Despite the fact that Hampton publicly denounced violence and intimidation, his lieutenants embraced both. Martin Gary drew up his "Plan of the Campaign" in 1876 in which he wrote, "never threaten a man individually if he deserves to be threatened, the necessities of the times require that he should die. A dead Radical is very harmless—a threatened Radical . . . is often very troublesome, sometimes dangerous, always vindictive." Gary did not hesitate to resort to the lowest measures in his quest to secure the election for Hampton, despite what the candidate said. To prevent black voters from showing support for the Republicans, Gary advised, "every Democrat must feel honor bound to control the vote of at least one negro, by intimidation, purchase, keeping him away or as each individual may determine, how he may best accomplish it." Alfred B. Williams, a Democrat and a reporter who traveled with Hampton as he toured the state, did not remain a disinterested bystander. Rather his commitment to good journalism was overwhelmed by his devotion to the candidate and the party. At Strawberry Ferry in Charleston County, he joined the Democrats as they terrorized a Republican meeting. The practice was common: attend in full force and shout down the speakers to subdue black voters. Williams, like many active Democrats, followed Gary's guidelines to the letter: "I waited until the Negroes had broken ranks . . . selected a large dark mulatto of middle age and got his attention. 'You see this gun[?]' He stared at it and said nothing. . . . 'Well take good notice and mind what I'm saying to you. My orders are to stick right by you all day and if any trouble is started here to shoot you until you're dead, first thing; and I'm going to do it.' . . . most of the 40 of us had a similar conversation with a chosen subject. . . . This sounds like very cruel bullying, but it was necessary for our own protection, and the best mercy for those people, misguided and betrayed." The violence escalated as the campaign progressed. In September Frank Thomas of Millett wrote to J. H. Aycock, "We thought it best to keep the hands here Friday and Saturday owing to some few squads of dispirate men that rode around hunting someone to kill & were not very particular who it was." Thomas chronicled the deaths of at least two local blacks that month, events that became commonplace throughout the state.[7]

The worst episodes of violence were the riots that consumed several counties over the course of the summer and fall. Hamburg erupted in early July. The "King Street Riot" in Charleston took place in September, as did the Combahee and Ellenton riots. Cainhoy and Barnwell exploded in October, and finally, the Charleston election-day riot began as voters gathered to cast their ballots on

"Hampton, Hon. Wade, Senator from South Carolina (General in Confederate Army)." From the Library of Congress, Prints and Photographs Division.

November 8. In each case whites were the aggressors; however, the freedmen did not passively turn the other cheek. They defended the privilege of suffrage with words, weapons, and even their lives. The use of the term riot following the attacks conveniently implied black-initiated violence, characterizing their pointed defense as the random actions of a brutish people. Most of these "riots" were directly related to the campaign and the election, but even those caused by economic struggles were set off by the atmosphere of fear and violence.

The "Red Shirts" that characterized the Hampton campaign were, in fact, the product of the Hamburg riot. When two white men were prevented from passing a black militia troop on the road into the town, armed whites, led by A. P. Butler of the Sweet Water Saber Club, retaliated by hunting down the militia and its leader. The whites were then arrested for the seven murders—including six executions—that followed. Before their day in court, Butler ordered a red shirt for each of his men at the suggestion of George Tillman—future member of the House of Representatives from South Carolina—and James George—future senator from Mississippi. Clad in their "bloody shirts," the white vigilantes marched in front of the judge, openly defiant of his authority and the law. The statement made by the shirts was also openly defiant of the Republican Party, which had been "waving the bloody shirt," or emphasizing the South's and the Democratic Party's complicity in the Civil War, in order to win the sympathy of voters in the recent elections.[8]

The final indignities heaped on the scales of justice took place on election day. Both sides resorted to fraud, but the Democrats proved their mastery of the art of intimidation. Throughout the state the Red Shirts used cunning, violence, and sheer numbers to keep black Republicans and their white allies from the polls. Charles F. Hard related his experiences that day to his daughter, Ellen. The Democratic chairman in the area of Citadel Green, Mr. Hugar, told Hard, "Lots of niggers will vote two or three times, and if you can challenge any of them and stop a few, do it. When any of them do vote the Democratic ticket, see that they are not annoyed or molested, and if they vote again we can't help it." But the balance of the illegal behavior belonged squarely to the Democrats. Hugar informed Hard and his allies, "If the vote goes at this place as I'm afraid it will, I want you to be ready to grab the box the minute the polls close, grab the box and toss it over the fence to some boys I'll have waiting there. . . . There will be U.S. soldiers stationed there, and you may get your head rapped with a refle [rifle] butt, but you can take that." Charles Hard followed his instructions, shouting "Hurrah for Hampton!" as he leapt the fence and ran off with the ballots. Frank Thomas reported to J. H. Aycock that, with the exception of twenty-one men, all of the black hands in their region of Ellenton were kept from voting on election day. He added that the Democrats had gained three thousand votes in their county since the last election, a feat almost certainly the product of fraud, intimidation, and violence.[9]

These acts of violence were long-standing postwar traditions by 1876, but an equally potent tradition by this time was the role of women in the struggle for their state. The election of 1876 was a battle waged by men and women of both races. In addition and perhaps more powerfully, the event itself was a deeply gendered ritual. Women were not always direct participants, but the issue of femininity was pervasive. The first and most obvious symbol of womanhood was South Carolina itself. It citizens routinely referred to their state as "she" and likened it to female figures such as wives and mothers: "When the sun goes down [on election day] . . . you will see the old flag of South Carolina, which will cover then a united, happy, and prosperous people, floating in triumph over your own Statehouse and our own mother, Carolina, risen from dust and ashes, spreading her arms over her children, blessing all her sons . . . who have come forth to save her." The Democrats, in particular, made good use of this language. The chairman of the Marlboro County Democrats rallied its citizens with letters designed to pique their sense of masculine indignation: "Our dear old commonwealth, with her noble record of the past, her fair fame and renown, has been violently and ruthlessly torn from us." Hampton himself embraced this effective and affecting rhetoric. In a speech delivered at Walhalla in which he criticized the North for its treatment of the South, he said of South Carolina, "though she is conquered, she is not humiliated. . . . She laid down her arms on honorable terms." Once they were victorious, however, their vision of South Carolina became decidedly more optimistic. John Leland, formerly imprisoned for Klan activities, chronicled the election for his memoirs. He was jubilant at Hampton's election and eventual inauguration, reflected most clearly in his domesticated description of events: "The Federal *Bayonet* was withdrawn from her throat, and she at once arose from her dust and ashes, and is even now, putting on her beautiful garments. . . . She smiles upon her battle-scared sons, who proudly love her with all the devotion of auld lang syne. And she clashs [*sic*] to her bosom her rejoicing daughters, who had watched around her couch of suffering, with such undying faith, and had scornfully resented all intrusion on the part of her heartless oppressors." By feminizing the state, the Democrats turned their campaign into a medieval knight's tale: they were the heroic champions who fought to save a woman imprisoned by dark forces. This was not original to the election of 1876. Southern men had always likened themselves to characters out of *Ivanhoe,* but the often grotesque and violent nature of the language as it evolved reflected a new tradition, born of desperation.[10]

The imagery chosen by the Democrats in 1876 depicted South Carolina as an oppressed and helpless woman, but they went further by portraying her as sexually victimized. Playing on fears of black men raping white women, the Red Shirts coined metaphors designed to promote a fury among South Carolinians. As John Leland wrote of his home, "She has been brought low—very low . . . but worse than this, more these than all, are her writhings under the humiliation, the spoliation, the unremitting efforts at degradation, for the last ten years." When Whipper and Moses were nominated for the bench, Leland compared the insult to a physical assault: "Meetings were simultaneously called all over the state and the unanimous sentiment of these meetings has been that their crowing outrage *shall never be consummated.*" Sometimes Democrats went beyond comparing South Carolina to an endangered woman, feminizing her citizens in language designed to berate and provoke: "So long as we are apathetic, and lie supinely on our backs. So long as we cherish the vain hope that relief must and will come from our Northern fellow men, we depend upon a snare." Hampton himself, despite his public rejection of violence, incorporated the language of rape to deliver the most powerful message possible to the white men of the state. He told an audience in 1876 that South Carolina had submitted to the will of the Union, but that "she is not degraded." Such statements increased the sense of immediacy among white men and inspired crowds of Democrats to fight the political dominance of Republicans and blacks with greater passion.[11]

Rape was a powerful metaphor because white men traditionally thought of themselves as the caretakers of white womanhood. This role defined southern masculinity before the war, and the noblest example of such a man was the white southern soldier. For South Carolinians fighting a battle on which, they believed, their lives depended, the additional metaphor was appropriate. Southern soldiers had failed to defend the Confederacy but looked to the election of 1876 as a second chance. The language and symbols of manly warriors were therefore ever-present in Democratic rituals. An obvious example was the use of military titles in addressing the nominee and leadership. Democrats referred to Wade Hampton, a Confederate veteran, as "General Hampton," despite the fact that the war had ended more than ten years earlier and he had served with distinction in the South Carolina General Assembly and as a state senator—both roles more relevant for the governorship than his military service—before the war. Martin Gary was similarly "General Gary" in public demonstrations and even private correspondence. The entire Democratic ticket, in fact, reflected the party's choice to fall back on ancient symbols of manhood. Mark Reynolds wrote to his son, away at school that fall, "Hampton has, as you may have heard, been nominated for Governor and the whole 'State ticket' which has been presented by the convention which met in Col[a] at the time you were there, is not only *democratic* but *military*. The convention has brought the Generals & the Cols & the Captains which figured in the late war to the front." This trend was only magnified by the revival of the white rifle clubs. The clubs were generally responsible for the violence committed at Republican rallies and were commonly hip-deep in the major riots of the summer and fall. Following the Hamburg massacre, "Captain" A. P. Butler of the Sweet Water Sabre Club was arrested and ordered to appear on charges including the murder of several black militiamen. His lawyer, "General" M. C. Butler—present purely in a legal capacity, but referred to by his military title nonetheless—told the judge that "these men might have to sacrifice their homes and firesides, but they would never give up their guns." The Democrats adopted this violent, defiant, and unapologetic tone throughout the campaign. The notion of fighting to the death for a heroic cause appealed to most white citizens, and they rose to the challenge. By November white South Carolina had embraced the martial spirit, and the metaphor of militarism was increasingly less of a metaphor: "No army was ever under better or more rigid or beautiful discipline than the white people of the state were during those eight crowded and dangerous months intervening between the first faint, fluttering longings for rescue and the astounding triumph of valor, patience and faith." This army, however, included both men and women.[12]

The Democratic leadership recognized the mythical overtones the military carried in South Carolina, and its appeal would draw white men into the fray, as intended. But the call for citizen soldiers similarly appealed to women: "The women had not understood much of the puzzles and cross currents of the trades and mixes with the hated 'Radicals' but they could understand a headlong man-like onward rush led by a dashing soldier, and men daring consequences for wives and children and they were for that, and said so, distinctly." Ironically this attraction would bring South Carolina's white women closer to the political process than ever before, a development decidedly different from its gendered intentions. In the meantime their men set about establishing the parameters of the coming conflict.[13]

In order to reclaim manhood for whites only, South Carolina Democrats had to assert their definition of masculinity. The "heroic" antics of militant Democrats and white vigilantes were an important step, but masculinity was meaningless to white South Carolinians if it was enjoyed by black men as well. Violence was, of course, the easiest way to cow former slaves and their allies, but whites were creative in their use of more mundane gestures and language. As in the years immediately following the war, whites exploited the economic weaknesses of the black community to prey upon its members. To keep blacks from the political process and deny them their rights as citizens and especially as men, whites "boycotted" black laborers. White Democrats refused to hire black laborers if they said they would vote Republican; landowners refused to rent land to black Republican voters; those who were already tenants faced eviction at the end of their contracts; and merchants refused service or denied credit to active Republicans. The simple act of attending a political meeting—although such meetings were often rendered fruitless by the disruptive Red Shirts anyway—provoked whites to punish blacks economically. Once again the inability to control their economic circumstances left black Republicans at the mercy of white Democrats, and without the federal government to protect them, their voting power suffered as well. This power remained as potent a symbol of masculine dominance as the right of suffrage.

The use of dehumanizing language did little to effect change at the polls in 1876, but it went a long way toward bolstering whites' confidence, which ultimately went hand in hand with their victory in the election and their renewed sense of manhood. In public and private documents, whites referred to blacks and Republicans in general as animals and savages. At a Republican meeting at

Edisto, Charles Hard was responsible for stalking one of the white candidates, whom he described as, "a long lanky Yankee, with a scrawny neck that he craned like a turkey." Such mocking images were an ideal companion to the violence and intimidation that they followed. "'I am going to stay right by you,'" Hard told the candidate, "'even when you get up to speak, and if there is any shooting, someone else might get killed first, but I promise you will be second.' And I patted my pocket with it's peacemaker. He scuttled off sideways like a crab." The intimidation worked, but Hampton's victory was not yet secure. Widespread fraud cast doubt over the election, and Chamberlain refused to relent as a result. Republicans in the legislature were similarly defiant, and for several days, a turf war waged between incumbents and their Democratic usurpers within Carolina Hall itself. Representatives of both parties camped out by their desks, refusing to give ground. This near victory frustrated the Democrats, but they saw the Republicans' weak footing and the reluctance of the federal government to intervene. This sense of superiority, engendered by blacks' near defeat and the power they knew was at their fingertips, prompted even more brutish comparisons from whites: "It was hard service for these gentlemen to be thus shut-up with these unwashed 'hands of the nation', sending forth a stifling native perfume." White Democrats, described in accounts as martyrs, suffered largely because, according to those same accounts, the conditions were not fit for humans but tolerable and even pleasant to blacks: "The piercing cold. . . . Sleeping too on dirty floors, each with a single blanket . . . their heads and frames ached. . . . In all this the negroes had the great advantage, as they were just in their element. The perfume seemed to but stimulate them to song and jollity, and a blanket big enough to cover the head, was all that each needed." By dehumanizing the competition, whites reasserted the kind of definitions that were common under slavery. Thus their eventual political victory was equally a victory for antebellum values and, in turn, white manhood.[14]

The most ironic—and, as some contemporary white men might argue, tragic—effect of the election of 1876 was the continued rise of the political woman in South Carolina, even as white manhood took center stage once again. Both black and white women participated as never before. Their roles were diverse and often indirect, but they were active. South Carolina's white women attended meetings, chronicled events, and worked themselves into a frenzy for their candidates. Black women were, once again, more easily accepted into the political realm by their community. They turned out in full for Chamberlain and in smaller numbers even for Hampton. Overall the election returned white men to power in South Carolina, "redeeming" their state as well as their sense of the "natural" racial order. But, even as they worked to redefine masculinity in their own image, they inadvertently promoted the continued evolution of womanhood and femininity.

Black women remained among the most passionate political operatives within the freed community. They attended meetings and encouraged their husbands to do the same: "Indeed, the whole evidence indicated that the women were more interested in the political canvass than the men." Black women of all classes, "prepared meals for the participants, danced, sang 'spirituals,' arranged the stands, and rode in processions." In some cases black women pressured reluctant family members and neighbors who had been turned away by apathy or white intimidation to return to the Republican fold. They were particularly tough on black Democrats, whom they viewed as traitors to their communities and race. During the congressional investigation into the allegations of fraud surrounding the election of 1876, several black Democrats testified to the fierce loyalty of female Republicans. Jonas Weeks of Richland County told the South Carolina committee that his wife "cussed me; and I had on a dirty shirt and she wouldn't give me no clean shirt to put on" because he was not a good Republican. Ashbury Green of Abbeville claimed that black women kept him from attending church because he supported Hampton, and that they "persuaded with my wife to quit me." In the committee's final report to the U.S. House of Representatives, they reported, "Women utterly refused to have any intercourse with men of their own race who voted against the republicans." In addition they considered the relative absence of black women at Cainhoy to be evidence of the Republicans' intention to start a riot and kill white Democrats: since black women were so active, only a premeditated plan for violence could have kept them away. Such partisan behavior reflected their adoption of the political process as their own, and their determination, despite the absence of women's suffrage, to influence the vote as they saw fit. Democrats greeted this behavior with distain, often referring to these outspoken women as "wenches" and accusing some of "prostituting their persons." Whites assumed that the label of "whore" would hurt and hinder black women. In these gendered attacks, they attempted to strip black women of their potency; to intimidate them into submission by denying them the privileges of womanhood and femininity. The strategy failed, largely because black women did not subscribe to white standards. They chose to define themselves through partisan activism and in some cases violence. Supported by the Republican leadership, they fought on. Sympathetic journalists aided the women by, on occasion, turning the gendered tide in their favor. The *Columbia Daily Union-Herald* mocked a local Democrat who had threatened the black community and its political women by responding, "Edward Henderson, of Abbeville, notifies the colored women that he will be down upon them with the full penalties of the law if they try to abuse or intimidate the members of his democratic club. Poor fellows, the girls must not frighten them." This exchange and the active role of black women in the election demonstrated the simultaneous battle for political and sexual power in South Carolina.[15]

The most dramatic female presence in the election of 1876, however, was that of white women. As in the past, they became historians of state and local events, kept friends and family apprised of details, and supported their cause from the confines of the domestic circle. However, the election of 1876 propelled white women into the fray as never before. The passion of the participants, the draw of the candidates, and most important, the significance of the issues at stake inspired public participation by white women that was even welcomed by their male counterparts. This development was deeply ironic, given that the power to define gender roles—or reassert traditional roles—was the prize awarded the victor. As these women took longer and faster strides into the political world of South Carolina on behalf of antebellum notions of masculinity and femininity, they irrevocably altered the meaning of southern womanhood.

White women continued to act as informal historians of political developments and purveyors of information in South Carolina. As a young woman in 1876, Mary Aiken kept a faithful, if choppy, record of events. When she was an older women, over twenty-five years later, her reminiscences took on the tone of a public account, one in which she included and celebrated the participation of her father, David Wyatt Aiken: "During the big campaign he made many telling speeches—the most effective being on the celebrated "Big Tuesday" in Abbeville. . . . The Abbeville Press and Banner said this of him about this time, 'Owing to his energy and courage to do the right under any and all circumstances . . . no man contributed more to the glorious victory of that year [1876].'" A more sophisticated young woman named Lizzie Geiger of Lexington County wrote to her beau often about developments in Hampton's campaign. He welcomed her accounts and they often exchanged opinions. At the end of October, she wrote: "The mind of every person seems to be taken up with Hampton. I don't think there ever was as much excitement through the country about an election as at this time. Oh, if Gen. Hampton can only be elected and our proud old state redeemed. . . . I read a piece in one of our Charleston papers yesterday, of a meeting that took place in Beaufort where Hampton and other distinguished men were to speak. The radicals tried to provoke a riot with the democrats, finally Hampton arose and told the speakers and audience that they would close their meeting, and also told the rads that there were a half dozen United States officers present in citizens dress and had witnessed their behavior, don't you think they fell out?" In return he told her of events in his area, including the murky reality of election fraud: "I hope the Election passed quietly down on the River side as it has here. We nearly doubled the rads at our precinct. One hundred and sixty nine votes were taken one hundred and twelve for Hampton . . . About four Negroes voted our ticket." In much the same vein, Mary Reynolds wrote to her brother Mark of disturbing developments during the contest and her predictions for the future of the state: "No doubt you have heard of the last blow, that is the plot of arresting hundreds of our men & imprisoning them until after the election. Well I will not trust myself to say anymore but my state of hope for Hampton is now slowly fading. Now I won't say that either but I hope to the end." These women were as invested in the outcome of the election as their men, and while the nature of this indirect participation was not new, they did not hesitate to escalate their role for the benefit of Hampton and the return of the white, male hegemony of the past.[16]

South Carolina's white women took their enthusiasm for their candidate and his platform out of the world of letters and diaries and into the traditionally male arena of political meetings, rallies, demonstrations, and even coercion. White women were a constant and accepted presence at Democratic functions throughout the state. At Winnsboro a flyer for an October meeting announced that a number of seats were "reserved for the ladies" and guarded by an armed Democrat. At the opening of the Democratic speaking tour in Anderson in early September, "Every vehicle was sent to carry the women and children." The *Charleston News and Courier* commented, "A striking feature of the day was the decoration of the windows along the line of march. These, without exception, were adorned with sweet fair faces of women and children. From eager lips came shrill hurrahs. . . . Snowy handkerchiefs were waived by hands that never seemed to tire." The cries of the women, in fact, stood out in the memories of a number of witnesses. Ordinarily decorous, these well-bred white women seemed to abandon the lessons of proper behavior for Wade Hampton. Strangely such displays in 1876 were welcomed by husbands, fathers, and friends. Journalist Alfred B. Williams wrote years later that at the idea of a Democratic convention in the summer of 1876, "the women loosed their tongues. Matrons living now with never a thought of fear for themselves or their descendants know that their own childhood and girlhood were lived in the shadow of daily, deadly dread." Hampton himself seemed to generate such an excited response from the crowds he addressed that both men and women often lost their composure: "When General Hampton advanced to deliver his first speech of the campaign, he was forced to stand a long while and look and listen. He saw a far spreading tumult of whirling hats and hands and handkerchiefs and flags and heard the yells of men frantically screaming their heads off and the shrieked love and frenzy of women."[17]

This devotion was evident in other dramatic public displays of political and personal loyalty. Women wrote to local newspapers to proclaim their support for Hampton and their distain for the Republicans. One such woman, who signed her letter "An Old Fashioned Christian," wrote to announce the gathering of a number of women to pray in protest following Chamberlain's declaration outlawing the rifle and saber clubs. These prayer circles were common and often statewide. Mary Reynolds reported to her brother Mark that Thursday, October 26, was "set aside for fasting and prayer all over *this State* on account of the political troubles of course. Everybody tried to attend service, & we had quite a number out." Women participated in the economic boycotts designed to pressure blacks into voting Democrat or keeping away from the polls on election day. As arbiters of the household economy, white women were, in many ways, the people best suited for this job. Alfred Williams reported: "White women did their own washing and ironing and housework if they could not find a colored woman with Democratic affiliations, or, at least, willing to 'keep her mouth off' male colored Democrats, or a Democratic white woman willing to undertake such jobs. Charleston women set the fashion of patronizing only Democrats at market stalls." Women worked on all fronts of the Democratic movement, and while many of their activities could be characterized as largely feminine in nature, the cause to which they dedicated themselves was only newly feminized.[18]

Perhaps the most common and overt political role for South Carolina's white women was in the rituals of Democratic gatherings throughout the state. It was also the clearest sign that southern politics was embracing the female influence. To almost every Democratic meeting and rally, white women brought their sense of presentation and decoration. Flowers adorned podiums, banners in brightly lettered words proclaimed Hampton's future victory, and, what is most significant, women and girls themselves became living representations of the cause for which they were fighting. Journalists traveling with Hampton were amazed by the extent to which these women went on behalf of their candidate: "Even in late October the women in the Low Country found flowers somehow. There developed a regular system of something like a ritual of flower funerals. If we left a place by train the accumulated tokens of womanly devotion and patriotism would be dropped from car windows." Mary Reynolds told her brother Mark that she and her friends had been busy with preparations for Hampton's arrival in early October: "Banners, flags, etc. are being made for the different clubs." White women seemed to be constantly sewing and painting for the Democrats. Their work was evident everywhere, and even the state's most prominent newspapers included detailed descriptions of their efforts in their accounts: "Every lady and every child, who could get one, bore a flag, the Stars and Stripes, inscribed with the name of Tilden and Hedricks and Hampton. . . . In the center was a venerable white silk banner, embroidered with a palmetto tree, surmounted by a scroll bearing the insurrectionary inscription: 'Our Liberties and Our Homes.'" Other appealing phrases included, "Hampton—We Love, Welcome, and Honor Him" and "While There's Life There's Hope." The women also used paintings to represent the struggle of white Democrats and often included ironic images of the freedmen: "A large cartoon represented the palmetto prostrate and white and Negro men, working together to lift it." The act of decoration seemed to become a source of inspiration, as if the sacrifices of the women were a sign of the desperation of the times and the need for men of action.[19]

Beautifying the stage set for their candidate, however, was only part of the process. The women of South Carolina went a dramatic—or perhaps melodramatic—step further in urging the Democrats to victory. Known as "tableaux," these deeply symbolic scenes created by the women incorporated them further into the public ritual of politics. At a stop in Orangeburg, Hampton encountered "three impressive tableaux along the route of the procession. . . . 37 young women were grouped on an elevated stand posed like statues representing the states and surrounded a crouched figure in mourning and rags. General Hampton was in a carriage arranged with flowers and flags to represent a chariot . . . and as he appeared a young woman waved a wand, 'Prosperity,' and the prostrate figure arose, rags and mourning falling from her, and turned a smiling face toward the leader as 'Peace and 'Plenty' advanced and stood at her side. Miss Cora Wannamaker was the South Carolina." Even children participated, although almost always girls rather than boys. At Charleston, "a noteworthy feature of the procession was the truck of Hook and Ladder No. 1. . . . It contained thirteen little girls dressed in white, with blue sashes and golden tiaras studded with stars. . . . Ella Hewitt, of South Carolina, represented the Goddess of Liberty." Although intended to represent the thirteen original colonies, these little girls were far more significant to their audience. They were innocent and weak, much as South Carolinians felt their state had been. But the symbolism went beyond political realities: the little girls represented nascent womanhood, abused by the federal government and in need of rescue by revitalized southern manhood. As that same tableau progressed,

> Little Miss Mary Forbes, aged seven years, approached Gen. Hampton bearing upon her brow, in glittering letter, the words "South Carolina," and in her hands a bouquet of flowers. This fair little representative of the state then . . . addressed Gen. Hampton as follows: "Gen. Hampton, our beloved chieftain, in behalf of my little companions, our fathers, mothers, and the

people of Charleston, permit me to present to you this token of our esteem and love, with our prayers and their prayers; in you rests our hope, and may the God of all mercies grant that, through you, our beloved State will be freed and redeemed." . . . Gen. Hampton then imprinted a kiss upon the brow of the little South Carolinian, and said, . . . "I thank you, little ladies, for these beautiful flowers. Make it your highest aim to grow up and be as noble and true as your mothers of Carolina. . . . *It only remains for you, men of Charleston, to do your duty as you have done to-day, as your brothers and sisters are doing in every county of the State.*"

Their duty, of course, was in the realm of sexual politics: to redeem the state and preserve the feminine virtue on display. Ironically the act of reinforcing these stereotypes only violated them. Even as women perpetuated the image of helpless womanhood, their participation in the election of 1876 wildly defied it. They became stronger, more vocal, and more integral to the traditionally male arena of politics. As John Leland wrote, "There was one potent influence in inspiring and urging forward this wild excitement and jubilant greeting . . . and that was the *Women* of the state! However gloomy and despondent their husbands and brothers many have become, *they* had never 'despaired of the Republic'; but were as unyielding and defiant . . . as when the Confederate flag waved over Fort Sumter. . . . The candid historian must record, that if it had not been for the women of the state, her early redemption from Radical rule would have been impossible." In fact, by bolstering white masculinity, the white women of South Carolina may indeed have weakened it.[20]

The last assault on black claims to political power and manhood was violent, and the election of 1876 was a showcase for abuses committed by both sides. Finally energized and organized, whites pushed hard to reclaim their power. In response blacks acted defensively, although sometimes without immediate provocation, to preserve what was left of their rights. In the middle of the fray were the women of both races, each working on behalf of their side to secure their respective goals. All hands were bloodied in the process. As in the 1860s and early 1870s, women's roles in both politics and violence evolved as the two intertwined, altering the definition of femininity and the definition of masculinity that the two were supposed to characterize.

Once again white women were participants in and victims of racial violence, but the strong emotions that accompanied the election intensified their support of such measures. Whites considered their women particularly vulnerable targets of black anger; it both excused the measures they took to win the election and shored up their own insecurity. As a result they took extreme measures to spread these fears and "preserve" the sanctity of white womanhood. Charles Hard told his daughter that in the weeks before the election, white women were particularly visible at Democratic meetings in Charleston, but that their presence made many nervous: "Lots of the ladies wore red dresses or scarves, and some of the children were dressed in red. We were worried about having so many ladies and children to look after, and afraid the niggers might start fires in different places and cause a panic while the men were off guard." The *Charleston Journal of Commerce* was similarly suspicious of black activities but, like much of the white community, blamed outside influences and corrupt leaders for them: "I am convinced that the great masses of negroes in South Carolina . . . are perfectly peaceable and harmless. It is only when their leaders stir their passions and appeal to their prejudices that they are vicious or dangerous." The paper was nonetheless chiefly concerned about the fate of white women: "I was at Capt. Croft's house in Aiken at nine o'clock at night . . . when two ladies who had been visiting him passed out, and getting into their buggy drove off alone in the moonlight, living nearly two miles away. . . . Surely the ladies of few counties will trust the masses of their people to go out riding alone at night." These men used such situations to reinforce white masculinity: violence had always been an outlet for and proof of southern manhood, particularly when it came in defense of white womanhood. Ironically women contributed to the panic, indicating that even they looked to traditional gender roles for comfort. Most did not believe the area around Farmhill, the Reynolds home, to be secure. Mary Reynolds noted in a letter that all of the balls and parties in the months leading up to the election were cancelled as "the ladies won't be out after dark." Such remarks satisfied white men's need to be needed by their women. An Aiken man stated it most plainly to a reporter when he explained the reason for the trust many of the women in his county had in their security and the docility of the black community: "Them women was safe, because we've taught the nigger down here that our women is one thing they can't tetch. It's sartin death to a nigger to put his hand onto a woman." But, even as they reverted to the security of gender roles that presumed female fragility and provided the luxury of male protection, women again defied those roles by demonstrating a resistance to victimization and a desire to victimize.[21]

White women made easy targets, but in violent situations women didn't always surrender as easily as white men assumed they would. Many, in fact, were proud of their ability to "defend" themselves against their black adversaries. Mrs. Alonzo Harley of Silverton claimed that she was sick at home with only her young son for company when two black men entered her house. She told the authorities that the men knocked her down and beat her, apparently with the intention of robbing the family. Mrs. Harley allegedly managed to evade her

"Tableaux vivant." From the Henry Spanner Family Collection, D. H. Ramsey Library Special Collections, University of North Carolina, Asheville.

attackers long enough to grab her husband's (unloaded) gun and drive the men out of her home. Her remarkable—and suspicious—account of the events of September 1876 proclaimed her survival instincts, her strength, and her bravery. She was apparently unabashedly proud of her valiant defense of her home, but her story sent her husband and the men of the community into a violent and vengeful rage, as she must have known it would. They caught a black man by the name of Peter Williams, whom they dragged back to Mrs. Harley. The woman calmly identified him as one of the assailants, knowing full well the consequences. Mr. Harley beat Williams and several of the posse shot him as he allegedly tried to escape. Accounts then differed as to whether or not he survived, but, assuming he had been killed, blacks gathered to avenge his death. The Ellenton riot—"the most vicious demonstration of racial violence in Reconstruction South Carolina"—lasted several days and left up to one hundred blacks and three whites dead, and a woman was at the heart of it. Women demonstrated their support for violence in other ways as well. The simplest was implicit acceptance that violent measures were appropriate tactics in the war for South Carolina. W. A. Leaphart wrote cheerfully and even proudly to Lizzie Geiger of his own contributions to racial violence: "Last night the negroes made a fire in front of the store. . . . I gave Jake Hook a handful of powder to throw in the fire. The negroes fell backwards off their seats when it flashed." In response Lizzie Geiger related events in her county. Politics and racial violence were no longer subjects for men alone, but those that even women commonly and calmly discussed. Following election day she informed Leaphart: "Much excitement still exists in Orangeburg, the Democrats speak of contesting the Election, we have just heard that a riot is expected at my Uncles in the upper part of Orangeburg Co., a colord Democrat was severely beaten and had his house burnt by a colord rad. . . . Mr. Maynard Spigener spent Saturday night with us, he thought we ought to be satisfied with Hampton, said it would be too much to have Tilden too." Women were also more directly involved. They cheered, supported, and even helped rally white men in their violent mission: "It was man or boy to mount and ride . . . and the farmer . . . sent his son, daughter or wife to stir the near neighbors and call out every man or boy who could sit in a saddle and buckle on a gun." They were willing to threaten and intimidate. Present at the beginning of the Red Shirt movement, women fulfilled a common domestic role in uncommonly public demonstrations. Captain A. P. Butler requisitioned a red shirt for each of the men of his company once they had been ordered to appear in court on charges relating to the Hamburg riot. The men wore the shirts, but the women prepared them and other accoutrements, carefully and conscious of their larger meaning: "The ladies of Aiken soon made 40 red shirts and the armed uniformed prisoners marched into Aiken to court. The women made a large red shirt which was tacked to a cross with negro faces and kinky heads. . . . On one side was 'awake, arise, or be forever fallen' in black letters. On the other was emblazoned in black letters 'none but the guilty need fear.'" These threats—the cross and the slogan—revealed a strongly partisan and ruthless side to South Carolina's white women. The election of 1876 had stirred them to further embrace racial violence. It would be the solution to what they perceived as the "problems" of Reconstruction: black empowerment and an altered social hierarchy. As in the past, white women accepted and even encouraged violence, but perhaps as a result of the passions aroused by the election and potential "redemption" of the state, many became more active participants, transforming the traditionally female role of victim into one of coconspirator.[22]

Black women were even more directly involved in the violent racial conflicts of 1876; they were often their instigators. Witnesses frequently commented on the passionate response of black women to Republican rallies and the interference of white Democrats. In fact they were commonly singled out as the most vitriolic of the Republicans' allies. Some of their activities were indecorous but relatively harmless. For example South Carolina's black women did not hesitate to use the worst possible language in their interactions with Democrats: "Among these were a number of Negro wenches who . . . were stationed at the corner of King and Calhoun streets . . . and at various points along the line. They filled the air with foul and blasphemous language. . . . Said one of the Negro women: 'I wish dat stage would break down and break dat ____ Hampton neck.'" Their language also occasionally bordered on the overtly sexual. Tom Lomax of Abbeville County told the congressional committee that a group of black women called several Democrats, "damned fools" and instructed them to "kiss my arse" as they hoisted their coats over their heads and lifted their legs. Their fury was evident at each meeting they attended and actually seemed to escalate as the year progressed. By election day, "the women were very boisterous and noisy. . . . In one instance I saw one woman shake a club in the face of a man that was there and curse him for a red-bearded son of a bitch." Language, however, was a weapon of the past. Black women escalated the conflict by embracing violent retribution. At Four Mile Church Precinct on election day, according to William R. Wheelock, about twenty black women gathered, "armed with knives, or bayonets, or clubs. . . . One woman in particular, that I knew, had a large butcher-knife stuck in her apron belt." A. M. Latham of Charleston County commented, "There was hardly a woman that hadn't a bludgeon, and they were, if anything, worse that the men." More than one went so far as to attack the candidates themselves. At a procession in Georgetown, an "old woman hurled a brick at Hampton himself, missing her aim . . . but arousing the temper of the whites to the danger point." As a result the black women found themselves in the middle of some of the worst racial conflicts of the campaign. During the Ellenton riot, a number of blacks took refuge in a swamp. To flush them out, the white vigilantes sent in a black woman with possible terms of surrender. She disappeared into the trees, electing to remain with and support the besieged band. A witness to the Cainhoy massacre named Smith testified that a group of three black women were responsible for telling the black militia that the Democrats had seized their weapons. These activities removed black women from the sidelines of violent exchanges and placed them squarely in the fray. The election of 1876 made both black women and white women of South Carolina accomplices with their men in the bloodier battles for political power.[23]

Black women reserved the worst treatment by far, however, for members of their community who chose to reject the Republicans and vote the Democratic ticket. Their abuse of black Democrats ranged from individual intimidation to indiscriminate rage. At a Democratic rally in Strawberry Ferry, Charleston County, black women focused their attention on one particularly offensive participant: "Thomas Fraser, colored Democrat, who went up and returned on the boat, was allowed to speak undisturbed, except for bitter abuse and derision from the women. It is safe to say that but for the presence of the armed force protecting him he never would have spoken nor come away alive." The *Charleston News and Courier* reported this behavior, portraying the women as animals in a senseless fury: "The conduct of some gangs of colored Radicals on the line of march was outrageous; but they were less violent than the colored women. They seemed bent on causing a disturbance . . . at this point seemed frenzied with rage, when a colored man was observed riding on the same mule with a white man, and they rushed at him, and tried to pull him off the animal." But what the paper—and most whites for that matter—failed to understand was that black women were acutely aware of what was at stake in the election. It was not simply political power that hung in the balance but the power to define and defend themselves, and for black women that was indeed a valuable commodity. For that reason even husbands were not spared their violent wrath. A black man named Edward Henderson of Abbeville County testified that wives vowed to starve their husbands to death and that one who wished to vote for General McGowan, a Democratic candidate, was attacked by his wife in broad daylight: "his wife whipped him in the street, took his hat, and tore his coat off, and took him up by the school-house, to make him vote the republican ticket." Even these black men missed the significance of the election for the women of their community. Aaron Mitchell, another black Democrat from Abbeville County, testified to his own assault at the hands of black women, and he too characterized them as animals, not seeing the justifiable concern that motivated their actions: "They passed on straight like bulls, and they looked so blood-thirsty I was afraid, and I got down out of the way; and . . . they cried out, 'There's that damn democrat nigger, knock him, knock him down, knock him to hell in a minute.'" The passion of black Republican women on behalf of their party and their people was unparalleled, except perhaps by men like Martin Gary, because like white Democrats, they saw stakes beyond mere political office and monetary gain.[24]

These acts of violence also took on distinctly sexual overtones because black women also recognized the overtly gendered nature of the election and chose to use threats of emasculation to browbeat black men who wanted to vote the "wrong way." The best way to publicly humiliate black Democrats was to strip them, literally, of what made them Democrats and distinguished them as men. The most obvious target was the red shirt, but black women tore the pants from as many as they could reach: "One Negro man was riding a mule behind a white man and the women made a rush at him, with frantic outcries, and tried to pull him to the ground. He held fast to the white man and escaped, but his clothes were torn off." Preston Taylor of Richland County made the mistake of shouting "Hurrah for Hampton" as he left the polls. In response "the women jumped on me and tore off all my clothes; just stripped me and tore off all my clothes." They left him on the ground, naked. Jonas Weeks, also of Richland County, was assaulted—or so he claimed—every day by the women in his community because he supported Hampton, to whose father he had once belonged. His attackers did not waste their time with his shirts, however. He testified before congressional representatives that "they called me all kinds of names, and they would pull off my breeches and call me a devil." By stripping the men, they humiliated them, denying them their claims to masculine authority and dignity, the very thing on which the election of 1876 rested.[25]

Unfortunately, black women were also victims of the racial violence that characterized the election. As in the past, they were rarely the primary targets, but by abusing black women, blacks' enemies once again chipped away at the masculine prerogative of protecting virtuous womanhood, regardless of race. Democrat Edward Henderson's wife and daughter were both threatened by black Republicans. His enemies whipped his daughter while she was at school and did the same to his wife at—of all places—church. He told the congressional committee that "the parties were arrested for whipping my girl; and I was going home to dinner one day, and they were after my wife, and they called her bad names, 'a dirty bitch,' etc." Fortunately the party fled when they saw Henderson coming. Aaron Mitchell and his wife were attacked late one night in their home. Republicans had already forced Mrs. Mitchell to close her business and had chased the couple from their church. The attack involved between fifty and one hundred angry Chamberlain supporters: "They were hollering, and yelling, and cursing around there, and they finally fired one pistol. My wife was all in a tremble. . . . The second shot struck the plate about five feet from the eaves. . . . We sat there perfectly quiet . . . and [t]hey cursed, and yelled, and abused us . . . and we slept none." Black women, however, were also often heroic. When James Grant, another black Democrat, was attacked at the polls on election day, he was chased and beaten until a black woman named Rebecca Bennett threw herself on top of him, "trying to cover me with her clothes." Bennett protected him to the best of her ability but could not save him entirely from the blows of the black men and women who ran them down. Ultimately, however, most wives and daughters of black Democrats were victims rather than champions. At a Republican meeting on James Island, the wife of a black Democrat was shot by the black militia. Although the woman recovered, she bore the scars of the election for the rest of her life. Ironically she would share that with the black women of the South Carolina Republican party once Hampton took office and the redemption of the state commenced.[26]

Once concluded, the 1876 battle for South Carolina left its black citizens at a distinct disadvantage. Political power, for the most part, passed back into the hands of elite white Democrats and left the black community without the means to protect what limited social and economic gains they had made since the war. That alone was dramatic enough change, but the election forever altered the nature of masculinity and womanhood in South Carolina. White men had indeed reclaimed the power to rule and therefore the power to define themselves as they chose. They looked to traditional guidelines as they did with so much else. Political activity, violence, and the defense of white womanhood ranked high among them. As much as they sought to reinforce these stereotypes, however, more modern interpretations intruded. The women of South Carolina transformed their gender forever with their partisan support for their candidates. As historians, vocal disciples, symbolic representations, and promoters of violence, black and white women created a place in southern politics for women and a place in femininity for political activity. As desperate as white men (and many white women) were to restore the antebellum gender balance, South Carolina's women made it impossible. It would take a more extreme and cruel phenomenon to do that.

5.

Strange Fruit Hanging from the Palmetto Tree

Lynching in South Carolina

The 1876 "redemption" of South Carolina brought the white, native-born men of the state back to the fore of political power. Having won the governor's seat, the state legislature, and assurances from the federal government that noninterference was their new official policy, the victors set about restoring the control they had once had over most areas of life. The federal government's removal of the last of its soldiers in 1877 facilitated their efforts. Interestingly, and perhaps expectedly, however, the essential goal of restoring traditional gender roles was unfulfilled. Political power did not translate as easily into sexual power. The women of both races had been too much altered for easy reversals, and black men held on tightly to the gains they had won in the preceding decade. In the election of 1876, white South Carolinians had discovered the efficacy of political organization supported by acts of intimidation and violence. Now that they were firmly in control with little risk of interference from outside the state's borders, whites embraced a campaign of unbridled brutality to assert themselves over those issues that still vexed them.

In the twenty-five years following Hampton's election, whites reclaimed total control over much of what they had lost in the Reconstruction era. Although black men continued to vote and accumulate property into the early twentieth century, they lacked the leverage necessary to hold onto their fair share of either the elective franchise or the state's economic growth. What remained to them were some of the social changes that had taken place over the preceding ten years. A sense of strength and pride borne of emancipation and the reconstruction of community and family lingered long past Chamberlain's defeat. These intangible luxuries were more difficult for the white community to strip from them; they were the things onto which the black men and women of the state clung most tightly. Among them were the newly redefined gender roles that combined qualities unique to the black community with traditionally white southern rituals and evolved throughout the Reconstruction years. Masculine pride and feminine virtues did not necessarily require political or economic power to thrive among the freedmen, but what they would sadly discover is that they had great difficulty surviving the unchecked rage of a South Carolina lynching bee.

Lynching—extralegal execution via shooting, burning, hanging, or torture, that was often mob driven—in nineteenth-century South Carolina never achieved the levels that it did in other southern states. The state ranked only eighth of the eleven former Confederate states in numbers of lynchings between 1881 and 1940, an interesting and perhaps contradictory fact when compared to the violence practiced in South Carolina in the decade following the Civil War. South Carolina was also relatively unoriginal when it came to the targets of its lynch mobs. The freedmen and freedwomen were not the exclusive victims; occasionally a white man was on the receiving end of mob "justice," but black men and women were a disproportionate majority in the Palmetto State as they were throughout the South. South Carolina, however, did not lag behind in terms of the brutal nature of the lynchings it witnessed. Victims suffered a range of cruelties, justified by a series of accusations and crimes, but a single consistent thread ran through each incident. Lynching was, above all, a sexually charged ritual, and the last attempt of white men to assume exclusive control over southern manhood.[1]

In general, lynchings in South Carolina rose dramatically from the 1880s through the 1890s, which was the worst decade by far, and declined slowly thereafter into the 1930s. The worst region of the state overall was the Western Piedmont, home of Edgefield County, and the five predominantly black regions of the state witnessed more than 60 percent of the state's lynchings. The stated reasons for lynchings in South Carolina ranged from arson to murder to the most electric of accusations, rape. In many cases the lynchers claimed that they acted because they felt the law could not. Governor "Pitchfork" Ben Tillman, a notorious racist who had publicly advocated violence to prevent blacks from voting, made this argument in a speech in 1894: "It appears to me that South Carolina has the best system of laws and rules of court to enable men to shirk the gallows that can possibly exist anywhere. The consequence is, the people have lost all patience and almost all faith in the administration of justice. This lamentable . . . condition is the direct and almost sole cause for the prevalence of lynch law in our midst." Others complained of the inconvenience. Representative Arthur Kibler told his friend Mamie Salter of Athens, Georgia, "Do they lynch people over in GA as they do in S.C.? If they do not, they are behind, not up to date. Just lynched a white man over in Kershaw County a few days ago. Did not want to go to the expense of having a trial. You know courts and juries cost something, and why go to the expense when a few men with a good rope can do the business in so short a time." Such statements encouraged a casual, and therefore permissive, attitude toward extralegal "justice."[2]

The lack of substantive opposition to lynching also led to the development of particularly brutal methods for exacting revenge. Victims were shot over and over, or hanged and then shot in exaggerated statements of hatred and vengeance. Torture became prominent in the process, and those actions that caused the greatest fear and pain in the target were favored. One mob tied a rope around their intended victim's neck and ordered him to climb the tree to which it was attached. Once out on a limb, the mob shot the man until he fell. Unfortunately the rope broke, and the man was forced to repeat the exercise. One poor victim was tied, gagged, and tortured to death. The mob scalped him, cut off his ears and genitals, cut out his eyes and tongue, and stabbed him repeatedly. They finally tied him to a grate and threw him in the Santee River. This level of brutality was a reflection of the rage of the white community, but that rage was not simply a response to the alleged crime. It was prompted by their insecurity and desperation. That, of course, was not the message they intended to send. They wanted to convey a sense of white manhood's superiority; the more cruelly a black man's dignity and life were taken from him, the clearer they believed the message was. In addition, the more public a lynching, the more effectively it sent that message. Bodies were often left by the side of a road as a warning to passersby. Richard Puckett was hanged from a railroad trestle for all to see. Lawrence Brown was found "dangling from the danger signal where the old stage road crosses the railroad" in the small town of Stilton in 1897. The danger signal was an obvious but effective metaphor. These public displays, however, reached beyond the confines of South Carolina. Even curious and appalled observers overseas commented on the excesses of the era. Reverend C. F. Aked of England wrote that 1894 was "the worst year, in point of numbers and bloodthirstiness, since the days of the Ku Klux." And there appeared to be no end in sight. As black minister Abraham Middleton of the Methodist Episcopal Church bemoaned in his diary in 1893, "Everywhere in our land there is murder and bloodshed, lynching."[3]

There were those who tried to stem the tide of the lynching phenomenon, largely without success. In the early 1890s, one of the last remaining black delegates in the state legislature pushed a bill to allow the governor to remove any local official who allowed a mob to take and hurt his prisoner. Although ultimately defeated, it reflected the courage of those black citizens who remained in government despite the best efforts of the Democrats. Eventually the state government adopted a similar measure when it rewrote the state constitution in 1895. The new constitution was not favorable to the black community, adopting criteria—though never explicitly racial—to keep black men from the polls. However, the 1895 constitution did include a section that punished those officials and counties that allowed the lynching of prisoners and provided a measure of relief to the victims' families: "In the case of any prisoner lawfully in the charge, custody or control of any office, State, County or municipal, being seized and taken from said officer through his negligence, permission or connivance, by a mob or other unlawful assemblage of persons, and at their hands suffering bodily violence or death, the said officer shall be deemed guilty of a misdemeanor, and upon true bill found shall be deposed from his office pending his trial, and upon conviction shall forfeit his office, and shall, unless pardoned by the Governor, be ineligible to hold any office of trust or profit within this State." Section 2 of the law awarded no less than two thousand dollars to the families of the victims. The county was liable, unless an arrest was made, in which case local authorities could sue the perpetrators' families for remuneration. Strangely the force behind the new constitution was Ben Tillman. As governor from 1890 to 1894 and senator from 1894 to 1918, Tillman pushed for changes to overturn the Reconstruction constitution of 1868. That attraction was understandable, but more confusing was his advocacy of the antilynching statutes. Perhaps he recognized the potential efficacy of the new suffrage limitations and believed they would go unnoticed if the same document tried to quash a greater injustice. Perhaps he resented extralegal justice as an abridgement of his power as the state's highest authority. Regardless, the gesture was largely empty, lynching went on relatively unabated for several years, and Tillman continued to be an advocate of the violent oppression of the black populace. His influence also grew with time. As lawyer J. Altheus Johnson of Washington, D.C., commented in 1896, "Tillman may be a madman, but he is eminently successful in inoculating others with the same madness that he has." Lynching remained a popular response to alleged crimes committed against the white community. The *Columbia State* editorialized in 1897: "*The State*'s criticisms of lynchings and lynchers have been denounced before, and they will doubtless be condemned again, for we do not expect lynchings to cease in South Carolina." The paper was correct.[4]

Ultimately even those who condemned lynching in South Carolina missed the underlying motive for such savage behavior. It was a decidedly gendered activity, designed to strip black men—once and for all—of any claims to manhood and assert the primacy of exclusively white masculinity over both women and the black community. Historians of the 1970s and 1980s favored this argument largely because they believed that accusations of rape dominated incidents of lynching. They argued that the frequency of such claims, justified or not, was an expression of the sexual insecurity of southern white men. But these historians focused almost exclusively on claims of rape and assault made by white women, an argument refuted more recently by those historians who note more common accusations of murder and arson in many if not most areas. Terence Finnegan has written: "These stories and historical accounts of sexual and gender tensions are a distortion. Although such tensions lay beneath many lynchings, many, many more had little or nothing to do with sexual concerns." He further argues that the tensions surrounding the black community's struggle for equality was the primary cause of the lynching phenomenon and that "white males resorted to lynching not only to preserve and protect the virtue of their wives and daughters, but, more immediately and more often, to protect the honor, property, and lives of themselves." While this is true, he fails to note that honor and masculinity (or sexual prerogative) were synonymous. Lynching did not require an assault against a woman or even a vague allusion to rape to be both deeply gendered and a reflection of white men's sexual insecurity. Lynching was indeed connected to the defense of white womanhood—southerners and South Carolinians often made that claim—but lynching was equally a defense of white manhood.[5]

Violence was a traditionally masculine pursuit in the South. Violence against the black community was an effective tool for asserting white authority, particularly white male authority. Lynching victimized black men more than any other group; black men were struggling to hold onto the dignity and pride won following emancipation and resented deeply by those who had lost such luxuries. Finally, a common excuse for lynching was indeed rape, attempted rape, or various forms of assault against white women, but perhaps more important, the protection of white women was the province of white manhood. Regardless of whether or not a woman was involved—and in South Carolina almost three-quarters of all lynchings did not involve women—lynching was an attempt by white men to complete the process begun following the war. It was the last stage in an erratic but successful campaign to restore white male hegemony over both women and black men.[6]

The stated, and seemingly nongendered, causes of lynching included theft, arson, and murder, but all were tied to the question of white authority and insecurity, and the threat posed by a confident black community. Again many claimed that lynching was "the outcry of a conservative and law loving people against the abuses of a system of criminal procedure which has become intolerably inefficient."

As a reader of the *Columbia Daily Register* wrote to the paper, "Judge Lynch is an abler judge and . . . a truer discerner of equity." But, since few of these dramatic cases actually reached past the initial indictment, most did not know whether or not the law would have failed them. In addition equity was rarely the goal; crushing the will of black manhood through violence and an arrogant disregard for the law was. Lawrence Brown was charged with arson but released from jail for lack of evidence. Rather than consider the possibility of his innocence, the mob came for him near his home in Stilton Station. He was lynched in a merciless demonstration of manly prowess, an arrogant exercise of white men's right to commit heinous crimes to defend their interests. The men responsible left a warning to the black community next to Brown's limp body: "Notice to all whom it may concern: Judge Lynch's court is in session tonight for the protection of our property, and by the help of God, he will convict and execute any man, woman, or child that burns or destroys our property." Another mob raided a York County jail in 1887, where they removed five black men accused of murder and lynched them all. There was no justifiable reason for the attack except that the crimes of the five men represented a threat to white authority: "it does not seem that there was either any doubt about their guilt or any doubt that they would be convicted and hanged in due course of law. . . . The mob hanged them simply because it could not wait for the law to take its course." The alleged weakness of the system was a red herring designed to obscure the true reason for extralegal justice.[7]

In many cases lynchers did not bother to defend their actions by hiding behind a "weak" legal system but took pride in their actions because they served what they believed was a greater purpose. The efforts they made to humiliate and degrade their victims were a sign of that purpose and the pleasure many white men took in it; it was also an effective tool for undercutting black manhood. Eight black men arrested for two separate murders were lynched in Barnwell in 1889. They were tied to trees by the side of the road and shot multiple times. When the weight of their bodies came down on the ropes holding them to the trees, they "occupied all sorts of grotesque and revolting positions." The victims were handled with such disdain that the coroner left the bodies at the side of the road after he examined them, their clothes torn away and their limbs flopped in all directions. The men had been in custody and their cases were proceeding apace, but their violations of the law were far more important as violations of the social order. As a result, their remains were treated as less than human, and the mob continued to strip away at black men's claims to both citizenship and manhood. Other lynchings did not require much of a crime but happened only because white men felt that their black counterparts were not heeding their warnings. In 1895 a black man named Isham Kearse was seized and lynched

Lynching victim Frank Embree, July 22, 1899. From the Without Sanctuary Collection, National Center for Civil and Human Rights, Atlanta, Georgia.

because a Bible and some furniture had been stolen from a local church. There was no evidence against him, except that he had admitted to recently being in the vicinity of the crime. The community justified his horrific death by arguing that recent attacks on white men and suspected cases of arson had plagued the neighborhood and that the larger message—one that cowed the black community—was more important than the truth. A citizen of the county wrote to the *Charleston News and Courier* to defend the white mob, but the *New York Times* took issue with his approach: "he does not pretend that the particular negro who was beaten to death had anything to do with the shootings or the stabbings or the fires. . . . The 'young men' who took upon themselves the task . . . seem to have been actuated by the belief that, if anything goes wrong, it is always safe . . . to kill a negro, and that any negro will do." The point of Kearse's death was to strike a blow at black citizenship and manhood, not create any real atmosphere of justice. For white South Carolinians, justice was a social order dictated by gender and race. Finally, historians have found that political and economic tensions continued to promote violence against blacks, lynching being the most fashionable practice. Political violence in the Piedmont in 1898 led to an election-day riot that lasted ten days and left at least nine blacks lynched. But, as these activities had always been deeply infused with gendered meaning, they went hand in hand with the rise of lynching in the last decades of the century.[8]

The fragile confidence of white manhood underlay lynching in South Carolina, and any violation of the accepted social order might have drawn the attention of a mob in the late nineteenth century, but lynching was particularly the response of insecure white men to powerful or assertive black men. Any hint that black masculinity survived the Klan or Redemption was anathema. In 1897 Frazier Baker, a black teacher, was made postmaster of Lake City. The mob that attacked his home and killed him was later acquitted. He had not committed, nor was he accused of committing, a crime. His offense was to occupy a position of power that elevated him above white men in his community. In January 1897 a black man was lynched in Orangeburg because a white man's barn had been burned by unknown parties: "there does not seem to be any evidence that the lynchee was concerned in burning it, but nevertheless he was a negro, and even 'a prominent negro,' whatever that may mean." A prominent black man was a contradiction in terms in white-dominated South Carolina, and such men could not be allowed the pretense of power. At the outbreak of the Spanish-American War, the federal authorities were concerned that the presence of black troops in South Carolina would spark an outbreak of lynchings. Although the *Washington Post* reported that the troops would probably pass through without incident, even outsiders recognized the fears that powerful black men created in white southern men. Samuel Turner of Johnsville was not an influential or overly successful black man, but by shooting and killing a white constable named Poston, he usurped his position, violated the local hierarchy—racial and civil—and showed a lack of respect for white authority. A mob came upon Turner and his wife, put several pistols to his head, and shot him. Although the murderers were not masked, "the Coroner's jury found a verdict of killing by unknown persons." Ultimately this response to black men who continued to assume—and in some cases violate—the rights of citizens and white men was the product of a white community convinced that gender roles adopted across racial lines were a threat to their personal power, their civil authority, and nature itself. As Ben Tillman stated in 1899, "I say the entire negro race is lower in the scale than the white man. God made them so, and they will always be so." In fact their definition of masculinity required it.[9]

The highly gendered nature of lynching was evident in the rituals that often accompanied the deaths of black men. The most deeply sexual act found in these murders was the castration of the victim: a literal and symbolic unmanning of a black man. This mutilation was in keeping with the deliberate brutality of many lynchings and a tradition of removing "souvenirs" from the body, but it was far more meaningful than the cutting of a finger or an ear. Neither did the crime that provoked the lynching need to be of a sexual nature to lead a mob to emasculate their victim. Keitt Bookard argued with a white man and allegedly threatened to "spank" him. The mob tortured him at length and eventually castrated him. Their actions demonstrated that while the defense of white womanhood was an attractive excuse for lynching, the fight for white manhood was a stronger motivation.[10]

Occasionally a white man threw this otherwise black-and-white system into disarray. The system worked best when the white community could define black men and women as the only transgressors of the natural hierarchy. When white men crossed the line, the lynch mob was forced to respond. White manhood's primary responsibility was the protection of its women. When white men violated that unwritten rule, they too needed punishment to keep them in line and ensure complete adherence to the gender code. Oliver Culbreath was lynched in 1885 for the murder of a young man courting his daughter, but Culbreath was known for abusing his wife—the daughter of a wealthy local man—and his own mother. His lynching was less about the poor dead boy than the bruised and battered women of his household. His abuse of women in the household disgraced white manhood. It took the extraordinary behavior of men such as Culbreath to provoke a white mob to act against a white man, whereas black men were lynched if a white man's barn burned, regardless of whether or not they were actually responsible. Black men were lynched for continuing to vote. Black men were lynched for holding particular jobs. It did not take much to incite the white community into killing a black man. It did, alternatively, commonly require the most heinous crimes, including evidence of guilt, to inspire the lynching of a white man. Murder was by far the most common reason white mobs lynched white victims. In South Carolina, however, lynch mobs targeting white men were not always successful. The police seemed more than willing to protect their prisoners when those prisoners shared their race. In 1890 George S. Turner, the owner of a cotton mill and a "general merchandise store," was among the richest men in Spartanburg County. Unfortunately he was also among the most hated and feared men in the county as well. In 1887 he killed an employee of the mill, a German man named Julius Metzkie, but was acquitted thanks to the testimony of his sister-in-law and her brother, Edward Finger. Finger and Turner, however, soon became enemies. Finger's sister accused Turner of "betrayal" and sued him for several thousand dollars, and a rift developed between the families. In the spring of 1890, Turner met Finger in the road and shot him. In custody for Finger's murder, Turner attracted a lynch mob of locals fed up with his abuse of power. The police, led by the mayor, fought back, capturing a cannon the mob had brought with them and planned to use to break into the jail. The authorities removed Turner to another town until his trial, when he was returned to Spartanburg. A lynch mob, two hundred men strong, made a second attempt but was again foiled when the sheriff placed an armed guard around the jail and posted sentries throughout the town. Turner's money may have bought his first acquittal, but the citizens of the county were unimpressed, and no black man would have merited the protection Turner received. In fact wealthy or powerful black men would probably have been in greater jeopardy. A similar situation existed in 1894 when D. C. Murphy was arrested for the murder of the Orangeburg County treasurer, Robert Copes. Held in Columbia for safekeeping, Murphy was followed there by the mob, who planned to "liberate" him in the early morning hours of December 8. To thwart the mob, the governor had Murphy stashed away in the state penitentiary and posted extra guards. In both cases the murder victims were white men. Had they been black, a lynch mob would never have bothered to seek "justice." However, in both cases, the murderers were also white, which was the only reason the authorities made such an effort to protect them and ensure that their cases came to trial. Turner, a bully and a murderer, was guarded by the mayor himself, who flew headlong into the fight to prevent his lynching. Murphy, the assassin of a state official, drew the attention and support of the governor. Rare was the black man who enjoyed such care, largely because white murderers broke only the law, while black criminals violated the social and sexual hierarchy.[11]

Ultimately women were central to the lynching phenomenon of the late nineteenth century. Regardless of whether or not women were actually attacked, white South Carolinians liked to revive the specter of the sexual menace of the black male and the image of the helpless female victim because they stroked the egos of white men and validated extralegal violence. In the 1880s the most violent region in South Carolina was the Eastern Piedmont, in which 70 percent of all lynchings were attributed to rape-related crimes: "signs or placards were often attached to a victim's body, warning African Americans that white men would protect the virtue of their wives and daughters with their lives." It was a convenient excuse for murder since most agreed that it was "the only crime for which lynching is justifiable," as Ben Tillman himself said on a number of occasions. He added six years later, "I would lead any lynching party to lynch any man who robbed a woman of her virtue. I have been in four negro riots and I'm proud of it." On one of the rare occasions when a white man stood up for the rights of a black man, a judge made an impassioned plea on behalf of true, and not vigilante, justice. The judge in the case of *The People v. Will Fair* in Spartanburg recognized the flimsy evidence against the accused and instructed his jury that "if it is not true beyond a reasonable doubt, then to write a verdict of 'Guilty,' in answer to anybody's demand would be to crucify the law, to degrade our courts and to stultify you men." However, even this otherwise rational, fair-minded judge raised the issue of endangered white womanhood by stating: "I know the awful peril our country women are subject to." The defense of white womanhood became such a common excuse during the lynching era that the impression of many outside the region was that rape dominated the crimes answered by lynchings. The truth is that rape-related accusations dominated—but were never a majority—in the state in the period from 1881 to 1895 and were dramatically overtaken from 1896 on by murder and assault.[12]

Nonsexual assaults on women attracted as much attention as a cry of rape because an assault upon a woman was, in these cases, more of an assault on white manhood than on white womanhood. In Charleston three black men were lynched for the murder of a white woman named Atkinson. The mob was so enraged that they even burned to the ground the property of a white man who had tried to talk the mob out of the lynching. Former governor Duncan Heyward kept a record of his experience at a lynching in Greenwood at the turn of the century. Heyward struggled to prevent the death of the targeted black man, but without luck. The man, Bob Davis, was accused of slitting the throat of a white girl for no apparent reason. The mob planned to burn him at the stake; since the girl had lived, the charges against Davis would not include the death penalty, and the crowd believed he deserved to die. Eventually they settled for shooting him repeatedly. What made Heyward marvel, however, was the ritualistic approach of the lynching bee and the ever-present reminders of the fragility of the female victim designed to enrage and inspire the men present. When he returned with the mob to the young woman's house, where she was forced to identify Davis, "I realized for the first time that on the railing of the piazza for almost its entire length was a woman's blood stained garments which I was later told had been displayed there for some time."[13]

In cases of rape and attempted rape, the reaction of the white community was unparalleled. The rape of a white woman by a black man was indeed a violation of the law, but more significantly, it was a violation of the racial and sexual order. Such actions met with a particularly cruel response from white men because their ability to protect their women—and hence their masculinity—hung in the balance. A crowd of 250 men tracked Will Burts fifty miles across South Carolina over three days in order to lynch him for the attempted rape of Mrs. C. L. Weeks. Three black men were lynched for the rape of a white woman in the Midlands in 1893. One was tortured and beaten until his eye nearly fell out. He was then shot so many times he was difficult to recognize. The other two men were stripped, tortured, hanged, and shot. The motivations behind such murders were reminiscent of the postwar Bushwackers, Klansmen, and Red Shirts, but the exaggerated overkill was driven purely by the only remaining insecurity of white men. The only absolute control they lacked was over black men's assertion of manhood, of which they believed rape and attempted rape were a sign. Lynching was designed to quell that "impulse." Following the rape and murder of Miss Bessie Wertz, "highly educated, accomplished, and very beautiful . . . a favorite in the neighborhood and a great belle," near Prosperity, two black men were hunted and lynched. Several hundred neighbors viewed her body in a dark ritual that culminated in the shooting of one of the accused. He was also tied to the tree behind which he was alleged to have hidden in wait for his victim. The second man was taken from jail by between five and six hundred people and lynched in the same manner. Two thousand men lynched Richard Puckett for attempted rape in Laurens. Although the victim failed to identify him, "blood hounds were then used to fasten guilt on him." When George Thomas was accused of forcing Miss Rosa Douberly, "to submit at the point of a pistol," near Hardeeville, he was arrested, but even the paper did not know if the authorities had managed to get him safely to the jail at Beaufort. In 1893 a white girl named Mamie Baxter was attacked "with an intent to commit rape" by an unknown black man in Denmark. More than twelve men were arrested, interrogated, and marched before Miss Baxter, who failed to positively identify any of them. Eventually the authorities tracked down John Peterson. Despite the fact that the victim herself stated that Peterson was not the man who had attacked her, the mob was impatient. Five hundred men lynched Peterson by hanging and shooting him. Clearly the lynching was not about justice for Mamie Baxter. Peterson's death was a defense of white manhood's right to claim the life of a black man with impunity. This atmosphere of terror and revenge pushed the black community further out of the public arena, but it did not secure South Carolina's women, in particular its black women.[14]

Although black men were more commonly the targets of lynch mobs in the Palmetto State, black women were often victimized by the phenomenon in an effort to demonstrate the weakness of black men and the power of white manhood. In Anderson County, Ruben Elrod was shot by a mob of fifty men who attacked his house late one night. Elrod was a "respectable old negro," and the papers did not have an explanation for the attack. Once their immediate goal was achieved, the mob then grabbed three black women who lived in the house, stripped them, and beat them nearly to death. Historian Terence Finnegan has argued that "whites used lynching to punish African Americans who advocated or sought social equality," that is, "for challenging the white caste system." But the lynching of a black woman served additional and perhaps more important purposes for the white community. First, it sent a message to black men that they were powerless to protect their own women—a necessary facet of manhood—and must therefore lack masculine qualities. Second, it gave white men the apparently unrestricted access to black women that they had enjoyed under slavery. And, third, it denied black women the shield of femininity and southern womanhood, reserving such luxuries exclusively for white women.[15]

In addition the lynching of black women was often particularly brutal and graphic. When Isham Kearse was lynched at Broxton Bridge for the theft of a Bible, the mob grabbed his mother and his wife as well. Hannah Walker, Kearse's mother, and his wife, Rosa, were stripped and whipped until Walker was dead and Rosa nearly so. The *New York Times* wrote of the cruel murder, "the excuse for lynching, in case of, 'the usual crime,' is that it is necessary that negroes should be terrified into respecting white women. But when this excuse fails, the spirit of the mob is seen to be mere savage desire to do murder." What the *Times* failed to recognize was that by grabbing wives and mothers, lynch mobs were making a calculated—if frenzied—decision to make a larger statement about sexual power in South Carolina: not merely that white women were entitled to respect, but also that black women were not. The murderers of Isham Kearse and Hannah Walker were eventually acquitted, even though they never denied responsibility. Rosa Kearse testified against them, but "one defense attorney described her as 'sassy' and said 'the woman wasn't whipped. Didn't get enough if she was.'" Such statements reflected a general disdain for black women and mocked their claims to the protection of womanhood. In addition, the act of stripping them, which was common in such events, was humiliating to the women and also deeply symbolic for the lynchers: the women could no longer claim feminine modesty, and the white mob reasserted its right to their bodies.[16]

When it came to violence against black women, not even the age of the target was respected. When Frazier Baker, the newly named black postmaster of Lake City, was attacked and killed, his family was with him. His wife managed to get most of the family to safety, but among the dead was their two-year-old daughter. On the other hand, Hannah Walker was elderly, as was Eliza Cowan, who was lynched in 1881 in response to the burning of a wealthy white planter's barn. The goal of such attacks was to cripple the confidence of the black community and assert a social and sexual hierarchy with white men at the top. But, as with every effort they made to reestablish such primacy, women and blacks changed the rules, altering them consciously and unconsciously by claiming the right to create their own gender roles, even in the nightmarish era of nineteenth-century lynching.[17]

Although lynching typically victimized the black community, members of that very community sometimes actively sought lynchings for blacks, and for many of the same reasons that white vigilantes did. Ironically both black men and black women saw lynching as a way to protect womanhood and promote honorable manhood; however, their definitions of these ideals included members of their race. During the Greenwood lynching at the turn of the century, Duncan Heyward noted the presence of a black woman in the crowd of white lynchers. She was the mother of a young girl who had been assaulted by Bob Davis before he slit the throat of the fair Miss Brooks. According to Heyward, she demanded that the mob burn Davis at the stake: "This woman was very much worked up and begged any man with a gun who came by to lend it to her, for she wanted, she said, to fire the first shot. There were several Negro men near where we were and their sympathies seemed entirely with the mother of the girl and it was very evident they wanted the Negro put to death." Black women had not enjoyed the luxury of such protections before emancipation; they were at the mercy of white men who raped them without consequences. Once free, they claimed the rights of virtuous womanhood: the right to say no and the right to have abuses avenged. For black men, punishing Davis was a way to separate his actions from themselves, in effect casting him out of the realm of black manhood. Most black-on-black lynchings occurred before the turn of the century, and the vast majority were for the crimes of murder and rape. E. M. Beck and Stewart Tolnay have argued that these events were prompted by the black community's understandable lack of faith in the white judicial system, but they add that equally powerful was the notion that black criminals threatened the stability and survival of their community. Black criminals, particularly accused rapists, discredited black manhood and often violated black womanhood. It was important for black South Carolinians to avail themselves of extralegal justice in several of these cases to preserve what few assets remained to them following Redemption.[18]

On rare occasions black men were even willing to resort to the lynching of white men—violations of the racial and social order—to exercise black manhood and protect black womanhood. In 1889 Harrison Heyward and William Williams became the first black men in the state of South Carolina to lynch a white man accused of the murder of a thirteen-year-old black girl. They were convicted of murder, but the public responded with demands that the governor commute their sentences. Heyward and Williams's supporters held mass meetings, distributed circulars, and signed petitions begging for clemency for the lynchers. According to newspaper accounts, they renounced lynching but "claim that many of their own color have been lynched upon little or no evidence, and in lynching Waldrop they only followed an example set them by the whites." By calling on

"The Mob at the Lake City Post Office—An Artist's Portrayal," the lynching of Frazier Baker. From the *Boston Post,* August 10, 1899.

the example of white lynch mobs, Heyward and Williams not only sought an excuse for their behavior in the hypocrisy of whites but also laid claim to the same defenses: the preservation of womanhood—black or white—and the rights of men—black or white—to do it. They did not make distinctions between the races and held fast to that rule. Sadly, few whites followed suit. Although some spoke of equality in such cases, few lived up to the rhetoric. Ben Tillman claimed, "I would lead a mob to lynch any man, white or black, who had ravished any woman, white or black," but Tillman also characterized black men as rapists and never pursued justice for black women assaulted by white men. Because most of the white community shared his view, black victims received little justice from white South Carolina; and because blacks enjoyed so little power following Redemption, they found as little assistance in black extralegal justice. As Representative George Henry White, a black Republican from North Carolina and the last black man to hold elected federal office in the nineteenth century, told

Congress in 1900, "if there were not outrages and assaults committed, not upon white women by black men, but by white men upon black women, these lynchings would be less than they are now." In South Carolina they would have been far fewer, but the fact of the rare black lynch mob demonstrated that civil power was not the only right worth defending.[19]

White women were equally disruptive when it came to reasserting traditional gender roles through lynching. In the atmosphere of terror established by white lynch mobs, it is not surprising that women came to accept and even encourage extralegal violence. Many became as bloodthirsty as their men. In her famous 1897 speech, Rebecca Latimer Felton concluded that if "it needs lynching to protect woman's dearest possession from the ravening human beasts—then I say lynch, a thousand times a week, if necessary." Tacit acceptance, however, was the most common response, and since women were often the excuse for lynchings, they were drawn into the middle of the fray by the very men who claimed to want to keep them from it. In cases of assault and rape, the ritual of the lynching bee included dragging the victim in front of his accuser for identification. This was not really considered necessary, however, as evidenced by the fact that the victims were commonly lynched even when the accuser failed to confirm them as the attacker. But, for the lynchers, the identification was also a way to demonstrate their masculine prowess: by bringing the accused before a vulnerable woman, they were in effect showing off captured prey to hungry and grateful diners. Women, however, often turned the tables on these manly rituals. Some saw the viewing as an opportunity for power: to make the men of a community act at their behest through accusations, identifications, or testimony. In 1890 the brother of Willie Leaphart's victim was overheard saying that his sister had cried rape in order to guarantee a conviction. At an 1899 lynching in Denmark, the lynchers organized a mock court at the scene of the murder where "a woman of low character . . . testified that she had seen Peterson quite near the place where the crime had been committed, and at the time." Such a woman would not ordinarily have the men of her community so responsive to her claims, but in the case against John Peterson, her word was sacrosanct. The *New York Times* commented that "the life possibly of every man, certainly of every black man, is throughout the Southern States at the mercy of every malicious woman. . . . The word of the woman is taken without cross-examination and without hesitation." Other white women became as enraged and hungry for a brutal death as their men, a decidedly unfeminine quality. "Bissie" wrote to W. L. McKeown in 1887 to defend a white lynch mob from Yorkville that had murdered five black men accused of killing a white boy. She was repulsed, she wrote, that the newspaper had maligned the "good law abiding citizens of York" and claimed that one of the black victims was "a desperate negro . . . possessed of whole Indian characteristics shrewd, daring, and revengeful." Some were even willing to commit the crime themselves. At the lynching of Bob Davis, the young victim's stepmother invited Duncan Heyward into their home to dissuade him from stopping the lynching. She went even further by saying, "if those men out there are not men enough to burn him, I am woman enough to take a gun and shoot him." For Mrs. Brooks, womanhood now incorporated violence, revenge, and outgunning the men if necessary.[20]

For other women their powerful role in lynchings provided an opportunity to promote justice. Some women refused to identify their attackers, or rather insisted that the mob capture the right man before they would consent. The alleged victim of John Peterson insisted that he was innocent until threatened by her father. He harassed the poor girl until she was willing to lay the blame at Peterson's feet. The guilty man was eventually found in Georgia. In some cases men made appeals to women to help put a stop to the lynching phenomenon. At the turn of the century, a group of Confederate veterans called for southern women to use their influence to prevent the practice: "We appeal to all Confederate veterans, their wives and daughters, and to that great and glorious organization the Daughters of the Confederacy . . . to . . . help put a stop to this diabolical, barbaric, unlawful, inhuman and ungodly crime of burning human beings." Many men recognized the power of women in these situations. The fact that they were central to lynching positioned them to stop it. But, even in those cases where a woman was not directly involved, the gendered nature of the ritual gave women leverage. Ironically the gendered nature of lynching had also altered the very gender roles it was designed to enforce. Women were made powerful and occasionally violent in the process: qualities that were certainly not in keeping with the demure antebellum ideal.[21]

Ultimately many of the very people lynching was designed subordinate were those who made the greatest strides in the nineteenth century toward ending the practice. In the South, women and the black community were the earliest active opponents of lynching. Various newspapers and politicians spoke out against it, but the first organized efforts were made by the victims of the phenomenon. Among the black community, the standard bearer was Ida B. Wells, a journalist who dedicated her life and sacrificed her safety to speak out against the injustice of lynching. Wells's wise strategy was to twist the argument white southern men had been making to endorse it. She redefined lynching as a perversion of manhood and indeed humanity. She characterized it as barbaric, stripping it of masculine honor and leaving savagery and ignorance in its place. She also pointed out that the common cry of rape was often made in cases of consensual relationships between black men and white women and that it was white men who felt victimized by them to the extent that they resorted to lynching to restore their desired racial-sexual order: "There have been many such cases throughout the South . . . the southern white men in insensate fury wreak their vengeance without intervention of law upon the Negro who consorts with their women." Wells exposed the myth white men had been promoting but acknowledged the gendered nature of the practice. And, as historian Gail Bederman has argued, Wells made her appeals to insecure northern men who had long tolerated this southern ritual: "Wells attacked the idea that lynching showed the continuing power of manliness. Instead, she argued, Northern men could only regain their manliness by stopping the lynching." Her work was revolutionary, and although the lynching era was far from over, she denuded it of many of its pretenses and gave others who might join her the leverage they needed.[22]

Black women, however, found two avenues for protest. The first was at the side of Wells, considered more radical and—ironically—"unfeminine" for her bold public discussions of sexuality. The second was among the black middle-class clubwomen who chose to embrace white gender roles and assume the mantle of respectable womanhood in order to represent their community and—they believed—protest more effectively in the wider world. The National Association of Colored Women, for example, worked for community uplift, and they saw themselves as a vehicle for improved interracial relations. Members adopted white standards because "change the behavior, they reasoned, and white people would stop the abuse." Or, as Josephine Ruffin stated in an 1895 speech, "it is . . . 'our bounden duty' to stand forth and declare ourselves and our principles, to teach an ignorant and suspicious world that our aims and interests are identical with those of all good aspiring women." Ultimately, however, black women like Mary Church Terrell "politicized" the N.A.C.W. by rallying black women's groups against lynching and eventually organizing the Anti-Lynching Crusaders, which tried to draw in the support of white women. The Crusaders operated under the umbrella of the N.A.C.W., which resolved in 1896, "In view of the fact of the numerous lynchings and the many victims burned at the stake, extending even to women . . . we, the representatives of Negro womanhood, do heartily deplore and condemn this barbarous taking of human life, and that we appeal to the sentiment of a Christian world to check and eradicate this growing evil." As their antilynching work evolved, their public activism became more in keeping with that of the politicized freedwomen of the 1860s and 1870s, despite their claims to an ideal of demure and deferential womanhood favored by white men.[23]

In South Carolina the earliest signs that opponents of lynching were willing to speak up generally came from the judicial system. Gradually the authorities began to pursue, indict, and prosecute white mobs who resorted to extralegal justice. As early as 1884, the Edgefield authorities filed indictments against thirty-three men for lynching a man named Culbreath. Following the murder of postmaster Frazier Baker in 1898, thirteen white men, all merchants and farmers, were indicted in the U.S. Circuit Court. The judge commented that the crime was "one of the blackest ever perpetrated in South Carolina," and even a black man named Henderson Williams was brave enough to testify against the lynchers. Unfortunately not all were as enlightened. The attorney for the defendants argued that they were not responsible for the lynching. He blamed President McKinley for appointing a black man to the post in the first place. That same year Horry County managed to arrest, try, and convict two black men for assaults on white girls without a lynching. The judge commended the residents for allowing the law to run its course: "Such a spectacle is worth a thousand lynchings. Lynch law means the destruction of the law." He further embraced the rhetoric of Ida B. Wells by stating, "Behind the hand of the lynchers may be the power of Samson, but in the exercise of that power . . . they would hurl the country into the lap of barbarism." In a remarkable turn of events in 1913, a Spartanburg jury actually acquitted Will Fair of assault on a white woman, "despite the positive statement of a respectable white matron of high intelligence that he had assaulted her." The jury had initially been deadlocked but eventually determined that the woman was delusional because of her physical condition. Weeks earlier the local sheriff and his deputy had saved Fair from a mob trying to lynch him. The mob had blown up the jail with dynamite, but the sheriff faced them down. By 1899 even the governor had begun making genuine statements opposing lynching. Governor Ellerbe told the legislature, "In new settlements it is sometimes necessary to use this method as a remedy . . . for the ruthlessness of desperados. . . . We have no such pretext for the demoralizing savagery that breaks out now and then in our state."[24]

The court's record was still erratic through the turn of the century, but small victories emboldened others, particularly those members of South Carolina's black community, to fight lynching more aggressively. Former black congressman from South Carolina George Washington Murray formed the National Protective Association of Colored Men. The association was a national organization that made routine appeals to Congress and the president for justice in the courts as well as voting rights. On the local level, mass meetings of black citizens elected delegates to make direct appeals to the governor. By 1897 Ellerbe was willing to meet with them. Well-known individuals like Francis J. Grimke, a pastor of the Presbyterian Church and a member of the famous abolitionist family, were equally vocal. Grimke used, among other media, the pulpit and the press to make his case. In 1897 he wrote to the *Washington Post* to thank the paper for condemning lynching: "I express the sentiments of every colored person in the country. . . . It is only by such plain outspoken denunciation of wrong that such barbarities, such blots upon our civilization, are to be prevented." The rhetoric of humanity and masculinity was repeated in many of these appeals. Perhaps drawing on Wells or perhaps understanding better than most what lay beneath the surface of lynching, the black community tried to call attention to the true intention of the ritual: "Since the first day of January [1899] there have been twenty-eight cases of lynching in the South, and everyone of them colored. This is not only an unwarranted outrage upon them, but demoralizing to the white race. It terrorizes and *unmans* the former. It familiarizes the latter with lawlessness and crime, creating in them a contempt for lawful authority and desire for mob rule." But even many of these men backed down when the specter of rape arose. Rather than call white women liars and deny its frequency—as Wells often did, and maybe could more easily do because she was a woman and seemed to pose less of a threat to white manhood—they addressed it as an accepted truth: "We deplore, condemn, and denounce, in unmeasured terms, assaults upon women. . . . All we ask is that the regular machinery of justice be employed." It was the potency of rape that kept lynching a popular remedy for crime. Even though the incidence of rape accusations in South Carolina had declined by the turn of the century, the idea of rape still cast a shadow over the state, illustrating just how powerfully gender issues had embedded themselves in the lynching phenomenon.[25]

Despite its leadership in Klan violence and the skills of its Red Shirts, South Carolina was only average among the southern states when it came to late-nineteenth-century lynching. For the first time in decades, the Palmetto State did not necessarily set the standard. However, neither did South Carolina lag behind. Black men and women were many times on the wrong end of a gun or a noose throughout the 1880s and 1890s. South Carolina's remedies for alleged crimes were often among the most savage on record. Historians have argued that lynching arose because white southerners were willing to resort to such brutalities in order to restore and preserve the racial and political order, but in South Carolina, there was little need. Whites had reclaimed control over the civil life of the state in 1876. Economic control followed apace, and with those two in their pockets, social domination was not far along. The right to determine gender roles and who would be able to enjoy them, however, was one of the few elusive fundamentals that remained contested. Lynching was, at least in part, designed to give white men the right to dictate definitions of manhood and womanhood. The ritual was infused with gendered rhetoric and meaning from the start, and punishments were often sexually explicit. The result, however, was far from what white southern men intended. The black community fought hard for the right to enjoy the luxuries and responsibilities of masculine and feminine designations. In fact they invoked these responsibilities to defend their resistance to white authority. By turning the tables on white arguments, they temporarily fended off a loss like that of 1876. In addition, by making white women central to lynching, white men accidentally made them powerful, more so than they had ever been. With this power, some white women indulged in vengeance and violence, but others used it for nobler purposes. By 1930 Jesse Daniel Ames and a host of female representatives from the southern states had formed the Association of Southern Women for the Prevention of Lynching. In its declaration and pledge, the women promised to no "longer permit . . . those bent upon personal revenge and savagery to commit acts of violence and lawlessness in the name of women." Ames even hosted a meeting with black women club leaders in 1931 to discuss the sexual exploitation of black women and the "*double standard of ethical and moral* conduct based upon race," during which they concluded that, "as a corollary to this conception of Negro women in terms of animal wantonness, white public opinion conceived all white women in terms of angelic purity." Although the association never publicly discussed the double standard, Ames encouraged greater respect for black women. Eight years later journalist Lewis Nordyke commented on the association's powerful renunciation of white manhood's alleged defense of white women. He wrote: "To outsiders the most surprising thing about the anti-lynching drive is that southern women are responsible for it. The remark of one northerner who heard for the first time of the association's program was, 'Why that *is* peculiar. Isn't the primary purpose of lynching to protect white women?' To this question thousands of southern women have answered for nearly ten years with an emphatic, 'NO.'" Empowered southern women who contradicted them publicly were not what husbands and fathers had in mind when they began the long process of reclaiming their position of power in South Carolina shortly after the end of the Civil War. It was, however, the result of their efforts. As with most aspects of postwar life in the state, the freedmen and white women were unable and in many cases unwilling to revert to antebellum roles. But many of these changes were, ironically, made possible by the desperate white men themselves.[26]

Conclusion

The Civil War laid waste to gender roles as South Carolinians understood them. Men were defeated, women had become more independent, and blacks were free and empowered. The foundations of white manhood—the ability to protect virtuous white womanhood, the domination of emasculated black men, and the right to the bodies of black women—no longer existed as they once had. White men had lost the war, their wealth, their property, and their dignity; in many ways, the last was the bitterest pill to swallow. Their response was to defiantly reclaim what they had lost. In the first months after the war, South Carolina's white elite did their best to rebuild their society in its antebellum image. They wrote a state constitution that returned the freedmen to near slavery, they elected former political officials to office, and they set about restoring an economic and social hierarchy with themselves at the top. They were nearly successful. Once Congress took control over Reconstruction, however, white southern men were stripped of their power once again. The "Radical" Reconstruction decade witnessed dramatic changes for black men and women. While material gains were more elusive, the black community won less tangible—but no less important—benefits. Black men now enjoyed both freedom and the power to reclaim their families, labor, and the opportunities of citizens and men. Black women reasserted their rights to their children and their own bodies. Unfortunately the white community was utterly unwilling to concede defeat and compromise. South Carolina's white men once again set about restoring an economic, political, and social order that was far more favorable to their own interests. Their efforts were erratic at first: knee-jerk reactions to disappointment and frustration. Nevertheless, as time passed, they became methodical, organized, and more determined than ever.

At the heart of their efforts was violence against the black community. A traditional element of the system of honor that had characterized their class in the years before the war, violence was the right and indeed the responsibility, under certain circumstances, of white men. It defined them as both powerful and masculine. Violence was the tool for restoring their authority and the gender roles that would assuage the losses of the war and their slaves. But the white men of South Carolina failed to see that the gender roles to which they so clung were already long gone. White women and the black community were irreversibly altered by their recent experiences; their roles in the violence of the postwar era did more to further those changes than eradicate them. In the process a new southern man and a new southern woman—black and white—were born.

The first postwar challenge concerned land and labor: who owned it and who performed it. Assuming that antebellum relationships were best suited to the southern economy, whites attempted to drive the freedmen back into the fields under inflexible conditions. Using contracts, they manipulated plantation laborers to meet their own needs and resorted to violence to enforce their will. They were hindered, however, by the federal government and the freedmen themselves, who were determined to work for nothing less than their real value and hoped to one day become independent of white oversight. The combination of resistance from blacks and the dominion of the Freedmen's Bureau further enraged white South Carolinians and created an explosive situation. More threatening, however, was the behavior of black women who not only denied white men the right to control their families, bodies, and labor, but who lashed out when threatened, fighting back in a manner not often seen before the war. Their aggression provoked violent retribution, but not without consequences. White men were now suddenly accountable for actions taken against black women, framing the latter in a new feminine light. Ironically the struggle over labor stripped white women of much of what had defined them as feminine before the war, even as the definition came to include their black counterparts. White women were landowners and employers throughout South Carolina, and as such, they too had a vested interest in dominating black workers. This meant that many practiced and endorsed violence. In some cases white women fought black women—a battle not simply over labor, but over the right to call oneself a real woman and enjoy the privileges of womanhood. In the process the definition of a southern woman acquired new dimensions.

More threatening to the white men of South Carolina than the independent black laborer was the aggressive black voter. Once politicized, the black community grabbed suffrage with both hands and refused to let go. They paraded, rallied, voted, and celebrated victories until—terrified by the changes around them—whites predictably lashed out. Democratic clubs encouraged their members to coerce black men using first their economic weaknesses and later violent retribution. Whites used threats, beatings, and even assassination to keep black men from enjoying what had traditionally been the province of white men exclusively. Both politics and violence were part of the decades-old tradition of "honor" in the South, and they went hand in hand very comfortably during Reconstruction. Both were also attributes of southern masculinity, and if white men could use them to control the black community, they would be firmly in control, once again, of gender roles. Unfortunately for them, the freedmen fought back. Joining the Union League and the state militia, blacks asserted their hard-won right to participate in the political process and call themselves both citizens and men. The result was a clash of riotous proportions, and the prize was the right to claim both political and masculine power. But manhood was not the only gendered trophy: womanhood also hung in the balance because both white and black women suddenly joined the fray, forever changing the meaning of the feminine. Black women were as eager for their community to enjoy the vote as their husbands and sons. They too attended rallies and meetings of the Union League and occasionally snuck in a ballot of their own. They also proudly cheered their militiamen and even took up arms themselves when necessary. Having embraced violence in defense of their families and their right to choose the nature of their labor, black women continued to use it to ensure a political voice for black South Carolina. White women followed suit. Many had discovered politics, independent of their husbands, during the war, and still more developed political skills to support their families' interests after the conflict. Although most did not yet commit violence themselves, they supported it as an effective tool for reclaiming the franchise and restoring white supremacy. These developments further altered the meanings of manhood and womanhood in South Carolina. Black men refused to yield, and women of both races continued forward, even as some fought to move backward.

Having failed to restore the prewar hegemony in the economic and political arenas, white men looked to organized violence as a solution to their problems. The birth of the Ku Klux Klan reflected both the powerlessness felt by the white community and the gender insecurity of the men responsible. From its inception the Klan was designed to return white men to positions of power in the civil life of South Carolina, but it was also intended as a voice for downtrodden white manhood. Its immediate goals were to return black laborers to the fields and keep black voters from the polls. But the Klan also concerned itself with the "protection of [white] womanhood," and the enforcement of a social order of its own design. The Klan viewed itself as a mediator of appropriate behavior in South Carolina, political, economic, and sexual. As a result, black men were targeted for threatening white men and white manhood with their fierce defense of their rights. The Klan, however, also targeted women. White women who violated social mores brought the Klan down upon their heads. But, as always, black women were far more popular victims. They were substitutes for their husbands, sons, and fathers in hiding, but more importantly, they were threats to the social order in their own right. Black women had proved to be active in the decision making of the larger freed community, particularly in the political arena. The Klan chose to punish this violation of white authority and appropriate gender roles, but black women did not blithely sit back and suffer the abuse. They fought back until finally aided by the federal government. The Klan trials, ironically, empowered the last group from which to be heard. White women shone as supporters of Klan violence throughout the organization's tenure, but they were truly altered once hundreds of Klansmen found themselves in jail. Their wives and daughters kept the home front intact, often soliciting aid in their loved ones' defense. But recent experiences pushed them further. They defiantly demonstrated support for the "suffering" accused, some embracing violence as a solution to their woes. For the white men who brought the Klan to South Carolina, its greatest tragedy was not its inability to restore white supremacy, but its impact on gender roles. The Klan did not merely fail to assert its own social and sexual hierarchy; it helped create a new, authoritative southern woman, one who certainly did not conform to the ideals most Klansmen had in mind. In the meantime, black men continued to work, to vote, and to claim the rights of manhood as their own.

By 1876 violence alone had not helped white men retake South Carolina. The political climate indicated that the time was ripe for counterrevolution, but past efforts had failed, and many were uncertain as to how to proceed. A small group of unrepentant Democrats, however, conceived a plan. They traded desperation and relative disorganization for a political machine so finely tuned it marshaled a disconsolate populace to the victory they had sought for ten years. The election of 1876 was a violent victory for white supremacy, but in keeping with recent failures, it was not necessarily a victory for white manhood. The Democrats managed to elect Hampton to the governor's office, and they retook the state legislature, but the process pushed changes in gender roles even further. From the beginning, the campaign and election were deeply gendered events, from the feminized symbolism of the state itself, to the violence committed in the name of masculine prerogative, to the activities of the women of South Carolina. The state was portrayed as a woman, imperiled by a corrupt government, and in imminent danger of being ravished by the horde—either federal or freed. Such language and imagery became a part of every stage of Hampton's efforts, including the tableaux that graced his entrance at all major rallies. Responsible for these images, appropriately, were the white women of the state. These new Democratic constituents participated in the campaign at unheard-of levels. They decorated, sewed, cheered, performed, and pushed the juggernaut forward. Black women were equally active. They too attended rallies and supported their candidate. But the two groups ultimately had more in common: they each embraced a new aggressive female role in the struggle for South Carolina. White women endorsed and excused violence committed in the name of Hampton. At the same time, black women took matters into their own hands, attacking their political enemies even when they were members of their own community. Such behavior meant that even though white Democrats had defeated the black voter, their political success did not go hand in hand with a return of the gender roles they had long hoped to restore. Black men resisted the idea that political power equaled complete social control, and women of both races were long past the idealized notion of the demure, politically naïve southern lady. Once again, the efforts of South Carolina's white men were self-defeating.

In South Carolina the rise of lynching was the final stage in the white man's campaign to completely expel blacks from the world of southern manhood and restore the gender roles they failed to see were all but extinct. Lynching combined the masculine attachment to violence with the gendered symbolism prevalent in both politics and Klan activities. Lynching was also the most direct and explicit way to tell black men that they were unwelcome in the world of men. For a variety of crimes ranging from perceived insults to murder, black men were tortured and killed as a reminder that, in South Carolina, only white men were entitled to the privileges of power and dignity. But lynching was also a direct attack on black women. As a punishment for their strengths and their claims to the rights of womanhood, white men routinely assaulted black women. It was a message to the black community that they were helpless to guard against abuses of their women, and a message to the women themselves that they did not warrant the protections enjoyed by ideal womanhood. Lynching therefore imposed antebellum gender standards better than any other method in the late nineteenth century, but as effective as it seemed to be, once again, women changed the rules. Black and white women best distorted those antebellum roles by embracing lynching as their own crusade. From Ida B. Wells to Josephine St. Pierre Ruffin and from Rebecca Latimer Felton to Jesse Daniel Ames, women adopted a role for themselves that was both public and political, and despite their claims to refined and privileged womanhood, it was a definition of their own making.

The Reconstruction era in South Carolina failed to create permanent changes in the political and economic life of the state. The black community was left downtrodden—but not without hope—by the turn of the century. What remained to them was intangible but important: the right to consider themselves the social equals of whites, not in terms of class, but gender. The black community persisted in the notion that although their vote was largely gone and their economic opportunities never there, they were, by virtue of freedom, men and women on par with their white counterparts. Although white men did their best to dispel such ideas, their methods only led to greater changes for both men and women. Masculine power and feminine virtue—as proponents and victims—found common ground in the activities of vigilantes, Klansmen, Red Shirts, and lynch mobs. Southern violence had once been the province of men, designed to promote mutually exclusive roles for the sexes and the races, but in the postwar tumult, violence became a universal and interracial tool. In South Carolina, men and women changed the nature of violence, and violence changed the nature of men and women.

Notes

Introduction

1. Tolnay and Beck, *A Festival of Violence*, 9.

2. The so-called revisionist school of Reconstruction historians was a product of the mid-twentieth-century civil rights movement. Revisionists praised the efforts of Congress and liberal southerners to create a new social, political, and economic order. They stressed educational achievements, the expanded definition of citizenship that followed the Reconstruction amendments, and the attempts to redistribute land and grant the freedmen greater economic power. They lauded black political gains but dismissed the notion of a "black Reconstruction" vilified by the Dunning school. More recently, however, postrevisionists have criticized this idealized view of such a tumultuous period. Many historians of the 1970s and 1980s argued that Reconstruction was in fact far too conservative and that blacks enjoyed few genuine changes. Racism, they claimed, was not exclusively southern, and northern occupation forces, more often than not, thwarted the freedmen's efforts to liberate themselves from white oversight. The most advanced of these recent general studies was *Reconstruction: America's Unfinished Revolution*, by Eric Foner. Foner combined many of these earlier histories when he concluded that—as his title suggests—Reconstruction was indeed revolutionary in theory, but for every step forward, there was an equally powerful step back. Congress, he claimed, was cautious, and the reactionary impulse of most white southerners was strong. Foner further introduced a new central character into the story of Reconstruction: the freedman. His study chronicled freedmen's efforts to renew family ties, educate themselves, and support their families. Foner also illustrated the political power they wielded, although he too rejected the myth of absolute black power. He concluded that the "Redemption" of the South was set in motion by violent forces in reaction to the social freedoms granted the black population.

3. Thompson, *Ousting the Carpetbagger from South Carolina*, 20; Simkins and Woody, *South Carolina during Reconstruction*, 11 n.; Rable, *But There Was No Peace*, 71; histories of Reconstruction in South Carolina have focused—for better or worse—on the fact that the black population in the Palmetto State outnumbered its white counterpart. The Dunning writers remarked on the "Africanized" nature of South Carolina's Reconstruction government and characterized it as wildly corrupt. Revisionists Francis Butler Simkins and Robert Hilliard Woody tried to liberate the freedmen and the state from these negative assessments in their book *South Carolina during Reconstruction*, and they criticized native whites for the violence they used to curtail the rights of Republicans of both races. Joel Williamson continued in this vein in *After Slavery: The Negro in South Carolina during Reconstruction*. He illustrated the meanings of freedom from the perspective of the freedmen and described Reconstruction in South Carolina as a "period of unequalled progress" (63). Richard Zuczek's recent study *State of Rebellion: Reconstruction in South*

Carolina criticizes Williamson's optimism and brings the story of Reconstruction violence to the forefront. Zuczek concludes that violence was endemic to the state from the beginning of the nineteenth century. He argues that the violent reaction to black achievements during Reconstruction was merely another phase in whites' struggle to "protect their state," similar to their behavior during the Nullification Crisis and following the election of Abraham Lincoln. Zuczek writes that "the North stopped fighting—physically and mentally—in 1865; the South, however, did not," and he blames the violent predilections of southerners for the failure of Reconstruction (6). These histories of Reconstruction have grown to include the perspectives of multiple actors and increasingly embraced new approaches. However, despite the fact that gender issues have consistently shaped social, economic, and political conditions throughout American history, historians have only recently begun to examine Reconstruction through this particular lens. Both Joan Scott and Joel Williamson have argued the centrality of gender roles in defining relationships and power structures. Current historians of the nineteenth century have emphasized this essential component in their examinations of Reconstruction, Redemption and the rise of Jim Crow. Nina Silber has written that the outcome of the war itself was gendered by the victorious North. Immediately following the war, the language used by northerners, she argues, portrayed the South as feminine and therefore weak. They played upon Jefferson Davis's flight, allegedly in women's clothes, and mocked as "shrewish" and uncivilized those southern women who lashed out at northern soldiers. Silber concludes that gender was a "central metaphor" in the dialogue between the regions, one that encouraged Reconstruction measures and ultimately led to reunification and the celebration of the "Old South" (6). In *Gendered Strife and Confusion: The Political Culture of Reconstruction,* Laura Edwards claims that the question of manhood and womanhood—who could claim it and how to define it—was central to the social and political battles of the Reconstruction era. She argues that the private world of home and family shaped public debates and chronicles the shifting terrain of gender roles.

4. Jane Turner Censer's *The Reconstruction of Southern White Womanhood, 1865–1895* builds upon Scott's groundbreaking work. Censer studies the varied responses of elite women, venturing to argue that some even questioned the developing racial order of the period. She also breaks the late nineteenth century down into three generations of white women with increasing degrees of independent spirit. Although she characterizes the public efforts of white women as "nonpolitical," she stresses the dramatic changes in gender roles (278). LeeAnn Whites, however, has criticized these conclusions. In *Gender Matters: Civil War, Reconstruction, and the Making of the New South,* Whites writes that gender "constructs individuals' sense of themselves and their place in the social order" but concludes that white women's postwar memorialization of the Confederacy and its fallen soldiers was more of an effort to reestablish antebellum gender proscriptions than to break into the "public" realm of politics and social power (1). In her analysis of apprenticeship laws and custody battles, Karen Zipf has concluded that black women rewrote definitions of womanhood in their struggles to rebuild the black family ("Reconstructing 'Free Women,'" 8).

5. Catherine Clinton brought the significance of the violence committed against freedwomen into light and at the same time demonstrated the struggle of black women to salvage their much-maligned public image and create "the opportunity to express themselves, pioneering new avenues for individual and collective identity." Although her analysis of the "sexual terrorism" of white men against black women implies that the latter suffered more often than they persevered, other historians have interpreted the events

surrounding violence against black women more affirmatively (332); Hannah Rosen adds that rape was an attempt by white men to undermine black women's—and men's—assertion of their citizenship, but black women claimed the rights and protections of free womanhood by insisting that sexual assaults against them were indeed a crime (Rosen, "'Not That Sort of Women,'" 267).

6. LeeAnn Whites's examination of the southern household during the Civil War illustrates that the home served to define "free men" (*The Civil War as a Crisis in Gender,* 17–18). Stephanie McCurry's study of the yeoman class in the South Carolina lowcountry comes to the same conclusion: the domestic prerogatives of those with control over their dependents—wives, children, slaves—were denied to black men but brought the white men of the yeomanry into an alliance with the elite to defend their hegemony in this arena (*Masters of Small Worlds,* 213). Whites, McCurry, and Peter Bardaglio agree that manhood was defined by dominance within the home (Bardaglio, *Reconstructing the Household,* 120); Bederman, *Manliness and Civilization,* 121.

7. For an excellent account of the reconstruction of the Sea Islands during the war, see Rose's *Rehearsal for Reconstruction;* Wright, *Old South, New South,* 18–19; Eric Foner's analysis of the Reconstruction era argued that one of the great failures of the period was the death of "free labor ideology," the labor theory that dominated the antebellum battles between the North and the South. Before the war northerners stressed the superiority of their system, which allowed for social mobility and encouraged workers to aspire to more. Foner concludes that devotion to the system declined after the war and was replaced by a fear of class differences. This fear encouraged the federal government to abandon the drive for true equality and retrench into a world of labor contracts and other forms of control over the southern worker. Resistance to this control would initiate the violence that would come to characterize the late-nineteenth-century South (see Foner, *Reconstruction*). Julie Saville's *The Work of Reconstruction* ventures that blacks in fact rejected northern free labor systems or at least the idea that working for wages constituted genuine freedom. She argues that labor disputes and the negotiations that followed were the origins of black political organization and central to the broader changes that swept the postbellum South.

8. Jones notes that the unfortunate result was the devaluation of their labor and the illusion that they withdrew from the workforce (*Labor of Love, Labor of Sorrow,* 59); Schwalm goes so far as to claim that the struggle between blacks and whites to control the public world was echoed within the black home as husbands and wives worked to determine private gender roles (*A Hard Fight for We,* 260).

9. One of the earliest examinations of the politics of Reconstruction in South Carolina, Thomas Holt's *Black over White: Negro Political Leadership in South Carolina during Reconstruction,* blamed the collapse of the state's Republican party on divisions among the freedmen themselves. Holt argued that a class- or caste-based schism stunted the advances made possible by a powerful black majority. More recently, however, Steven Hahn has emphasized the lasting influence of black politicization in African American life. Hahn finds political significance in the everyday actions of both slaves and freedmen and shows how the latter linked political activity with the potential for land ownership, resulting in widespread participation (*A Nation under Our Feet,* 212); Elsa Barkley Brown, "Negotiating and Transforming the Public Sphere: African American Political Life in the Transition from Slavery to Freedom," in Dailey, Gilmore, and Simon, eds., *Jumpin' Jim Crow,* 35; Dunlap, "The Reform of Rape Law and the Problem of White Men," 353–54; Hodes, *White Women, Black Men,* 166.

10. Zuczek, *State of Rebellion,* 5; Rosen, "'Not That Sort of Women,'" 274.

11. The earliest histories of the Ku Klux Klan attributed its rise to the corruption and social disarray created by "black Reconstruction." They portrayed the Klan as a justifiable response to the racial imbalance created in the South by the federal government but argued that the Klan was never intended to overthrow Reconstruction. In the 1920s Francis Butler Simkins was the first historian to describe the goals of the Klan as insidious and destructive ("The Ku Klux Klan in South Carolina, 1868–1871"). Simkins was bothered by the flattering accounts that preceded his, but he concluded that the Klan was only marginally important in the story of Reconstruction. In the 1960s Herbert Shapiro contradicted Simkins when he argued that the Klan was indeed powerful and, at least in part, responsible for the reversal of Reconstruction measures ("The Ku Klux Klan during Reconstruction"). It wasn't until the 1970s that Allen Trelease produced the first major modern treatment of the Ku Klux Klan, *White Terror.* Trelease argued in favor of a direct relationship between southern politics and Klan violence. He concluded that the Klan was the military arm of the Democratic Party and an effective force in the battle against Reconstruction waged by southern whites. Trelease dismissed the notion that the Klan was either justified or motivated by corruption, and he demonstrated the widespread support for the organization among whites of all classes. J. C. A. Stagg ("The Problem of Klan Violence") followed Trelease's analysis with an examination of the Klan in South Carolina. Stagg, however, argued that the Klan's origins were in labor troubles but that it became politicized once blacks got the right to vote. Alternatively some historians like George Rable (*But There Was No Peace*), Edward Ayers, and Bertram Wyatt-Brown have argued that the Klan's motives were less exclusively political. Together with Lou Williams, author of *The Great South Carolina Ku Klux Klan Trials,* they argue that social control and racial anxieties were at the heart of the Klan's rise and successes. Richard Zuczek's recent analysis of Reconstruction in South Carolina returns to a modified version of Trelease's assessment by crediting political struggles with giving rise to the Klan, but only because, he argues, whites saw political power as the route to social control. These historians have restored the nuance of the Klan to modern histories, but they stop short of the gender analysis that is such a necessary component of this story; Simkins and Woody, *South Carolina during Reconstruction,* 444. Several historians have found that Klan activities involved women of both races and were driven by gender or sexual anxieties. LeeAnn Whites has written that many of the early accounts of the Klan were authored by women and often stressed the participation of white women. She further argues that the women of the South won the fight for Redemption through their support of the Klan. See Whites, *Gender Matters,* 93. Martha Hodes has found that the Klan linked the political rights of black men with sexual access to white women, and that they often used sexual mutilation to punish their victims, even when the "crimes" had nothing to do with sexual issues. The Klan, she contends, sought to police sexual activity in the South, forever uniting sexuality, politics, and violence. See *Sex, Love, Race;* "The Sexualization of Reconstruction Politics"; and *White Women, Black Men.* Scott Nelson further demonstrates the connection between economics and sexuality, arguing that the Klan feared and conflated changes with both of these: when black men entered the marketplace as equals, white men interpreted their access to the economy as sexual access to white women. He adds that the Klan was known to have engaged in "rituals of manhood, sexual power, and gallantry," including homoerotic initiation practices and the symbolic and literal emasculation of black men. See *Iron Confederacies* and "Livestock, Boundaries, and Public Space in Spartanburg," 111. Elaine Frantz Parsons has discovered a wealth of gendered symbolism in the costumes

and cultural tropes of the Klan. Seeking to reassert white manhood, she claims, Klansmen often adopted women's clothing and blackface in an effort to "appropriate the identities . . . of those who were not masters" and "transcend" their humiliation. See "Costume and Performance in the Reconstruction-Era Ku Klux Klan," 831.

12. Many studies of lynching focus on the influence of demographics, politics, and economics. Arthur Raper's 1933 study, *The Tragedy of Lynching,* claimed that lower-class, relatively powerless whites were largely responsible for lynching in the South. Raper also examined the Black Belt, in which, he believed, fewer lynchings took place because the social, political, and economic hierarchies of the region were more well defined. Sociologists Stewart Tolnay and E. M. Beck have similarly found a direct connection between patterns of lynching and economic changes. They conclude that cotton prices, white landlessness, and the question of control over black laborers drove lynching into the early twentieth century. See *A Festival of Violence.* More recently, however, Terrance Finnegan attributes the popularity of lynching to political motives: "lynching," he writes, "was political terrorism." Although lynching in the states in his study declined after disfranchisement, Finnegan finds that it was then driven by the persistence of black participation in the court system and other "political" issues. Unfortunately—and perhaps tellingly—Finnegan defines "political" broadly, including economic, social, and cultural matters under that more limited heading. Such a definition reflects the fact that lynching cannot be confined to strictly political motives and was inseparable from more personal and intangible issues. See Finnegan, "Lynching and Political Power in Mississippi and South Carolina" in Brundage, *Under Sentence of Death,* 191. Also see Finnegan, "'At the hands of parties unknown.'" Fitzhugh Brundage has produced the analysis that best embraces the variations that helps lynching to so often defy generalizations. He concludes that the methods and causes of lynching depended on a multiplicity of factors including location, the nature of the economy, and the character and background of the participants. Notably, however, Brundage draws attention to the influence of gender, in particular, changing gender roles as a driving force behind the phenomenon. See *Lynching in the New South.*

13. Brundage, *Lynching in the New South,* 264, appendix A6.

14. See Wells-Barnett, *On Lynchings.* More recently historians have echoed Wells's work by examining the connection between lynching and constructions of manhood. Joel Williamson, playing upon Wyatt-Brown's description of antebellum southern honor, has blamed lynching on the inability of white men to feel sufficiently confident in their role as manly protector of women. See Williamson, *The Crucible of Race.* Glenda Gilmore has written that, "when white men created and aggravated the danger of black rapists, they underscored white women's dependency on white men, a tactic that put both black men and white women in their places." This attempt to contain their former dependents was resisted in various ways by both parties and, as Gilmore argues, was echoed by black women who claimed both the rights of womanhood and the power of a public voice. See *Gender and Jim Crow,* 96. LeeAnn Whites asserts that white women like Rebecca Latimer Felton used lynching to resurrect white manhood. By promoting the idea of the black rapist, white women demanded protection from white men according to traditional gender roles. But Whites adds that women also called attention to the threat of the black rapist to punish white men for their failure to defend them during the Civil War. The failure of southern manhood empowered southern womanhood; however, Whites denies any desire on the part of white women to do anything other than reclaim the private sphere. See Whites, *Gender Matters.* Gail Bederman asserts that lynching was, for whites, the punishment of excessive black sexuality by restrained, and therefore civilized, white

manhood. Ironically, she adds, the act itself was as bestial and uncivilized as the rape they condemned: in effect, too much manliness. See *Manliness and Civilization.* Finally, Robyn Wiegman writes that "lynching guarantees the white mob's privilege of physical and psychic penetration" while simultaneously "feminizing" the black victim. She adds that lynching targeted the work of the Freedmen's Bureau in particular: by designating the man the head of the black household, the bureau had given freedmen the prerogatives of "free men" and, therefore, claims to southern manhood. See Wiegman, "The Anatomy of Lynching," 455; White, *Rope and Faggot.*

Chapter 1: Land, Labor, and Violence

1. Wyatt-Brown, *Southern Honor,* 357.

2. For a description of the contributions of black women to South Carolina labor systems from the antebellum era through Reconstruction, see Schwalm, *A Hard Fight for We.*

3. Holt, *Black over White,* 43.

4. For a more detailed account of slave resistance to the experimental labor systems created by northern occupation forces in the Sea Islands during the war, as well as in the upcountry following the surrender, see Julie Saville, *The Work of Reconstruction.* Saville further describes the politicization of land and labor issues among the freedmen following federal occupation of the state; Eric Foner's seminal work, *Reconstruction,* argues that control over their labor represented the realization of the freedmen's definition of freedom, while white's negative response to emancipation and federal intervention was motivated by both their fear of an empowered black populace and their need for a well-controlled labor force.

5. C. W. Moise to F. W. Dawson, September 15, 1885, F. W. Dawson Papers, Duke University, as quoted in Williamson, *After Slavery,* 275–76.

6. Wright, *Old South, New South,* 18–19; Morris, "Equality, 'Extraordinary Law,' and Criminal Justice," 30.

7. "Edgefield District Labor Contracts, 1866–1867," Freedmen's Bureau R.G. 105, National Archives and Records Administration (hereafter NAB); Post, "A 'Carpetbagger' in South Carolina," 25; "Edgefield District Labor Contracts, 1866–1867," Freedmen's Bureau R.G. 105, NAB.

8. "Greenville Reports of Outrages," Freedmen's Bureau R.G. 105, NAB; "Reports from the Central Office of the Freedmen's Bureau," Freedmen's Bureau R.G. 105, NAB.

9. "Edgefield District Labor Contracts, 1866–1867," Freedmen's Bureau R.G. 105, NAB; "Reports from the Central Office of the Freedmen's Bureau," Freedmen's Bureau R.G. 105, NAB.

10. "Marion Testimony of Witnesses," Freedmen's Bureau R.G. 105, NAB; "Reports from the Central Office of the Freedmen's Bureau," Freedmen's Bureau R.G. 105, NAB.

11. Leslie Schwalm has determined that black women throughout the lowcountry in South Carolina created new methods of resistance to white authority in the postwar era. See *A Hard Fight for We,* 177; "Unionville Register of Complaints," Freedmen's Bureau R.G. 105, NAB.

12. "Moncks Corner Testimony, Reports, and Other Records," Freedmen's Bureau R.G. 105, NAB; "Moncks Corner Registers of Complaints," Freedmen's Bureau R.G. 105, NAB; "Darlington Miscellaneous Records Relating to Complaints," Freedmen's Bureau R.G. 105, NAB.

13. For a more detailed description of black women and their role in the postwar labor force, see Jones, *Labor of Love, Labor of Sorrow.*

14. Karen Zipf's article "Reconstructing 'Free Women'" described the battle freedwomen waged within southern legal systems to reclaim control over their children. Zipf concludes that through these custody suits, black women fought the political and economic power of whites; "Darlington Misc. Records Relating to Complaints," Freedmen's Bureau R.G. 105, NAB; "York Registers of Complaints," Freedmen's Bureau R.G. 105, NAB; "Orangeburg Register of Complaints," "York Registers of Complaints," Freedmen's Bureau R.G. 105, NAB; "York Registers of Complaints," Freedmen's Bureau R.G. 105, NAB; "Darlington Journal of Complaints, 1866–67," Freedmen's Bureau R.G. 105, NAB.

15. "Darlington Misc. Records Relating to Complaints," Freedmen's Bureau R.G. 105, NAB; "Reports from the Central Office of the Freedmen's Bureau," Freedmen's Bureau R.G. 105, NAB; "York Registers of Complaints," Freedmen's Bureau R.G. 105, NAB.

16. Schwalm, *A Hard Fight for We,* 173; "Newberry Register of Complaints," Freedmen's Bureau R.G. 105, NAB; "Orangeburg Register of Complaints," Freedmen's Bureau R.G. 105, NAB.

17. Hannah Rosen writes that black women's use of the authorities to fight for their rights proves that they both embraced citizenship as eagerly as black men and that they believed they were, as citizens, entitled to justice and protection from the government. She adds that these actions undermined the power of elite white men and asserted their claims to womanhood. See Rosen, "'Not That Sort of Women,'" in Hodes, ed., *Sex, Love, Race,* 270. Karen Zipf claims that black women pushed the boundaries of the legal system to rewrite the meaning of "freedwomen" to more closely resemble the rights of "free women." In the process, they created legal protections and won greater visibility and independence (see "Reconstructing 'Free Women,'" 16, 26); "Unionville Register of Complaints," Freedmen's Bureau R.G. 105, NAB; "Abbeville Register of Complaints," Freedmen's Bureau R.G. 105, NAB; "Reports from the Central Office of the Freedmen's Bureau," Freedmen's Bureau R.G. 105, NAB; "Newberry Register of Complaints," Freedmen's Bureau R.G. 105, NAB; "Darlington Misc. Records Relating to Complaints," Freedmen's Bureau R.G. 105, NAB; "Moncks Corner Registers of Complaints," Freedmen's Bureau R.G. 105, NAB; "Greenville Reports of Outrages," Freedmen's Bureau R.G. 105, NAB.

18. Stanley, "Conjugal Bonds and Wage Labor"; "Orangeburg Register of Complaints," Freedmen's Bureau R.G. 105, NAB; "Newberry Register of Complaints," Freedmen's Bureau R.G. 105, NAB.

19. "Diary of Eugenia R. G. Leland, 1865–1868," Leland Papers, South Caroliniana.

20. "York Registers of Complaints," Freedmen's Bureau R.G. 105, NAB; "Newberry Register of Complaints," Freedmen's Bureau R.G. 105, NAB; "Darlington Journal of Complaints," Freedmen's Bureau R.G. 105, NAB.

21. "Abbeville Register of Complaints," Freedmen's Bureau R.G. 105, NAB; "Unionville Register of Complaints," Freedmen's Bureau R.G. 105, NAB; "Moncks Corner Registers of Complaints," Freedmen's Bureau R.G. 105, NAB; "Barnwell Reports of Outrages," Freedmen's Bureau R.G. 105, NAB.

22. "Summerville Registers of Complaints," Freedmen's Bureau R.G. 105, NAB; "Rockville Registers of Complaints," Freedmen's Bureau R.G. 105, NAB; "Columbia Register of Complaints," Freedmen's Bureau R.G. 105, NAB; "Chester Register of Complaints," Freedmen's Bureau R.G. 105, NAB; "Anderson Court House Reports of Outrages," Freedmen's Bureau R.G. 105, NAB; "Darlington Journal of [Business and]

Complaints," Freedmen's Bureau R.G. 105, NAB; "Anderson Court House Reports of Outrages," Freedmen's Bureau R.G. 105, NAB; "Moncks Corner Registers of Complaints," Freedmen's Bureau R.G. 105, NAB.

23. "Moncks Corner Registers of Complaints," Freedmen's Bureau R.G. 105, NAB; "Anderson Court House Reports of Outrages," Freedmen's Bureau R.G. 105, NAB.

Chapter 2: Black Politics and Violence

1. Leland, *A Voice From South Carolina,* 13.

2. Saville's *The Work of Reconstruction* argues this point and adds that labor struggles during the war were the first sign of political activism among the black community; Abbott, "Freedom's Cry"; Thomas Holt illustrated the immediate political activism of South Carolina blacks in his book *Black over White.* Recent work by Steven Hahn has shown that this powerful reaction to the potential for political power and social change was embraced by all classes of blacks, from the urban mulatto elite to the darker-skinned rural poor. See *A Nation under Our Feet.*

3. See Eric Foner, "Reconstruction Revisited," 89. Foner further writes that every black institution was politicized in this era, drawing freedmen spanning economic divisions, geography, and gender into the political battles of the day. See Foner, *Reconstruction,* 282–83, 290.

4. McPherson, *Ordeal by Fire,* 557; Hahn, *A Nation under Our Feet,* 218. Hahn adds that by electing of blacks to multiple important local offices, the towns and counties of the South "experienced political transitions and inversions of an immediacy and magnitude unprecedented in the region, nation, or hemisphere."

5. Holt, *Black over White,* 18.

6. Julie Saville argues that the vote "gave an explicitly political form to social divisions between employer and employee," and that while whites used economic issues to pressure blacks politically, blacks used employment as the centerpiece of their early activism (*The Work of Reconstruction,* 179); "York Registers of Complaints," Freedmen's Bureau R.G. 105, NAB.

7. "Newberry Register of Complaints," Freedmen's Bureau R.G. 105, NAB; "Abbeville Register of Complaints," Freedmen's Bureau R.G. 105, NAB.

8. Zuczek, *State of Rebellion,* 48; "Marion Statements Relating to Complaints," Freedmen's Bureau R.G. 105, NAB; "Greenville Register of Complaints," Freedmen's Bureau R.G. 105, NAB; "Reports from the Central Office of the Freedmen's Bureau," Freedmen's Bureau R.G. 105, NAB; "Abbeville Register of Complaints," Freedmen's Bureau R.G. 105, NAB; "Report of Outrages Committed by Whites against Freedmen in Abbeville County," Freedmen's Bureau R.G. 105, NAB; "Greenville Register of Complaints," Freedmen's Bureau R.G. 105, NAB.

9. "Abbeville Register of Complaints," Freedmen's Bureau R.G. 105, NAB; "Reports from the Central Office of the Freedmen's Bureau," Freedmen's Bureau R.G. 105, NAB; "Abbeville Register of Complaints," Freedmen's Bureau R.G. 105, NAB.

10. "Proceedings of Colored People's Convention of South Carolina," 24–25, as cited in Hahn, *A Nation under Our Feet,* 122. However, even as Hahn cites a number of deeply gendered statements and activities—white and black—he focuses on political change rather than the fluid nature of gender roles; "Testimony of Alexander P. Wylie," *Report of the Joint Select Committee,* vol. 5, 1425; Nelson, "Livestock, Boundaries, and Public Space in Spartanburg" 324.

11. "Abbeville Register of Complaints," Freedmen's Bureau R.G. 105, NAB.

12. Foner, *Reconstruction,* 283; also see Foner for a more detailed discussion of activities of the Union League; and for more information on the league in South Carolina, see Holt, *Black over White.*

13. "Newberry Register of Complaints," Freedmen's Bureau R.G. 105, NAB; "Greenville Reports of Outrages," Freedmen's Bureau R.G. 105, NAB; "Greenville Register of Complaints," Freedmen's Bureau R.G. 105, NAB.

14. "Marion Testimony of Witnesses at Several Court Cases," Freedmen's Bureau R.G. 105, NAB; "Orangeburg Register of Complaints," Freedmen's Bureau R.G. 105, NAB; "Darlington Misc. Records Relating to Complaints," Freedmen's Bureau R.G. 105, NAB; "Orangeburg Register of Complaints," Freedmen's Bureau R.G. 105, NAB.

15. Trelease, *White Terror,* 350; "Summerville Registers of Complaints," Freedmen's Bureau R.G. 105, NAB; "Reports from the Central Office of the Freedmen's Bureau," Freedmen's Bureau R.G. 105, NAB; "Orangeburg Register of Complaints," Freedmen's Bureau R.G. 105, NAB.

16. Columbia, S.C. *Daily Phoenix,* October 25, 187; Leland, *A Voice from South Carolina,* 56; Columbia, S.C. *Daily Phoenix,* October 25, 1870; Foner, *Reconstruction,* 427.

17. "Greenville Register of Complaints," Freedmen's Bureau R.G. 105, NAB; "Abbeville Register of Complaints," Freedmen's Bureau R.G. 105, NAB.

18. Brown, "Negotiating and Transforming the Public Sphere," 35.

19. Zuczek, *State of Rebellion,* 34.

20. "E. B. Munro to her mother," November 9, 1876, J. B. Grimball Papers, Duke University, as cited in Williamson, *After Slavery,* 344; Thompson, *Ousting the Carpetbagger from South Carolina,* 129; Columbia, S.C. *Daily Phoenix,* October 25, 1870; "Abbeville Register of Complaints," Freedmen's Bureau R.G. 105, NAB; "Testimony of E. W. Seibels," *Report of the Joint Select Committee,* vol. 3, 123.

21. "Abbeville Register of Complaints," Freedmen's Bureau R.G. 105, NAB; "Testimony of Hariet Hernandes," *Report of the Joint Select Committee,* vol. 3, 586; Formwalt, "Petitioning Congress for Protection," 318.

22. Hine and Thompson, *A Shining Thread of Hope,* 206; Foner, *Reconstruction,* 98; J. Smith, *Black Voices from Reconstruction,* 111–12; "Abbeville Reports of Outrages," Freedmen's Bureau R.G. 105, NAB; "Greenville Reports of Outrages," Freedmen's Bureau R.G. 105, NAB; McPherson, *Ordeal by Fire,* 574.

23. "Letter from A. L. Close to B. F. Butler," March 6, 1871, House R.G. 233, NAB; Zuczek, *State of Rebellion,* 31; Tindall, *South Carolina Negroes,* 223; Shapiro, *White Violence and Black Response,* 9.

24. For a thorough account of the activities of white southern women during the war, see Faust, Drew Gilpin, *Mothers of Invention: Women of the Slaveholding South in the American Civil War* (New York: Vintage Books, 1996).

25. "Testimony of C. H. Brownings," January 23, 1867, House R.G. 233, NAB; "Testimony of C. H. Brownings," January 23, 1867, House R.G. 233, NAB.

26. Laura Edwards has written that although elite white women tended to shy away from public political activism in the early postwar years, poor white women—like their black counterparts—embraced politics openly. However, she claims that black and white women who ventured into the political arena became pawns in the battle between black and white men (see *Gendered Strife and Confusion,* 151, 12); Shapiro, *White Violence and Black Response,* 74, 73.

27. Ella Aiken Smart, Memoir 1902, David Wyatt Aiken Papers, South Caroliniana; Shapiro, "The Ku Klux Klan during Reconstruction," 35–36; Ella Aiken Smart, Memoir

1902, David Wyatt Aiken Papers, South Caroliniana; Shapiro, "The Ku Klux Klan during Reconstruction," 35–36.

Chapter 3: Getting Organized

1. Early Klan histories focused on the political agenda of the first Ku Klux Klan. Allen Trelease argued that the organization was a "counterrevolutionary device to combat the Republican Party and Congressional Reconstruction policy in the South" (*White Terror,* xi). George Rable built on Trelease's premise when he asserted that the Klan's goals were not only to keep blacks from the polls but to promote white solidarity, political, social, and economic (Rable, *But There Was No Peace,* 94–95). Recent histories, however, have focused more deeply on the Klan's social and economic motives, including the question of gender and sexuality. Scott Nelson finds an economic cause in the unstable conditions created by the rise of the railroad in the South, but he adds that much of what drove Klan violence was the shifting gender roles and sexual anxieties produced by economic instability (*Iron Confederacies*). Further, Martha Hodes writes that the Klan sought to police sexual activity in the South because the Klan saw a direct connection between manhood and sexuality and politics. She adds that the violence promoted by the Klan served the dual purpose of subjugating black men and white women (*Sex, Love, Race*).

2. "A Hundred Years of Terror."

3. Elaine Frantz Parsons claims that the "tricks," costumes, and rituals used by the Klan were themselves a sign of the sexual anxieties that riddled white southern men. She argues that Klansmen chose tropes that would help them reclaim their lost masculinity ("Costume and Performance in the Reconstruction-Era Ku Klux Klan," 819, 828).

4. Williamson, *A Rage for Order,* 38. Williamson further argues that this confusion led to powerful sexual insecurities, and that the birth of the second Klan shifted the source of those insecurities from potent black men to powerful industries and Jews (244); Williamson, *A Rage for Order,* 39; Randel, *The Ku Klux Klan,* 254; Foner, *Reconstruction,* 433–34.

5. L. Williams, *The Great South Carolina Ku Klux Klan Trials,* 19; Zuczek, *State of Rebellion,* 55; Allen, *Governor Chamberlain's Administration in South Carolina,* 310.

6. "Rice Hope Plantation Register of Court Cases," Freedmen's Bureau R.G. 105, NAB; "Columbia Register of Complaints," Freedmen's Bureau R.G. 105, NAB; "Abbeville Reports of Outrages," Freedmen's Bureau R.G. 105, NAB; Zuczek, *State of Rebellion,* 30; "Orangeburg Register of Complaints," Freedmen's Bureau R.G. 105, NAB; "Greenville Register of Complaints," Freedmen's Bureau R.G. 105, NAB.

7. "Letter from J. K. Chambers," June 28, 1868, Iredell Jones Papers, South Caroliniana; *New York Times,* March 21, 1871; "Letter from 'Head Quarters,'" c. October 1868, Iredell Jones Papers, South Caroliniana; Shapiro, "The Ku Klux Klan during Reconstruction," 36.

8. "Letter from 'Head Quarters,'" c. October 1868, Iredell Jones Papers, South Caroliniana; Foner, *Reconstruction,* 426; Zuczek, *State of Rebellion,* 57; "Letter from J. K. Chambers," June 28, 1868, Iredell Jones Papers, South Caroliniana; *Report of the Joint Select Committee,* vol. 1, 85; Trelease, *White Terror,* 115.

9. "South Carolina—Reports from the Central Office of the Freedmen's Bureau," Freedmen's Bureau R.G. 105, NAB; Post, "A 'Carpetbagger' in South Carolina," 59; "Testimony of James H. Goss," *Report of the Joint Select Committee,* vol. 3, 68; Trelease, *White Terror,* 353; *New York Times,* March 21, 1871.

10. Rable, *But There Was No Peace,* 96; Stagg, "The Problem of Klan Violence," 308.

11. Shapiro, "The Ku Klux Klan during Reconstruction," 38; "Testimony of Leander Bigger," *Report of the Joint Select Committee,* vol. 1, 273–88; "Testimony of Hariet Hernandes," *Report of the Joint Select Committee,* vol. 3, 589.

12. "Testimony of E. W. Seibels," *Report of the Joint Select Committee,* vol. 3, 97; "Testimony of Landon M. Gentry," *Report of the Joint Select Committee,* vol. 3, 189; "Testimony of James Steadman," *Report of the Joint Select Committee,* vol. 4, 1022; "Testimony of Lewis Merrill," *Report of the Joint Select Committee,* vol. 5, 1480; In his account of the Klan's activities during Reconstruction, Allen Trelease notes more than once that the significant majority of Klan victims in South Carolina were black (*White Terror,* 115, 361).

13. Scott Nelson has written that the Klan targeted those black men who worked for white women because they "made the pilgrimage between public and private," representing their interests in the wider world and interacting with them on a threateningly intimate level. See Nelson, "Livestock, Boundaries, and Public Space in Spartanburg," 43; "Testimony of Joseph Herndon," *Report of the Joint Select Committee,* vol. 3, 214; "Testimony of Alexander P. Wylie," *Report of the Joint Select Committee,* vol. 5, 1428; Trelease, *White Terror,* 367; "Testimony of Joseph Gist," *Report of the Joint Select Committee,* vol. 4, 1052.

14. Randel, *The Ku Klux Klan,* 62; Post, "A 'Carpetbagger' in South Carolina," 51 n.; Simkins, "The Ku Klux Klan in South Carolina, 1868–1871," 622; "Testimony of William Champion," *Report of the Joint Select Committee,* vol. 3, 366; Simkins, "The Ku Klux Klan in South Carolina, 1868–1871," 625.

15. Catherine Clinton has written about the extensive violence committed against black women and concluded that they were more vulnerable to sexual violence after the Civil War because control over their bodies became symbolic of political and social power ("Bloody Terrain," 330–31, 332); "Testimony of John Lipscomb," *Report of the Joint Select Committee,* vol. 4, 666; Tolnay and Beck, *A Festival of Violence,* 8; "Testimony of Andrew Cathcart," *Report of the Joint Select Committee,* vol. 5, 1592; "Testimony of Elias Hill," *Report of the Joint Select Committee,* vol. 5, 1406; "Testimony of Samuel Bonner," *Report of the Joint Select Committee,* vol. 3, 577; Stephanie McCurry has written that control over a household and its dependents defined "free men," and Laura Edwards writes that the household dictated relationships—social and political—in the wider world (McCurry, *Masters of Small Worlds,* 6; Edwards, *Gendered Strife and Confusion,* 8). Peter Bardaglio further contends that attacks on female members of the household meant that the attackers "not only exercised control over the woman but also undercut the public authority of her husband or father." In the case of the Klan, attacks on black women were intended to deny black men control over their households, and therefore the rights of free men and the privileges of southern manhood (*Reconstructing the Household,* 189).

16. "Testimony of Samuel Poinier," *Report of the Joint Select Committee,* vol. 1, 27; "Testimony of Clem Bowden," *Report of the Joint Select Committee,* vol. 3, 380–81; "Testimony of Lucy McMillan," *Report of the Joint Select Committee,* vol. 2, 604–11; Stagg, "The Problem of Klan Violence," 315; "Testimony of Lucretia Adams," *Report of the Joint Select Committee,* vol. 5, 1577.

17. "Testimony of Isham McCrary," *Report of the Joint Select Committee,* vol. 3, 539–40; Trelease, *White Terror,* 363–64; "Testimony of John Lipscomb," *Report of the Joint Select Committee,* vol. 4, 667; Simkins, "The Ku Klux Klan in South Carolina, 1868–1871," 622–23; "Testimony of Jane Surratt," *Report of the Joint Select Committee,* vol. 3, 524–26.

18. "Testimony of Alexander P. Wylie," *Report of the Joint Select Committee,* vol. 5, 1430.

19. Simkins, "The Ku Klux Klan in South Carolina, 1868–1871," 627.

20. "A Hundred Years of Terror"; "1870: Enforcement Act of 1870"; "Civil Rights Act of 1871" ; the congressional records include a verbatim account of the testimony of South Carolina's witnesses before Congress. See *Report of the Joint Select Committee,* vols. 1–5; for a thorough account of the Klan trials in South Carolina see Williams, *The Great South Carolina Ku Klux Klan Trials.* The complete transcripts of the first series of trials were published in *The Great Ku Klux Trials: Official Report of the Proceedings before the U.S. Circuit Court.*

21. Foner, *Reconstruction,* 458; Zuczek, *State of Rebellion,* 108.

22. Zuczek describes Foner's distinctive argument, as well as his own in *State of Rebellion,* 103; Williams, *The Great South Carolina Ku Klux Klan Trials,* 113; Trelease, *White Terror,* 362.

23. Williams, *The Great South Carolina Ku Klux Klan Trials,* 63.

24. *New York Times,* March 21, 1871; "Testimony of Christina Page," *Report of the Joint Select Committee,* vol. 4, 1142; "Testimony of Laura Gowan," *Report of the Joint Select Committee,* vol. 4, 1068; Davis, *Authentic History,* as cited in Randel, *The Ku Klux Klan,* 7.

25. Trelease, *White Terror,* 367; Post, "A 'Carpetbagger' in South Carolina," 60; "Testimony of William K. Owens," *Report of the Joint Select Committee,* vol. 4, 1365; Trelease, *White Terror,* 367.

26. "Public Meeting of the Whites," from the Yorkville *Enquirer,* April 6, 1871, as cited in *Report of the Joint Select Committee,* vol. 5, 1541, 1543; "Testimony of James R. Bratton," *Report of the Joint Select Committee,* vol. 5, 1348.

27. C. D. Melton, esq. to John S. Bratton, December 25, 1871, Bratton Family Papers, South Caroliniana; John S. Bratton to his wife, c. 1871, Bratton Family Papers, South Caroliniana.

28. R. H. Phillips to Mrs. Bratton, February 5, 1872, Bratton Family Papers, South Caroliniana; T. L. J. to John Bratton, March 28, 1872, Bratton Family Papers, South Caroliniana.

29. S. P. Hamilton to Harriet Bratton, January 11, 1872, Bratton Family Papers, South Caroliniana; T. J. Robertson to Rev. James B. White, June 28, 1873, Bratton Family Papers, South Caroliniana.

30. Leland, *A Voice from South Carolina,* 91; "Journal of a Reputed Ku Klux," April 5 and April 6, 1872, John Leland Papers, South Caroliniana.

31. "Journal of a Reputed Ku Klux," April 22, 1872, John Leland Papers, South Caroliniana; Leland, *A Voice from South Carolina,* 128; "Journal of a Reputed Ku Klux," April 25 and May 3, 1872, John Leland Papers, South Caroliniana.

32. Randel, *The Ku Klux Klan,* 98, 96; Post, "A 'Carpetbagger' in South Carolina," 38.

33. Post, "A 'Carpetbagger' in South Carolina," 51 n.; "Testimony of John J. Neason," *Report of the Joint Select Committee,* vol. 3, 44; Simkins, "The Ku Klux Klan in South Carolina, 1868–1871," 635–36; "Testimony of Alexander P. Wylie," *Report of the Joint Select Committee,* vol. 5, 1428; Foner, *Reconstruction,* 430.

Chapter 4: Sin and Redemption

1. Mary Gayle Aiken, "Journal," Aiken Family Papers, South Caroliniana; W. Scott Poole's analysis of the election of 1876 in South Carolina, "Religion, Gender, and the Lost Cause in South Carolina's 1876 Governor's Race: 'Hampton or Hell!,'" uses gender in his examination of the events surrounding Hampton's victory. Poole demonstrates the power

of female and religious imagery in the campaign and concludes that the election marked the inauguration of late-nineteenth-century celebrations of the Confederacy. Those images created a "gendered language of insurgency" against federal and Republican authority (Poole, 587, 598). However, Poole's argument does not extend to issues of violence, nor does it see women's roles as actively or intentionally political. Nina Silber's work illustrates the use of gendered imagery in the relationship between the North and the South, and particularly in the celebrations of antebellum figures that followed the election of 1876. She argues that shifting ideas and representations of male and female, masculine and feminine, helped the regions work through their own tortured courtship (Silber, *The Romance of Reunion,* 6–7).

2. Zuczek, *State of Rebellion,* 142–43; and Foner, *Reconstruction,* 542–43. Corruption was certainly not confined to the Republican Party in South Carolina, but as the party in power, the activities of its leaders were more easily scrutinized and its reputation was more important for the survival of Reconstruction measures (Foner, 387); Zuczek, *State of Rebellion,* 137; Zuczek, *State of Rebellion,* 140.

3. Foner, *Reconstruction,* 543–44.

4. Zuczek, *State of Rebellion,* 146.

5. *Charleston News and Courier,* January 21, 1876, as cited in Zuczek, *State of Rebellion,* 153.

6. Williams, "Eyewitness to 1876" Scrapbook, September 26 and September 12, 1926, South Caroliniana; Foner, *Reconstruction,* 543; Williams, "Eyewitness to 1876" Scrapbook, January 9, 1927, South Caroliniana.

7. Simkins and Woody, *South Carolina during Reconstruction,* 576, 56; Williams, "Eyewitness to 1876" Scrapbook, October 2, 1926, South Caroliniana; Frank Thomas to J. H. Aycock, "Letter," September 25, 1876, Aycock Family Papers, South Caroliniana.

8. F. W. P. Butler, "Origin of Red Shirt for South Carolina," Butler Family Papers, South Caroliniana.

9. Charles F. Hard to Ellen Hard Lownes, undated, Charles F. and Ellen Whilden Hard Papers, South Caroliniana; Frank Thomas to J. H. Aycock, "Letter," November 13, 1876, Aycock Family Papers, South Caroliniana.

10. *Charleston News and Courier,* October 31, 1876, Reconstruction Scrapbook, South Caroliniana; Joshua Hilary Hudson, "Letter to the Citizens of Marlboro County," September 4, 1876, Joshua Hilary Hudson Papers, South Caroliniana; "Wade Hampton on the Crisis," *Charleston News and Courier,* September 9, 1876, Mrs. Edward LeRoy Reeves Papers, South Caroliniana; John Leland, "Post-script—Chapter 2 'Redemption and Home Rule,'" John Leland Papers, South Caroliniana.

11. John Leland, "Chapter 12 Centennial Sentiments,'" and "Chapter 11," John Leland Papers, South Caroliniana; Joshua Hilary Hudson, "Letter to the Citizens of Marlboro County," September 4, 1876, Joshua Hilary Hudson Papers, South Caroliniana; "Wade Hampton on the Crisis," *Charleston News and Courier,* September 9, 1876, Mrs. Edward LeRoy Reeves Papers, South Caroliniana.

12. Mark Reynolds Sr. to Mark Reynolds Jr., Letter, August 1876, Reynolds Family Papers, South Caroliniana; Dr. F. W. P. Butler, "The First Use of the Red Shirt . . . Interesting Reminiscences of 1876," 1910, Butler Family Papers, South Caroliniana; Alfred B. Williams, "Eyewitness to 1876" Scrapbook, September 12, 1926, South Caroliniana.

13. Alfred B. Williams, "Eyewitness to 1876" Scrapbook, August 15, 1926 South Caroliniana.

14. Charles F. Hard to Ellen Hard Lownes, undated, Charles F. and Ellen Whilden Hard Papers, South Caroliniana; John Leland, "Post-script—Chapter 2 'Redemption and Home Rule,'" John Leland Papers, South Caroliniana.

15. "Cainhoy Massacre Preconcerted?," House Select Committee, "Denial of Elective Franchise in South Carolina," February 21, 1877; Drago, *Hurrah For Hampton,* 40; Testimony of Jonas Weeks, Testimony of Ashbury Green, "Intimidation and Violence," and "Cainhoy Massacre Preconcerted?," House Select Committee, "Denial of Elective Franchise in South Carolina" February 21, 1877; *Abbeville Medium,* September 6, 1876, and *Columbia Daily Union-Herald,* September 14, 1876, as cited in Drago, *Hurrah For Hampton,* 42.

16. Mary Gayle Aiken, Memoir, David Wyatt Aiken Papers, South Caroliniana; Lizzie K. Geiger to W. A. Leaphart, Letter, October 30, 1876, and W. A. Leaphart to Lizzie K. Geiger, Letter, November 8, 1876, Lizzie K. Geiger Papers, South Caroliniana; Mary Reynolds to Mark Reynolds, Letter, November 3, 1876, Reynolds Family Papers, South Caroliniana.

17. Leaflet, Hampton Family Papers, South Caroliniana; Alfred B. Williams, "Eyewitness to 1876" Scrapbook, November 7, 1926, South Caroliniana; *Charleston News and Courier,* October 31, 1876, Reconstruction Scrapbook, South Caroliniana; Alfred B. Williams, "Eyewitness to 1876" Scrapbook, August 15, 1926, and November 7, 1926, South Caroliniana.

18. Alfred B. Williams, "Eyewitness to 1876" Scrapbook, January 2, 1927, South Caroliniana; Mary Reynolds to Mark Reynolds, Letter, October 26, 1876, Reynolds Family Papers, South Caroliniana; Alfred B. Williams, "Eyewitness to 1876" Scrapbook, November 7, 1926, South Caroliniana.

19. Alfred B. Williams, "Eyewitness to 1876" Scrapbook, November 14, 1926, South Caroliniana; Mary Reynolds to Mark Reynolds, Letter, October 2, 1876, Reynolds Family Papers, South Caroliniana; *Charleston News and Courier,* October 31, 1876, Reconstruction Scrapbook, South Caroliniana; Alfred B. Williams, "Eyewitness to 1876" Scrapbook, January 9, 1927, South Caroliniana.

20. Alfred B. Williams, "Eyewitness to 1876" Scrapbook, February 6, 1927, South Caroliniana; *Charleston News and Courier,* October 31, 1876, Reconstruction Scrapbook; John Leland, "Post-script—Chapter 1 'Hampton's Campaign,'" John Leland Papers, South Caroliniana; LeeAnn Whites finds that the white women of the South were as invested in traditional gender roles as their men, but that the war destabilized those roles and opened a public forum for women. She concludes that women were in a position to choose between pursuing more independent roles for themselves and bolstering white manhood, and chose instead to create a new "public domesticity" that bolstered traditional male hegemony (Whites, *The Civil War as a Crisis in Gender,* 212–13, 218–19). However, in reconstructing gender roles through a public display of political activism, women rewrote those roles permanently.

21. Charles F. Hard to Ellen Hard Lownes, undated, Charles F. and Ellen Whilden Hard Papers, South Caroliniana; "The True Story of the Race Conflict in Carolina," from the *Charleston Journal of Commerce,* October 14, 1876, reprinted in the *New York Herald,* James Aldrich Papers, South Caroliniana; Mary Reynolds to Mark Reynolds, Letter, October 26, 1876, Reynolds Family Papers South Caroliniana; "The True Story of the Race Conflict in Carolina," from the *Charleston Journal of Commerce,* October 14, 1876, reprinted in the *New York Herald,* James Aldrich Papers, South Caroliniana.

22. M. Smith, "All Is Not Quiet in Our Hellish County," 145; L. Williams, "Federal Enforcement of Black Rights in the Post-Redemption South," 172; M. Smith, "All Is Not Quiet in Our Hellish County," 152; Zuczek, *State of Rebellion,* 176; the numerous accounts of the Ellenton riot vary on several points, including its causes, its duration, and the number of victims; W. A. Leaphart to Lizzie Geiger, Letter, November 8, 1876, and Lizzie Geiger to W. A. Leaphart, Letter, November 13, 1876, Lizzie K. Geiger Papers, South Caroliniana; Alfred B. Williams, "Eyewitness to 1876" Scrapbook, September 12, 1926, South Caroliniana; F. W. P. Butler, "Origin of Red Shirt for South Carolina," Butler Family Papers, South Caroliniana.

23. *Charleston News and Courier,* October 31, 1876, Reconstruction Scrapbook, South Caroliniana; Testimony of Tom Lomax, in Drago, *Hurrah For Hampton,* 90; Testimony of John S. Horlbeck, Testimony of William R. Wheelock, and Testimony of A. M. Latham, House Select Committee, "Denial of Elective Franchise in South Carolina" February 21, 1877; Alfred B. Williams, "Eyewitness to 1876" Scrapbook, February 6, 1927, South Caroliniana; "The True Story of the Race Conflict in Carolina," from the *Charleston Journal of Commerce,* October 14, 1876, reprinted in the *New York Herald,* James Aldrich Papers, South Caroliniana; Testimony of Mr. Smith, House Select Committee, "Denial of Elective Franchise in South Carolina," February 21, 1877.

24. Alfred B. Williams, "Eyewitness to 1876" Scrapbook, October 3, 1926, South Caroliniana; *Charleston News and Courier,* October 31, 1876, Reconstruction Scrapbook, South Caroliniana; Testimony of Edward Henderson, in Drago, *Hurrah For Hampton,* 69; Testimony of Aaron Mitchell, in Drago, *Hurrah For Hampton,* 83–84.

25. Alfred B. Williams, "Eyewitness to 1876" Scrapbook, January 30, 1927, South Caroliniana; Testimony of Preston Taylor and Testimony of Jonas Weeks, in Drago, *Hurrah For Hampton,* 58–59.

26. Testimony of Edward Henderson, in Drago, *Hurrah For Hampton,* 68; Testimony of Aaron Mitchell, in Drago, *Hurrah For Hampton,* 80; Testimony of James Grant, House Select Committee, "Denial of Elective Franchise in South Carolina," February 21, 1877; Alfred B. Williams, "Eyewitness to 1876" Scrapbook, January 2, 1927. South Caroliniana.

Chapter 5: Strange Fruit Hanging from the Palmetto Tree

1. Finnegan, "'At the hands of parties unknown,'" 24. A number of writers have examined the connection between power, violence, and the body. Michel Foucault's discussion of executions in the eighteenth century and earlier determined that violations of the law were, by extension, a violation of the sovereign and that revenge therefore took the form of violence against the body of the criminal. The public execution in particular was a ritual that was not designed to restore law and order or judicial "balance" as much as it was an effort to illustrate "the dissymmetry between the subject who has dared to violate the law and the all-powerful sovereign who displays his strength" (Foucault, *Discipline and Punish,* 47–49). This explains the attraction of whites to lynching in the case of black "infractions" of the laws in the late-nineteenth-century South, although in the case of lynching, the laws in question were at heart social and cultural and revolved around the question of sexuality and gender.

2. Finnegan, "'At the hands of parties unknown,'" 11, 32, 27. For discussions of the "rape myth," see Sommerville, "The Rape Myth in the Old South Reconsidered"; "Tillman's Message to the Legislature," *New York Times,* November 29, 1894; Rep. Arthur Kibler to "Miss Mamie," Letter, October 17, 1904, Salter Family Papers, South Caroliniana.

3. In her discussion of torture, Elaine Scarry has argued that the pain inflicted on the bodies of victims of torture makes the power of the torturer seem "incontestably real," but the fact that the torture is taking place indicates the ultimate contestability of that power. Such is indeed the case with the power conferred on southern lynchers by their actions. The fact of the lynching does not support their claims to power but betrays its uncertain nature and the subsequent anxieties of white men. In this case, the power over black men's—and white women's—sexuality. Scarry also asserts that the act of torture "unmakes" the victim and fuels the torturer's sense of self (Scarry, *The Body in Pain,* 27, 41, and 56 In the case of the South, lynching was designed to strip—sometimes literally—the black man of his manhood and undermine the sense of self he developed following emancipation. It was also an attempt to bolster white manhood. The connection between the body, violence, power, and, in the case of the South, gender and sexuality, was manifested in the lynching phenomenon; "Negro Lynched to Avenge Assault on White Woman," *Washington Times,* February 18, 1900, in Ginzburg, *100 Years of Lynchings,* 30; Finnegan, "'At the hands of parties unknown,'" 70–71; "Negro Hanged to Trestle," *Montgomery Advertiser,* August 12, 1913; "Lynched as a Warning," *New York Times,* January 7, 1897; "Lynching Negroes South," *New York Times,* June 25, 1894; Abraham Middleton, Diary, March 8, 1893, Abraham Middleton Papers, South Caroliniana.

4. "Will Have a Law against Lynching," *New York Times,* October 18, 1895; "Measures Tillman Advocated," *Washington Post,* June 28, 1896; "Denounced but Not Scared," *Washington Post,* January 12, 1897.

5. Finnegan, "'At the hands of parties unknown,'" 4; Finnegan, "'At the hands of parties unknown,'" 20 and 31.

6. Peter Bardaglio writes that "rape challenged the power of the male household head to protect the women, children, and other dependents in his family, and damaged his standing in the community. . . . The rapist not only exercised control over the woman but also undercut the public authority of her husband or father" (*Reconstructing the Household,* 189); Land, "The Shame of South Carolina," C. B. Schultz Collection, South Caroliniana.

7. Taylor, "The True Remedy for Lynch Law"; Tindall, *South Carolina Negroes* as cited in Land, "The Shame of South Carolina," C. B. Schultz Collection, South Caroliniana; "Lynched as a Warning," *New York Times,* January 7, 1897; "Editorial No. 3," *New York Times,* April 6, 1887.

8. "Eight Hanging Bodies," *New York Times,* December 30, 1889; "Lynching in the South," *New York Times,* January 14, 1896; Finnegan, "'At the hands of parties unknown,'" 67.

9. Finnegan, "'At the hands of parties unknown,'" 83 and 85; "Editorial Article 7," *New York Times,* January 8, 1897; *Washington Post,* April 18, 1898; "Lynching in South Carolina," *New York Times,* December 30, 1897; "Tillman Talks of Negroes," *New York Times,* February 25, 1899.

10. Robyn Wiegman has written that castration was a way of denying a black man his manhood and therefore his citizenship, in effect, "allign[ing] the black male . . . with those still disfranchised" by feminizing him (Wiegman, "The Anatomy of Lynching," 224); Finnegan, "'At the hands of parties unknown,'" 70–71.

11. Finnegan, "'At the hands of parties unknown,'" 235–36; Beck and Tolnay, "When Race Didn't Matter," 141; "In Danger of Lynching," *New York Times,* August 3, 1890; "To Avoid a Lynching Bee," *The Washington Post,* December 8, 1894.

12. Finnegan, "'At the hands of parties unknown,'" 64; "Tillman on Lynching," *Washington Post,* September 30, 1893; "Tillman Talks of Negroes," *New York Times,* February 25, 1899; "Spartanburg Jury Acquits Negro Nearly Lynched," *Salisbury Piedmont Advocate,* September 27, 1913, in Ginzburg, *100 Years of Lynchings,* 86. In regions with black state legislators, lynchings related to rape accounted for 46.7 percent of the lynchings in South Carolina from 1881 to 1895 but declined to 20.8 percent between 1896 and 1910, whereas lynchings related to murder and assault rose from 13.3 percent to 41.7 percent of all lynchings. In regions without black state legislators, rape-related lynchings declined from 39 percent to 21.7 percent, and murder- and assault-related lynchings rose from 29.3 percent to 34.7 percent (Finnegan, "'At the hands of parties unknown,'" appendix: "Most Frequent Alleged Causes of Lynching").

13. "Fire Follows a Lynching," *Washington Post,* December 22, 1898; Duncan Clinch Heyward, "A Lynching That I Once Attended," Heyward Family Papers, South Caroliniana.

14. "Negro Lynched to Avenge Assault on White Woman," *Washington Times,* February 18, 1900, in Ginzburg, *100 Years of Lynchings,* 30; Finnegan, "'At the hands of parties unknown,'" 78–79; "Two Negroes Lynched," *New York Times,* January 21, 1881; "Negro Hanged to Trestle," *Montgomery Advertiser,* August 12, 1913, in Ginzburg, *100 Years of Lynchings,* 83–84; "Captured but Not Lynched," *Washington Post,* April 16, 1900; "Judge Lynch Commits Murder," *Washington Post,* April 28, 1893.

15. "Mob Lynched Negro Man, Flogs Three Negro Women," *Chicago Record-Herald,* July 2, 1903, in Ginzburg, *100 Years of Lynchings,* 59–60; Finnegan, "'At the hands of parties unknown,'" 227.

16. "Lynching in the South," *New York Times,* January 14, 1896; "A Failure of Justice," *New York Times,* March 1, 1896; Finnegan, "'At the hands of parties unknown,'" 233.

17. Finnegan, "'At the hands of parties unknown,'" 227.

18. Duncan Clinch Heyward, "A Lynching That I Once Attended," Heyward Family Papers, South Caroliniana; Beck and Tolnay, "When Race Didn't Matter," 140–41.

19. "To Save Two Lynchers," *Washington Post,* March 26, 1889; "Mob Law in the South," *New York Times,* June 3, 1894; "Debated Ballot Law," *Washington Post,* February 1, 1900.

20. Whites, *Gender Matters,* 181; Tindall, *South Carolina Negroes,* 241; "Visiting Southern Reporter Described Lynchings Seen," *Bangor Commercial,* September 5, 1899, in Ginzburg, *100 Years of Lynchings,* 20–21; "Mob Law in the South," *New York Times,* June 3, 1894; "Bessie" to W. L. McKeown, Letter, April 15, 1887, McKeown Family Papers, South Caroliniana; Duncan Clinch Heyward, "A Lynching That I Once Attended," Heyward Family Papers, South Caroliniana.

21. "Visiting Southern Reporter Described Lynchings Seen," *Bangor Commercial,* September 5, 1899, in Ginzburg, *100 Years of Lynchings,* 21–22; "Confederate Veteran Deplore Lynching Except for Rape," *New York Sun,* March 22, 1904, in Ginzburg, *100 Years of Lynchings,* 68.

22. Wells-Barnett, "A White Woman's Falsehood," *Red Record,* in *On Lynchings,* 110–11; Bederman, "'Civilization,' the Decline of Middle-Class Manliness, and Ida B. Wells's Antilynching Campaign (1892–94)," 15.

23. Schecter, "Unsettled Business," 304; D. Hine and Thompson, *A Shining Thread of Hope,* 183; Josephine St. Pierre Ruffin, "Address to the First National Conference of Colored Women," 13–15; D. Hine and Thompson, *A Shining Thread of Hope,* 200; National Association of Colored Women (NACW), "Resolutions," 1896.

24. "South Carolina Lynchers Indicted," *Washington Post,* November 12, 1885; "Lynchers to Be Tried," *Washington Post,* April 8, 1899; "Life Cheaper Than Cotton," *Washington Post,* April 20, 1899; "Judge Denounces Mob Law," *New York Times,* June 8, 1899; "Spartanburg Jury Acquits Negro Nearly Lynched," *Salisbury Piedmont Advocate,* September 27, 1913, in Ginzburg, *100 Years of Lynchings,* 85; "Sheriff Rescues Negro after Holding Back Mob," *Birmingham News,* August 21, 1913, in Ginzburg, *100 Years of Lynchings,* 84; "South Carolina Lynchings," *New York Times,* January 11, 1899.

25. Francis Grimke, "South Carolina Honor," *Washington Post,* March 3, 1898; "Appeal against Lynching," *New York Times,* June 11, 1899.

26. Nordyke, "Ladies and Lynchings," 683–86; Hall, "'A Truly Subversive Affair,'" 378–79; Nordyke, "Ladies and Lynchings," 683–86.

Bibliography

Unpublished Primary Sources

Abraham Middleton Papers, South Caroliniana Library, University of South Carolina.

Aiken Family Papers, South Caroliniana Library, University of South Carolina.

Alfred B. Williams, "Eyewitness to 1876" Scrapbook, September 26, 1926, South Caroliniana Library, University of South Carolina.

Aycock Family Papers, South Caroliniana Library, University of South Carolina.

Bratton Family Papers, South Caroliniana Library, University of South Carolina.

Bureau of Refugees, Freedmen, and Abandoned Lands, Record Group 105, National Archives and Records Administration, Washington, D.C.

Butler Family Papers, South Caroliniana Library, University of South Carolina.

Charles F. and Ellen Whilden Hard Papers, South Caroliniana Library, University of South Carolina.

David Wyatt Aiken Papers, South Caroliniana Library, University of South Carolina.

Eliza Hibben and Eugenia Rebecca (Griffin) Leland Papers, South Caroliniana Library, University of South Carolina.

Hampton Family Papers, South Caroliniana Library, University of South Carolina.

Heyward Family Papers, South Caroliniana Library, University of South Carolina.

Iredell Jones Papers, South Caroliniana Library, University of South Carolina.

James Aldrich Papers, South Caroliniana Library, University of South Carolina.

John Leland Papers, South Caroliniana Library, University of South Carolina.

Joshua Hilary Hudson Papers, South Caroliniana Library, University of South Carolina.

Lizzie K. Geiger Papers, South Caroliniana Library, University of South Carolina.

Mary Davis Brown Papers, South Caroliniana Library, University of South Carolina.

McKeown Family Papers, South Caroliniana Library, University of South Carolina.

Mrs. Edward LeRoy Reeves Papers, South Caroliniana Library, University of South Carolina.

Papers of the Georgetown Rifle Guards, South Caroliniana Library, University of South Carolina.

Papers of the United States House of Representatives, Record Group 233, National Archives and Records Administration, Washington, D.C.

Papers of the United States Senate, Record Group 46, National Archives and Records Administration, Washington, D.C.

Reconstruction Scrapbook, South Caroliniana Library, University of South Carolina.

Reynolds Family Papers, South Caroliniana Library, University of South Carolina.

Salter Family Papers, South Caroliniana Library, University of South Carolina.

Published Primary Sources

"Reconstruction and the Negro." *North American Review* 78 (February 1879): 161–73.

"Civil Rights Act of 1871." 17 Stat. 13 (1871). *Kansas State University Online,* accessed July 2010. http://www.arch.ksu.edu.

Columbia, S.C. *Daily Phoenix.*

Ginzburg, Ralph, ed. *100 Years of Lynchings: A Shocking Documentary of Race Violence in America.* New York: Lancer Books, 1962.

The Great Ku Klux Trials: Official Report of the Proceedings before the U.S. Circuit Court. Columbia, S.C.: Columbia Union, 1872.

Leland, John A. *A Voice from South Carolina.* Charleston: Walker, Evans and Cogswell, 1879.

Lerner, Gerda, ed. *Black Women in White America: A Documentary History.* New York: Vintage Books, 1972.

National Association of Colored Women. "Resolutions." 1896. *Facts on File Online,* October 24, 2000, http://www.fofweb.com.

New York Times.

Nordyke, Lewis T. "Ladies and Lynchings." *Survey Graphic* 28 (November 1939): 683–86. From *State University of New York, Binghamton Online,* January 11, 2002, http://womhist.binghamton.edu/aswpl/doc20.htm.

Post, Louis F. "A 'Carpetbagger' in South Carolina." *Journal of Negro History* 10 (January 1925): 10–79.

Rainey, Joseph H. "The Southern Situation." ca. 1872. In *Negro Orators and Their Orations,* edited by Carter G. Woodson. Washington, D.C.: Association for the Study of Negro Life and History, 1925. *Lexis-Nexis,*. March 4, 2004. http://cisweb.lexis-nexis.com

Ruffin, Josephine St. Pierre. "Address to the First National Conference of Colored Women." July 28, 1895. *Woman's Era* 2 (August 1895): 13–15.

Taylor, Hannis. "The True Remedy for Lynch Law." *American Law Review* 41 (March–April 1907).

Terrell, Mary Church. "Lynching from a Negro's Point of View." *North American Review* 178 (June 1904): 853–68.

Tourgée, Albion Winegar. *The Invisible Empire.* Fords, Howard and Hubert, 1880. Reprint, Baton Rouge: Louisiana State University Press, 1989.

U.S. Congress. House Select Committee. "Denial of Elective Franchise in South Carolina on the Recent Election in South Carolina." February 21, 1877. *Lexis-Nexis,* March 4, 2004. http://cisweb.lexis-nexis.com.

U.S. Congress. *Report of the Joint Select Committee to Inquire into the Conditions of Affairs in the Late Insurrectionary States.* 13 vols. Washington D.C.: U.S. Government Printing Office, 1872, vols. 1–5.

Washington Post

Wells-Barnett, Ida B. *On Lynchings.* New York: Humanity Books, 2002.

Secondary Sources

"1870: Enforcement Act of 1870." November 17, 2006. *Furman University Online,* accessed July 2010. http://facweb.furman.edu.

Abbott, Martin. *The Freedmen's Bureau in South Carolina, 1865–1872.* Chapel Hill: University of North Carolina Press, 1967.

———. "Freedom's Cry: Negroes and Their Meeting in South Carolina, 1865–1869." *Phylon* 20 (Fall 1959): 263–72.

Allen, Walter. *Governor Chamberlain's Administration in South Carolina: A Chapter of Reconstruction in the Southern States.* New York: Negro Universities Press, 1969.

Anderson, Eric, and Alfred A. Moss Jr. *The Facts of Reconstruction: Essays in Honor of John Hope Franklin.* Baton Rouge: Louisiana State University Press, 1991.

Ayers, Edward L. *The Promise of the New South: Life after Reconstruction.* New York: Oxford University Press, 1992.

———. *Southern Crossing: A History of the American South,* 1877–1906. New York: Oxford University Press, 1995.

Bardaglio, Peter W. *Reconstructing the Household: Families, Sex, and the Law in the Nineteenth Century South.* Chapel Hill: University of North Carolina Press, 1995.

Bederman, Gail. "'Civilization,' the Decline of Middle-Class Manliness, and Ida B. Wells's Antilynching Campaign (1892–94)." *Radical History Review* 52 (Winter 1992): 5–30.

———. *Manliness and Civilization: A Cultural History of Gender and Race in the United States, 1880–1917.* Chicago: University of Chicago Press, 1995.

Berkeley, Kathleen Christine. "Elizabeth Avery Meriwether, 'An Advocate for Her Sex': Feminism and Conservatism in the Post–Civil War South." *Tennessee Historical Quarterly* 43, no. 4 (Winter 1984): 390–407.

Bleser, Carol K. Rothrock. *The Promised Land: The History of the South Carolina Land Commission, 1869–1890.* Columbia: University of South Carolina Press for the South Carolina Tricentennial Commission, 1969.

Brown, Elsa Barkley. "Negotiating and Transforming the Public Sphere: African American Political Life in the Transition from Slavery to Freedom." *Public Culture* 7, no. 1 (1994): 107–46.

Brown, Richard Maxwell. "Legal and Behavioral Perspectives on American Vigilantism." *Perspectives in American History* 5 (1971): 95–144.

Brundage, W. Fitzhugh. *Lynching in the New South: Georgia and Virginia, 1880–1930.* Chicago: University of Illinois Press, 1993.

———. "Mob Violence North and South, 1865–1940." *Georgia Historical Quarterly* 75, no. 4 (Fall 1991): 748–70.

———. *Under Sentence of Death: Lynching in the South.* Chapel Hill: University of North Carolina Press, 1997.

Burton, Vernon. "Race and Reconstruction: Edgefield County, South Carolina." *Journal of Social History* 12, no. 1 (1978): 31–56.

Bynum, Victoria E. "'White Negroes' in Segregated Mississippi: Miscegenation, Racial Identity, and the Law." *Journal of Southern History* 64, no. 2 (May 1998): 247–76.

Carpenter, John A. "Atrocities in the Reconstruction Period." *Journal of Negro History* 47, no. 4 (October 1962): 234–47.

Censer, Jane Turner. *The Reconstruction of White Southern Womanhood, 1865–1895.* Baton Rouge: University of Louisiana Press, 2003.

Clinton, Catherine. "Bloody Terrain: Freedwomen, Sexuality, and Violence during Reconstruction." *Georgia Historical Quarterly* 76, no. 2 (1992): 313–32.

Dailey, Jane, Glenda Elizabeth Gilmore, and Bryant Simon, eds. *Jumpin' Jim Crow: Southern Politics from Civil War to Civil Rights.* Princeton: Princeton University Press, 2000.

Davidson, Osha Gray. *The Best of Enemies: Race and Redemption in the New South.* New York: Scribner, 1996.

Donald, David Herbert. "A Generation of Defeat." In *From the Old South to the New: Essays on the Transitional South,* edited by Walter J. Fraser and Winfred B. Moore. Westport, Conn.: Greenwood, 1981.

Drago, Edmund L. *Hurrah for Hampton: Black Red Shirts in South Carolina during Reconstruction.* Fayetteville: University of Arkansas Press, 1998.

DuBois, W. E. B. *Black Reconstruction in America 1860–1880.* 1935. New York: Free, 1998.

Dunlap, Leslie K. "The Reform of Rape Law and the Problem of White Men: Age of Consent Campaigns in the South, 1885–1910." In *Sex, Love, Race: Crossing Boundaries in North American History,* edited by Martha Hodes, 352–72. New York: New York University Press, 1999.

Edwards, Laura F. *Gendered Strife and Confusion: The Political Culture of Reconstruction.* Urbana: University of Illinois Press, 1997.

———. "Sexual Violence, Gender, Reconstruction, and the Extension of Patriarchy in Granville County, North Carolina." *North Carolina Historical Review* 68, no. 3 (July 1991): 237–60.

Faust, Drew Gilpin. "Southern Violence Revisited." *Reviews in American History* 13, no. 2 (June 1985): 205–10.

Finnegan, Terence R. "'At the hands of parties unknown': Lynching in Mississippi and South Carolina, 1881–1940." Ph.D. diss., University of Illinois at Urbana-Champaign, 1993.

———. "Lynching and Political Power in Mississippi and South Carolina." In *Under Sentence of Death: Lynching in the South,* edited by Fitzhugh W. Brundage, 189–218. Chapel Hill: University of North Carolina Press, 1997.

Fisher, William H. *The Invisible Empire: A Bibliography of the Ku Klux Klan.* Metuchen, N.J.: Scarecrow, 1980.

Fitzgerald, Michael W. *The Union League Movement in the Deep South: Politics and Agricultural Change during Reconstruction.* Baton Rouge: Louisiana State University Press, 1989.

Foner, Eric. *Reconstruction: America's Unfinished Revolution, 1863–1877.* New York: Harper and Row, 1988.

———. "Reconstruction Revisited." *Reviews in American History* 10, no. 4 (1982): 82–100.

Ford, Lacy K. "Rednecks and Merchants: Economic Development and Social Tensions in the South Carolina Upcountry, 1865–1900." *Journal of American History* 71, no. 2 (September 1984): 294–318.

Formwalt, Lee W. "The Camilla Massacre of 1868: Racial Violence as Political Propaganda." *Georgia Historical Quarterly* 71, no. 3 (1987): 400–426.

———. "Notes and Documents: A Case of Interracial Marriage during Reconstruction." *Alabama Review* 45, no. 3 (1992): 216–24.

———, ed. "Petitioning Congress for Protection: A Black View of Reconstruction at the Local Level." *Georgia Historical Quarterly* 73, no. 2 (Summer 1989): 305–22.

Foucault, Michel. *Discipline and Punish: The Birth of the Prison.* Translated by Alan Sheridan. New York: Vintage Books, 1995.

Fout, John C., and Maura Shaw Tantillo, eds. *American Sexual Politics: Sex, Gender, and Race since the Civil War.* Chicago: University of Chicago Press, 1993.

Gatewood, Willard B., Jr. "'The Remarkable Misses Rollin': Black Women in Reconstruction South Carolina." *South Carolina Historical Magazine* 92, no. 3 (1991): 85–98.

Gilmore, Glenda Elizabeth. "Gender and Jim Crow: Sarah Dudley Pettey's Vision of the New South." *North Carolina Historical Review* 68, no. 3 (July 1991): 261–85.

———. *Gender and Jim Crow: Women and the Politics of White Supremacy in North Carolina, 1896–1920.* Chapel Hill: University of North Carolina Press, 1996.

Gutman, Herbert G. *The Black Family in Slavery and Freedom, 1750–1925.* New York: Vintage Books, 1976.

Hackney, Sheldon. "Southern Violence." *American Historical Review* 74 (February 1969): 348–65.

Hahn, Steven. *A Nation under Our Feet: Black Political Struggles in the Rural South from Slavery to the Great Migration.* Cambridge: Harvard University Press, 2003.

Hall, Jacquelyn. "'A Truly Subversive Affair': Women against Lynching in the Twentieth-Century South." In *Women of America: A History,* edited by Carol Ruth Berkin and Mary Beth Norton. New York: Houghton-Mufflin, 1979.

———. "'The Mind That Burns in Each Body': Women, Rape, and Racial Violence." *Southern Exposure* 12, no. 6 (November/December 1984): 61–78.

Hennessey, Melinda Meek. "Racial Violence during Reconstruction: The 1876 Riots in Charleston and Cainhoy." *South Carolina Historical Magazine* 86, no. 2 (April 1985): 100–112.

Hine, Darlene Clark, and Kathleen Thompson. *A Shining Thread of Hope: The History of Black Women in America.* New York: Broadway Books, 1998.

Hine, William C. "Black Politicians in Reconstruction Charleston, South Carolina: A Collective Study." *Journal of Southern History* 49 (November 1983): 555–84.

———. "The 1867 Charleston Streetcar Sit-Ins, a Case of Successful Black Protest." *South Carolina Historical Magazine* 77, no. 2 (April 1976): 110–14.

Hodes, Martha, ed. *Sex, Love, Race: Crossing Boundaries in North American History.* New York: New York University Press, 1999.

———. "The Sexualization of Reconstruction Politics: White Women and Black Men in the South after the Civil War." In *American Sexual Politics: Sex, Gender and Race since the Civil War,* edited by John Fout and Maura Tantillo. Chicago: University of Chicago Press, 1993.

———. *White Women, Black Men: Illicit Sex in the 19th-Century South.* New Haven: Yale University Press, 1997.

Holt, Thomas. *Black over White: Negro Political Leadership in South Carolina during Reconstruction.* Urbana: University of Illinois Press, 1977.

"A Hundred Years of Terror." March 5, 1997. *The Southern Poverty Law Center Online.* Accessed December 12, 2001. http://www.iupui.edu/~aao/kkk.html.

Jarrell, Hampton M. *Wade Hampton and the Negro: The Road Not Taken.* Columbia: University of South Carolina Press, 1950.

Jones, Jacqueline. *Labor of Love, Labor of Sorrow: Black Women, Work and the Family from Slavery to the Present.* New York: Basic Books, 1985. Reprint New York: Vintage Books, 1995.

Katz, William Loren. "The People vs. the Klan in Mass Combat." *Freedomways* 20, no. 2 (1980): 96–100.

Land, Lorena. "The Shame of South Carolina." C. B. Schultz Collection, South Caroliniana Library, University of South Carolina.

Litwack, Leon F. *Been in the Storm So Long: The Aftermath of Slavery.* New York: Alfred A. Knopf, 1979.

———. *Trouble in Mind: Black Southerners in the Age of Jim Crow.* New York: Alfred A. Knopf, 1998.

Lowe, Richard. *Republicans and Reconstruction in Virginia, 1856–70*. Charlottesville: University Press of Virginia, 1991.

McCurry, Stephanie. *Masters of Small Worlds: Yeomen Households, Gender Relations, and the Political Culture of the Antebellum South Carolina Low Country.* New York: Oxford University Press, 1995.

———. "The Two Faces of Republicanism: Gender and Proslavery Politics in Antebellum South Carolina." *The Journal of American History* (March 1992): 1245–64.

McPherson, James M. *Ordeal by Fire: The Civil War and Reconstruction.* New York: Alfred A. Knopf, 1982.

———. "Redemption or Counterrevolution? The South in the 1870s." *Reviews in American History* 13, no. 4 (December 1985): 545–50.

Miller, Kathleen Atkinson. "The Ladies and the Lynchers: A Look at the Association of Southern Women for the Prevention of Lynching." *Southern Studies* 17, no. 3 (Fall 1978): 221–40.

Morris, Thomas D. "Equality, 'Extraordinary Law,' and Criminal Justice: The South Carolina Experience, 1865–1866." *South Carolina Historical Magazine* 83, no. 1 (January 1982): 15–33.

Nelson, Scott Reynolds. *Iron Confederacies: Southern Railways, Klan Violence, and Reconstruction.* Chapel Hill: University of North Carolina Press, 1999.

———. "Livestock, Boundaries, and Public Space in Spartanburg: African American Men, Elite White Women, and the Spectacle of Conjugal Relations." In *Sex, Love, Race: Crossing Boundaries in North American History,* edited by Martha Hodes, 313–27. New York: New York University Press, 1999.

Olzak, Susan. "The Political Context of Competition: Lynching and Urban Racial Violence, 1882–1914." *Social Forces* 69, no. 2 (December 1990): 395–421.

Parsons, Elaine Frantz. "Costume and Performance in the Reconstruction-Era Ku Klux Klan." *Journal of American History* 92. no. 3 (2005): 811–36.

Poole, W. Scott. Religion, Gender, and the Lost Cause in South Carolina's 1876 Governor's Race: "Hampton or Hell!" *Journal of Southern History* 68, no. 3 (August 2002): 573–98.

Rable, George C. *But There Was No Peace: The Role of Violence in the Politics of Reconstruction.* Athens: University of Georgia Press, 1984.

Randel, William Peirce. *The Ku Klux Klan: A Century of Infamy.* New York: Chilton Books, 1965.

Raper, Arthur F. *The Tragedy of Lynching.* Chapel Hill: The University of North Carolina Press, 1993.

Rapport, Sara. "The Freedmen's Bureau as a Legal Agent for Black Men and Women in Georgia: 1865–1868." *Georgia Historical Quarterly* 73, no. 1 (Spring 1989): 26–53.

Reynolds, John S. *Reconstruction in South Carolina, 1865–1877*. Columbia: State Company, 1905.

Rose, Willie Lee. *Rehearsal for Reconstruction: The Port Royal Experiment.* Athens: University of Georgia Press, 1999.

Rosen, Hannah. "'Not That Sort of Women': Race, Gender, and Sexual Violence during the Memphis Riot of 1866." In *Sex, Love, Race: Crossing Boundaries in North American History,* edited by Martha Hodes, 267–93. New York: New York University Press, 1999.

Saville, Julie. *The Work of Reconstruction: From Slave to Wage Laborer in South Carolina, 1860–1870.* New York: Cambridge University Press, 1996.

Scarry, Elaine. *The Body in Pain: The Making and Unmaking of the World.* New York: Oxford University Press, 1985.

Schwalm, Leslie A. *A Hard Fight for We: Women's Transition from Slavery to Freedom in South Carolina.* Urbana: University of Illinois Press, 1997.

Scott, Anne Firor. *The Southern Lady: From Pedestal to Politics, 1830–1930.* Chicago: University of Chicago Press, 1970. Reprint, Charlottesville: University Press of Virginia, 1995.

Shapiro, Herbert. "Afro-American Response to Race Violence during Reconstruction." *Science and Society* 36, no. 2 (Summer 1972): 158–70.

———. "The Ku Klux Klan during Reconstruction: The South Carolina Episode." *Journal of Negro History* 49, no. 1 (January 1964): 34–55.

———. *White Violence and Black Response: From Reconstruction to Montgomery.* Amherst: University of Massachusetts Press, 1988.

Silber, Nina. *The Romance of Reunion: Northerners and the South, 1865–1900.* Chapel Hill: University of North Carolina Press, 1993.

Simkins, Francis Butler. "The Ku Klux Klan in South Carolina, 1868–1871." *Journal of Negro History,* vol. 12, no. 4 (October 1927): 606–47.

Simkins, Francis Butler, and Robert Hilliard Woody. *South Carolina during Reconstruction.* Gloucester, Mass.: Peter Smith, 1966.

Smith, John David. "Racial Determinism and the Fear of Miscegenation Pre-1900." In *Anti-black Thought, 1863–1925,* vol. 11. New York: Garland, 1993.

———. *Black Voices from Reconstruction: 1865–1877.* Gainesville: University Press of Florida, 1997.

Smith, Mark M. "All Is Not Quiet in Our Hellish County": Facts, Fiction, Politics, and Race: The Ellenton Riot of 1876." *South Carolina Historical Magazine* 95, no. 2 (April 1994): 142–55.

Sommerville, Diane Miller. "The Rape Myth in the Old South Reconsidered." *Journal of Southern History* 61, no. 3 (1995): 481–518.

Stagg, J. C. A. "The Problem of Klan Violence: The South Carolina Up-Country, 1868–1871." *Journal of American Studies* 8 (December 1974): 303–18.

Stanley, Amy Dru. "Conjugal Bonds and Wage Labor: Rights of Contract in the Age of Emancipation." *Journal of American History* 75, no. 2 (1988): 471–99.

Taylor, Alrutheus Ambush. *The Negro in South Carolina during the Reconstruction.* Washington, D.C.: Association for the Study of Negro Life and History, 1924.

Taylor, Hannis. "The True Remedy for Lynch Law." *American Law Review* 41 (March–April 1907): 255–66.

Thompson, Henry T. *Ousting the Carpetbagger from South Carolina,* 2nd ed. Columbia: R. L. Bryan, 1927.

Tindall, George Brown. *South Carolina Negroes, 1877–1900.* Columbia: University of South Carolina Press, 1952.

Tolnay, Stewart E., and E. M. Beck. *A Festival of Violence: An Analysis of Southern Lynchings, 1882–1930.* Urbana: University of Illinois Press, 1995.

Trelease, Allen W. *White Terror: The Ku Klux Klan Conspiracy and Southern Reconstruction.* Baton Rouge: Louisiana State University Press, 1971.

Vandal, Giles. "Black Violence in Post–Civil War Louisiana." *Journal of Interdisciplinary History* 25, no. 1 (Summer 1994): 45–64.

———. "'Bloody Caddo': White Violence against Blacks in a Louisiana Parish, 1865–1875." *Journal of Social History* 25, no. 2 (1991): 373–88.

Vill, Karen, ed. "Women and Social Movements in the United States." December 1999. *The State University of New York at Binghamton Online.* Accessed January 11, 2002. http://womhist.binghamton.edu/aswpl/intro.htm.

White, Walter. *Rope and Faggot: A biography of Judge Lynch.* 1929. Notre Dame: University of Notre Dame Press, 2002.

———. "The Shambles of South Carolina." *Crisis* 33, no. 2 (December 1926): 72–75.

Whites, LeeAnn. *The Civil War as a Crisis in Gender: Augusta, Georgia, 1860–1890.* Athens: University of Georgia Press, 1995.

———. *Gender Matters: Civil War, Reconstruction, and the Making of the New South.* New York: Palgrave Macmillan, 2005.

Wiegman, Robyn. "The Anatomy of Lynching." In *American Sexual Politics: Sex, Gender, and Race since the Civil War* edited by John C. Fout and maura Shaw Tantillo, 223–45. Chicago: University of Chicago Press, 1993.

Williams, Alfred B. *Hampton and His Red Shirts: South Carolina's Deliverance in 1876.* New York: Books for Libraries Press, 1935.

Williams, Lou Falkner. "Federal Enforcement of Black Rights in the Post-Redemption South: The Ellenton Case." In *Local Matters: Race, Crime, and Justice in the Nineteeth-Century South,* edited by Christopher Waldrep and Donald G. Nieman. Athens: University of Georgia Press, 2001.

———. *The Great South Carolina Ku Klux Klan Trials, 1871–1872.* Athens: University of Georgia Press, 1996.

Williamson, Joel. *After Slavery: The Negro in South Carolina during Reconstruction, 1861–1877.* Chapel Hill: University of North Carolina Press, 1965.

———. *The Crucible of Race: Black-White Relations in the American South since Emancipation.* New York: Oxford University Press, 1984.

———. *A Rage for Order: Black-White Relations in the American South since Emancipation.* New York: Oxford University Press, 1986.

Woodman, Harold D. "Class, Race, Politics, and the Modernization of the Postbellum South." *Journal of Southern History* 63, no. 1 (February 1997): 3–22.

Woodward, C. Vann. *Origins of the New South: 1877–1913.* Baton Rouge: Louisiana State University Press, 1951. Reprint, 1994.

Woody, Robert Hilliard. "The South Carolina Election of 1870." *North Carolina Historical Review* 8 (1931): 168–86.

Wright, Gavin. *Old South, New South: Revolutions in the Southern Economy since the Civil War.* Baton Rouge: Louisiana State University Press, 1986.

Wyatt-Brown, Bertram. *Southern Honor: Ethics and Behavior in the Old South.* New York: Oxford University Press, 1982.

Zipf, Karen L. "Reconstructing 'Free Women': African-American Women, Apprenticeship, and Custody Rights during Reconstruction." *Journal of Women's History* 12, no. 1 (2000): 8–31.

Zuczek, Richard. *State of Rebellion: Reconstruction in South Carolina.* Columbia: University of South Carolina Press, 1996.

Index

Page references given in *italics* indicate illustrations or material contained in their captions.

About the Author

KATE CÔTÉ GILLIN is chair of the Department of History at the Pomfret School, a college preparatory school in Pomfret, Connecticut. She was awarded the Caroline Ray Hovey 1967 Master Teachership and the Award for Teaching Excellence from the Madeira School in McLean, Virginia. Gillin has been nominated for a National Honor Roll's Outstanding American Teacher Award and a Disney American Teacher Award. She has also been honored with the Recognition for Teaching Excellence from the National Society of High School Scholars.

CPSIA information can be obtained at www.ICGtesting.com
Printed in the USA
LVOW12*0045070114

368350LV00003B/3/P

9 781611 172911